THE TRADE OF NATIONS

THE TRADE OF NATIONS

BY

MICHAEL A. HEILPERIN

Second Edition, Enlarged

ALFRED A. KNOPF *New York* 1952

L. C. CATALOG CARD NUMBER: 51-11998

THIS IS A BORZOI BOOK,
PUBLISHED BY ALFRED A. KNOPF, INC.

Published January 1947
Second Edition, Enlarged, February 1952

TO THE MEMORY OF

MY FATHER AND MOTHER

FOR a thorough understanding of the general influence and effects that the commerce of nations is likely to produce, it is indispensable to realize clearly its connection with the fundamental condition of division of labor and consequent specialization of employment. Unless we bring ourselves to perceive that the movement towards an increase of trade relations between nations is parallel to, and accounted for in the same way as, the growth of domestic trade, and on the whole confers the same benefits, we are likely to be mistaken both in our interpretation of the facts of foreign commerce and in our judgments on matters of commercial policy.

C. F. BASTABLE : *The Commerce of Nations* (1892)

FIVE YEARS LATER

Preface to the Second Enlarged Edition

WHEN MY PUBLISHERS informed me, a few months ago, that *The Trade of Nations* was practically out of print and another printing of it was under consideration, I had before me three courses of action. One was to suggest that the book be reprinted again in exactly the same form in which it was originally published in January 1947. Another was to revise the book completely in view of the events and the literature of the five years that had passed since the original manuscript was completed. The third course, and one that after reflection I decided to follow, was to leave the main body of the first edition unchanged but to enlarge it by a new section on *Economic Reconstruction in an Insecure World,* some Appendix notes, and a new Preface.

The Trade of Nations represented, in the words of my original Preface, "an attempt to re-examine the problems of international trade, finance, and money, with special reference to the tasks of peace-making and to the particular responsibilities of the United States." When writing it, I was impressed by the fact that "to build a world economy in a highly nationalistic world is a difficult and delicate task." I was impressed by the fact that economic nationalism seemed to have survived the war. I expressed my ardent hope that peace would survive economic nationalism. Now, five years later, that hope is as ardent as ever, but it is mingled with regret over the failure to make peace more secure by launching in these first postwar years a determined campaign against economic nationalism.

This book, as I explained in introducing its first edition, stemmed "from my deep concern over the dangers that threaten our civilization unless we shunt the car of economic and political progress to the track of international collaboration, in the service of the ideals of human freedom and of peace-with-dignity for which people have so often been willing to die and for which they so rarely are willing to live. International economic organization involves the liquidation of economic nationalism. Politically this is, of course, a very difficult operation and it is also

[iii]

one that involves some short-run material sacrifices. . . ." It
was my conviction then and it is my conviction now that the
United States "is the only power in the world today that could
promote a movement towards economic internationalism. It is
the only nation that can play St. George to the deadly dragon
of nationalism." I might add, in retrospect, that we in our day
seem to have confused the role of St. George with that of Santa
Claus and that the dragon is just as alive now as it was in the
beginning of the postwar era, even if Santa has become both
wiser and sadder by experience.

Today the United States still must choose between its devotion
to liberal democracy, individual freedom, and free economic
institutions, and its attachment to the high tariff. Only by giving
up the latter can we effectively promote the former. The choice
must be made soon and it must be made by the public at large.
It was my conviction when I wrote *The Trade of Nations* that
American public opinion concerning the country's foreign
economic policy occupies a most crucial position in the international scene. This was why I addressed my book to the general
public rather than my fellow economists alone. Some reviewers
understood and applauded this decision to leave the ivory tower
for a while and appear in the "market place." Others regretted
my departures from the academic jargon that seems to be *de
rigueur* when economists write for each other, and criticized
my failure to present both sides of the picture with such im-
partiality that no relevant conclusion whatsoever might follow
from my presentation. Although in writing this book I have
never departed from the strictest canons of the search for truth,
I have been trying to uphold a thesis with all the vigor at my
command. It is that economic nationalism is the mortal enemy
of both human prosperity and international good will, and that
the traditional principles of international economics, while
adapted to the changing conditions of our disturbed world,
must be as honored in our days as they were honored in the
prosperous days of the past. It is the thesis of this book that the
United States alone among all nations has the opportunity of
leading the world from the wilderness of conflicting nationalisms into the promised land of international economic co-
operation. And, finally, it is the thesis of this book that world
trade based on the operations of free markets and on the per-

sonal enterprise of free men fosters the cause of international understanding, while trade straitjacketed by governmental controls and subject to authoritarian dictation from the top becomes a servant of nationalism and an abundant source of ill will, friction, and conflict.

Some of the critics of *The Trade of Nations* have deplored my impatience with compromise. Well, the history of the past five years has been frustrating precisely because there has been too much compromise floating around and too little understanding of what the reasonable limits of compromise are. If only people in responsible positions had read Lord Morley's brilliant essay *On Compromise* (1874), before going to international conferences or negotiations, they might have pressed more stanchly for the objectives of free international trade and payments, even if this had meant delaying the day of treaty signing. To seek compromise within its reasonable limits is the art of a statesman. The economist advising men of action must uphold the truth as he sees it and base his advice upon it. Whenever he acts differently, whenever he limits himself to providing intellectual equipment for the rationalizing of predetermined policy positions, he betrays his function and his trust.

The original manuscript of *The Trade of Nations* was completed in the spring of 1946. The five years that have elapsed since then have confirmed rather than denied the analysis and the conclusions of the book. The stultifying effects of national economic planning and its inability to solve any country's problems could now be abundantly documented from recent experience. The division of the world into an area of state-controlled trade and one of free-enterprise trade, which was anticipated in Chapter X, has become more and more a reality. Since the "Iron Curtain" descended across the middle of Europe in 1947, the uneasy peace has grown into a "cold war" that has become increasingly less "cold." Governmental controls over economic activity have gradually declined in continental Western Europe while Great Britain, where they remain strongly entrenched, has found itself both unable and unwilling to participate wholeheartedly in the movement toward the economic unification of Western Europe. And advocates of national economic planning have become more and more explicit in preferring bilateralism to multilateral trade—a development foreshadowed in *The Trade of Nations*.

When the manuscript of this book first went to press, a charter was being drafted for the projected International Trade Organization. I was alarmed by the excessive opportunity provided, in the earliest drafts of the Charter, for the survival of quantitative trade restrictions. My misgivings were fully borne out, alas, by the further course of the ITO negotiations; the Havana Charter of 1948 will remain a monument to economic nationalism. Cloaked in the heavy garments of technical jargon and declaiming insincere praises of freer world trade, the Charter forges new links in the chains that restrain the freedom and the growth of international economic relations.

My critical views on the full-employment planners and their approach to international economic relations (another source of displeasure among some of my reviewers) have been vindicated not only in the proceedings of the ITO Conferences but also in the report on *National and International Measures for Full Employment* published by five United Nations Experts at the end of 1949.[1] In discussing some problems of transition, I expressed the view that it is a matter of conjecture whether state monopolies of foreign trade can practice nondiscriminatory, multilateral trade. Some of my reviewers were quick to discover, between the lines of the book, my profound skepticism in the matter; some reproached me for it. After the experience of five years this ceases, however, to be a mere matter of conjecture. To the extent to which any such controversy can be settled by an appeal to historic experience, the conflict between state control of foreign trade and the practice of nondiscriminatory, multilateral trade has proved to be fundamental and inescapable.

In discussing—in 1946—Britain's postwar predicament, I expressed my conviction that: "a new wave of economic pioneering and risk-taking is necessary," and that "faith in the power of initiative and inventiveness of individual men and women, and the creation of conditions favorable to the exercise of these twin motors of dynamic economies, can do more for England in the end than faith in the miracles of state-ownership and state control." I still hold this view, and I think that the failure of

[1] Prof. J. M. Clark, Mr. Nicholas Kaldor, Prof. Arthur Smithies, M. Pierre Uri, and Mr. E. Ronald Walker.

Great Britain to liberate from restraints the dynamic forces of British society is more responsible than any other single factor for the slowness of Britain's recovery and for the frustrations the British people even now have to endure.[2] I also suggested that "there may be much scope for constructive collaboration between American and British industries: exchange of technological 'know-how,' market research, etc.," and I am glad to note that the Anglo-American Council on Productivity, established under ECA's auspices, has for the past three years been making significant progress in that direction.

Without going into further detail, it was my impression as I reread *The Trade of Nations* with a view to preparing its new edition that there was no need at this time to revise the main body of the book; there was, on the other hand, obvious need for bringing the story down to the present day. Important events had taken place since the first edition went to press: the inauguration of the Marshall Plan, the ITO Conferences, work done under United Nations auspices in the fields of full employment and economic development, the movement toward economic reconstruction, the changing pattern of American foreign economic policy—all of these made it advisable to expand the book by adding a new section to it, even though the first fourteen chapters be kept in their original form. Some of the additional material has been placed in appendixes.

Although I am bringing the book up to date in this new edition, I want to make it abundantly clear that a book of this kind must not be regarded as an *almanac,* one of the cardinal duties of which is to be entirely up to date! The broad outlines of basic problems change rarely, if ever, with the latest headlines, but there are moments in history which mark if not the end of an epoch at least the end of a chapter. Such a moment occurred when the outbreak of war in Korea forced the Western world to undertake a major rearmament program.

[2] In reviewing *The Trade of Nations* for *The Nation* (April 12, 1947) Mr. George Soule suggested that I "almost go so far as to imply that the British would be better off if they should give up their present heroic effort to stimulate their export surplus through import restriction and internal regulations." This is a very acute comment for, although I did not say so explicitly, this was very much my feeling at the time. Now, five years later, with the added benefit of hindsight, this feeling has become a certainty. For a very illuminating British discussion of these problems, see *Return from Utopia* by Richard Law, M.P. (London, 1950).

The five years between the first and second editions of this book are now a closed chapter. In many ways it is a disappointing chapter. It is so because St. George did not kill the dragon. He did not even inflict serious wounds upon the beast. Indeed, it seemed at times that he was persuaded by advocates of unlimited compromise that he could live happily by the dragon's side forever after. And, all through these years, economic nationalism successfully interfered with the course of world economic reconstruction. This dismal chapter is now finished.

The problem of military preparedness will be with us for many years to come. To salvage the greatest possible degree of international economic co-operation and to promote, at least throughout the non-Soviet world, the goal of free multilateral trade, will be a great challenge for both students and statesmen during the difficult years ahead.

Both the original contents of *The Trade of Nations* and the new material included in the present edition have greatly benefited by my conversations and discussions with many friends in the United States and Canada and throughout Western Europe. I could not hope to enumerate here all those to whom thanks are due. May those of my friends who will read this book and, in reading it, recall the discussions we have had at one time or another, find here the expression of my sincere appreciation for all they have contributed to my knowledge and understanding, and for the stimuli they gave to my thought.

The material presented in both the first and second editions of *The Trade of Nations* has been the object of three lecture series which I delivered in 1946, 1948, and 1950 respectively, at the Graduate Institute of International Studies in Geneva, an institution at which I earlier had the good fortune to be successively a student and a teacher, and which for a quarter century, through good times and harsh, has served the noble cause of scientific independence, of human liberty, and of international good will. May I reaffirm my perennial admiration and my grateful friendship to the founders and directors of that Institute, Paul Mantoux and William E. Rappard.

My thanks are due to The American Academy of Political and Social Science in Philadelphia, and to Time & Life, Inc., in New York for the use of material which appeared previously in my articles published, respectively, in *The Annals* and in *Fortune* magazine.

I cannot close this Preface without expressing my deep-felt gratitude to Henry P. Bristol, Lee H. Bristol, and William M. Bristol, Jr., of Bristol-Myers Company, New York. It is largely owing to their friendship, interest, and understanding that I was able to carry on my research and writing, under the most favorable conditions, during these recent years in which I have been living outside of all ivory towers.

M.A.H.

New York City

Acknowledgments

My THANKS are due to the following publishers for permission to quote from the books and publications named:

COLUMBIA UNIVERSITY PRESS: *A Price for Peace*, by Antonin Basch (1945).

HENRY HOLT AND COMPANY: *The Politics of Mercantilism*, by Philip W. Buck (1942), and *National Investment and Domestic Welfare*, by Norman Buchanan (1945).

HOUGHTON MIFFLIN COMPANY: *The Position of the Laborer in a System of Nationalism*, by E. S. Furniss (1920).

LITTLE, BROWN AND COMPANY and ATLANTIC MONTHLY PRESS: *You Can't Do Business with Hitler*, by Douglas Miller (1941).

McGRAW HILL BOOK COMPANY and COMMITTEE FOR ECONOMIC DEVELOPMENT: *International Trade and Domestic Employment*, by Calvin Hoover (1945).

THE MACMILLAN COMPANY: *Economic Progress and Social Security*, by Allan G. B. Fisher (1946), and *Economic Planning and International Order*, by Lionel Robbins (1937).

METHUEN AND CO., London: *The Commerce of Nations*, by C. F. Bastable (1923).

W. W. NORTON AND COMPANY: *Full Employment in a Free Society*, by William H. Beveridge (1945), and *America's Role in the World Economy*, by Alvin H. Hansen (1945).

PRINCETON UNIVERSITY, INTERNATIONAL FINANCE SECTION: *Essays in International Finance*, by Howard S. Ellis, Ragnar Nurkse, and Arthur I. Bloomfield (three pamphlets, 1945 and 1946).

G. P. PUTNAM'S SONS: *The Tariff History of the United States*, by Frank W. Taussig (1931).

SIMON AND SCHUSTER: *An American Program*, by Wendell L. Willkie (1944).

THE TWENTIETH CENTURY FUND: *Tomorrow's Trade*, by Stuart Chase (1945).

UNIVERSITY OF CHICAGO PRESS: *New Perspectives on Peace*, George B. de Huszar, editor (1944).

YALE UNIVERSITY PRESS: *International Relations as Viewed from Geneva*, by William E. Rappard (1925), and *National Self-sufficiency*, by J. M Keynes (*Yale Review*, 1933).

My thanks are also due to the following periodical publications from which material has been quoted by permission:

American Economic Review, published by the American Economic Association.
The *Atlantic Monthly*.
The *Banker*, London.
The *Economist*, London.
International Affairs, published by the Royal Institute of International Affairs, London.
Planning, published by P. E. P. (Political and Economic Planning), London.
The *Review of Economic Statistics*, published under the auspices of the Department of Economics, Harvard University.

To any publisher or author whose name may have been omitted through oversight from the above list I offer my sincere regrets.

Contents

[xiii]

BOOK FOUR. THE UNITED STATES AND
THE WORLD ECONOMY

BOOK FIVE. ECONOMIC RECONSTRUCTION
IN AN INSECURE WORLD   235

Introduction : An Old Problem
in a New Setting

Now that the war is over we are faced once again with the perennial quest for durable peace and stable prosperity. Victory affords to the victors an opportunity of establishing an international order which embodies their ideas and ideals. This opportunity of building a satisfactory world does not last forever. If it is not promptly and effectively used, it disappears, leaving in its wake forces of chaos and conflict and an environment receptive to seeds of another war. If the hard, cruel, and expensive lessons of the recent past have been learned, we know only too well that peace is not made secure by the mere fact of winning a war. We know that world economic relations do not settle down to peaceful ways spontaneously and automatically after having been torn to pieces by a major conflagration. We know that much thought and effort are necessary to build a society of nations upon the ruins left by war, and that this work must extend not only to political but also to economic matters.

At the end of World War I the belief was widely held that nationalism had been dealt a deathblow and that the world was a safe place for the normal peace-loving individual. How quickly did we wake up from that dream! Today we cannot but agree with that wise philosopher, Carl Becker, "that it is quite futile to discuss post-war reconstruction on the assumption that the sentiment of nationalism will be any less strong than it has been, or that nations will cherish their sovereign independence any less than they have, or be less disposed to define and promote their real or supposed national interests, or be less concerned with a balance of power that is advantageous to them."[1]

It is, therefore, in a world of intensified nationalism that we shall have to solve the great problems of international reconstruction. Nationalism will be more violent than ever, as a result of the war itself and the growth of collectivism or state socialism. War tends always to intensify the feeling of nationalism, and when the very existence of many countries is placed in jeopardy and

[1] Carl L. Becker: *How New Will the Better World Be?* (New York, 1944), pp. v–vi.

the war becomes a struggle for survival, this growth of national-ism is particularly strong. Centralized national economic plan-ning, on the other hand, results in an increased emphasis on national boundaries and an increasingly sharp differentiation between domestic and foreign transactions.

Nationalism, moreover, is stimulated by insecurity almost as much as by the more positive collective quest for power. The fear of war leads to policies aiming at economic self-sufficiency almost as much as does the preparation for aggressive war. This has been amply demonstrated between the two world wars when, in the words of Ernest Bevin, British Foreign Secretary: "We had become accustomed to a vicious circle whereby trade could not flourish because of lack of security, while security was endangered through lack of trade." [2] We can only prevent the reappearance of that vicious circle by dealing early and decisively with the problems of political security and of economic well-being. Both call for concerted international action. Peace and prosperity both are indivisible, and no single nation can long enjoy either of them when other nations are in the throes of either war or depression. Two world wars and one great world-wide depression must have brought home this truth to every one of us.

On the political side we have taken a decisive step towards the organization of peace through the adoption of the United Na-tions Charter. Obviously this is merely a first step. No document and no institutional arrangement will, by themselves, provide durable peace and stable order. Peace is a dynamic process, not a static condition; it involves continuous day-to-day adjustments between the different national attitudes and objectives of the various countries. Beyond the intentions expressed in documents and the instrumentalities of action provided by institutions, there is the overwhelming need for a *will to act*. Failing that will, good intentions will not be implemented, and institutions will not be made use of. If the League of Nations did not succeed in main-taining peace, this was largely due to the lack of a will to action on the part of the member states, rather than to any intrinsic weaknesses of the Covenant or of the existing institutional ar-rangements.

[2] Speech in the House of Commons delivered on August 20, 1945, as reported in the *New York Times*.

In the economic field the problem which we have before us now is very similar to that which we failed to solve after the last war. Economic nationalism was never subjected to a determined frontal attack since the end of World War I and consequences of that failure were not slow in appearing: eleven years after the Armistice the world was plunged into the greatest economic depression in its history. Economic nationalism stems from many causes and it is much more thoroughly entrenched nowadays than it was even in 1919. The problem of overcoming it and of establishing an integrated economy in a world politically divided into sovereign states is very ancient. It was well launched on the road to a solution in the latter part of the nineteenth century. Before that time, in the age of mercantilism, the world economy was sacrificed to nationalism. Afterwards, since 1919, nationalism was *not* sacrificed to the world economy. Now our problem appears in a new setting, owing to the growth of socialistic planning throughout the world. The Soviet Union, of course, is entirely wedded to a system of state ownership of instruments of production and trade, and her foreign economic relations are, in essence, a state monopoly. In many other countries the principle of national planning of economic life, combined with a larger or lesser degree of state ownership of industry, communications, and credit, results in a growing importance of the state as producer and trader. This change from nineteenth-century conditions will have far-reaching effects upon international commercial and financial relations. "If after the war," wrote Wendell Willkie in his last pronouncement on public affairs, "the industrial and commercial life of most of the countries of the world is either state-owned or controlled, then the whole problem of the survival of a free economic system, even in the United States, will be complicated." [3] Yet the preservation of a free economy, indeed its rejuvenation and revitalization, is, in the United States at least, one of the major objectives of the peace.

2.

In terms of the last one hundred and fifty years, the achievement of an integrated and closely-knit world economy is an old objective; the emergence of state socialism and of national planning

[3] Wendell L. Willkie: *An American Program* (New York, 1944), p. 19.

is a new setting in which this objective must now be sought. But if we should look further back into history, as it is occasionally useful to do, especially in times of great upheavals and momentous changes, we should find that state control of economic life is a very ancient condition whereas "One World" is a relatively recent social objective. It is the progress of travel and discovery and, more important still, the progress of technology that have brought about the realization that people are interdependent, regardless of where they live, that their problems are interwoven, and that their collaboration is necessary to bring about peace and prosperity for each and all of them.

The freedom of the individual, the philosopher's dream since time immemorial, has also become a widespread reality only in relatively recent times. It is challenged today in the name of an even greater freedom for all. "Hypocrisy," in the words of La Rochefoucauld, "is a homage which vice pays to virtue"; in our days collectivism is the homage which despotism pays to democracy. Even though individual freedom is on the defensive and nationalism stronger than ever, humanity is today striving with more determination than ever for freedom, for prosperity, and for peace. Ours is a difficult time in which to solve these problems; yet the penalty for failing to solve them will be greater than ever before on account of the social, physical, and technological conditions under which we live. In the age of collectivism the alternative to freedom is cruel slavery. In an industrial age the alternative to prosperity is acute and chronic distress spreading to the entire world. In the "atomic age" the alternative to peace is ruthless destruction. The stakes are high and the dice are loaded against us.

In this setting the position of the United States is peculiarly important and difficult. This country is the only major power definitely committed to the preservation of a free economy based on the operations of the market and on private enterprise and the only major economic unit which wants international trade to be conducted by individuals rather than by states. Nevertheless, while the public has come more and more to understand the importance of international collaboration, political as well as economic, it persists in clinging to the now obsolete high-tariff tradition inherited from older days. "For generations," said Cordell Hull some years ago, "humanity has built its life upon a recognition of the primary fact that trade is the lifeblood of economic activity. *This is equally true whether within or among nations.* Each nation has accordingly developed far beyond domestic requirements those branches of production in which it has special endowment or aptitude. Each nation has come to regard foreign markets as the natural outlet for its surplus output, and the surplus production of other nations as sources from which to supply its own deficiencies." [4] It would be hard to find a clearer and more succinct statement of the significance of foreign trade.

3.

America's position in the world economy changed so suddenly between 1914 and 1919 that the change long remained unacknowledged both by the public opinion and by national policy. In the years that have elapsed since 1919, America's economic pre-eminence in the world has become more and more pronounced, and, since 1941, it is linked with political and military pre-eminence as well. The task of constructing a world economy was very much easier twenty-five years ago than it is today. Today, however, under much more difficult circumstances, we have at least this great advantage—that we are increasingly aware of the urgent need to solve the problem. America's power to act has been greatly increased. The United States is capable of accepting the challenge and of taking bold and determined steps towards the building of a world economy. In order to be fully effective, the acceptance of the challenge must be based on a broad view of the long-range interest of America as a nation, and of the long-range objectives of Americans as individuals. A proper understanding of what the trade of nations consists of, of how it works, where its advantages lie, and what obstacles it has to surmount in order to develop and to flourish, is an indispensable condition for the development of an enlightened public opinion behind a consistent national foreign economic policy. To contribute, however modestly, to that understanding is the purpose of the present study.

[4] Cordell Hull: *American Foreign Trade Policies,* address delivered before the 24th annual meeting of the Chamber of Commerce of the United States, Washington, April 1946. *International Conciliation* No. 323, October 1936, p. 454 (Italics added).

BOOK ONE

The Trade of Nations

CHAPTER I

International Trade

INTERNATIONAL PROBLEMS, economic as well as political, arise out of the peculiar structure of our planet which, physically a single and indivisible unit, is divided politically into a number of separate states. Politically each of these states seeks independence and is jealous of its "sovereignty"; but owing to the uneven distribution of resources on the earth's surface—and underneath it —the various states are united by links of economic interdependence. The quest for better living conditions has driven men, since time immemorial, to travel, exploration, migration, and trade. In addition, man, like the elephant's child from Kipling's tale, is "full of 'satiable curiosity." To satisfy his insatiable curiosity he has set out upon a career of travel, visiting hitherto unknown regions and meeting new and strange people. Hunger and curiosity are the two powerful driving forces which made man, early in history, surrender the cosiness of his immediate surroundings for the sake of exploring the wide spaces of the world in which he might find adventure, wealth, and knowledge. Opportunities for intercourse between men belonging to different groups, tribes, city-states, and states grew steadily. Trade and war were the outcome of these inter-group and inter-state relations. And whereas we are more than ever anxious to eradicate from the surface of the world the scourge of war, we are very eager to develop and promote the peaceful relations between the peoples of the world. Among these none is more frequent and more important than trade.

Trade between separate human groups is as old as trade between individuals composing each particular group—or maybe even older. Many of the early communities were collectivistic in their mode of economic organization, exploiting in common, under the leadership of their chieftains, the resources of land and sea, of rivers, fields, and forests. But even these primitive groups were not entirely self-contained; whenever opportunity arose, they engaged in trade with other groups, and numerous types of such exchanges have been discovered and studied by anthropologists. Some of these early forms of barter or trade are present to this very day among primitive tribes. It is not our purpose here to describe the history of trade; but it is well to remember how ancient are its origins in order that we should avoid being too much perplexed by current problems of international commerce.

Trade occupies a great role in the life of nations and in relations between nations. It is therefore as regrettable as it is dangerous that the average person should shrink away from its problems, discarding them as either "dull" or "technical" and leaving them to the "experts." Economic problems are not really difficult to grasp, and the intellectual equipment necessary to grapple with them is child's play compared with that which is requisite to understanding the radio, or if we wish to be up-to-date, the atom. Economic problems are less difficult to understand than they are difficult to settle; this can be attributed to the complexity of our social environment and to the unmanageable character of man-in-society. Whereas we have made spectacular progress in all of the natural sciences, in the realm of social life we haven't moved far ahead—if we have moved at all—in the past twenty-five hundred years. How striking it is, when rereading the *Politics* of Aristotle or certain plays of Aristophanes, to find how much similarity, nay, identity there is between their preoccupations and ours, their perplexities and ours, the problems they could not solve and those we cannot.

In the realm of economic affairs part of the difficulty—and an important part at that—stems from the aloofness of the man in the street in the face of problems of trade, money, and finance. This aloofness may have regrettable consequences: the democratic societies of today, and the American society most of all, will be called upon in the next few years to make very important decisions in the realm of domestic as well as foreign economic policies. The question of foreign lending, of tariff policy, of monetary stabilization, and many others will have to be settled and much of our future peace and prosperity will depend upon the wisdom with which they will be settled. And, whereas most of these decisions will be taken either by Congress or by the executive branch of the government, their nature will reflect the state of the public opinion throughout the nation, for this is the way democracy works.

2.

All trade,[1] domestic as well as international, is the result of the uneven distribution of resources throughout the planet, of the unequal distribution of aptitudes and skills among men, and of the advantages in terms of productive efficiency which follow from a specialization of productive efforts and from a division of labor. No area of the planet can produce all the varied resources which could be put to good use by its inhabitants; the exchange of goods which are relatively plentiful for others which are either scarce or unavailable is therefore the first purpose of trade. These goods are often basic, essential commodities; but frequently they are goods needed for a greater enjoyment of life. Since the earliest days, luxuries and trinkets were not unimportant components of trade.

Primitive collectivistic groups were generally self-contained, providing as well as they might for the needs of their members, though, whenever opportunity arose, even they would seek to improve their material condition by engaging in trade. But no single individual can ever envisage self-sufficiency. The famed Robinson Crusoe not only was a fictional character, but was a man living in isolation, not a man living in society—a fact which has frequently been forgotten by writers on theoretical economics! An individual in society specializes in some pursuit, sells goods or renders services to other members of the community, and, with the income derived thereby, avails himself of goods and services produced by others and required for his own welfare and that of his dependents. The *division of labor* is a basic feature of life in society, though its extent can vary and be more or less considerable according to circumstances. With the growth of modern productive methods, specialization has very much gained in scope, thus increasing the efficiency of the productive processes. The connection between the division of labor, specialization, and efficiency has been first described one hundred and seventy years ago in the immortal opening pages of Adam Smith's *Wealth of Nations.*[2]

[1] The term "trade," as used here, includes not only trade in merchandise, but also trade in services (so-called "invisible trade") such as rail, shipping, and air freights, tourist expenditures, payment for banking services, and royalties.

[2] Adam Smith: *An Inquiry into the Nature and Causes of the Wealth of Nations,* first published in 1776, Book I, Chapter I: "Of the Division of Labour."

The principle of the division of labor applies not only to individuals living together in a small area, but also to groups of people inhabiting the various regions of the globe. It is one of the achievements of the "classical" economists that they translated the individual experiences concerning the division of labor into a language applicable to inter-group and inter-regional commercial relations. Among these wider relationships, those which take place between persons residing in different political units or states fall under the notion of *international* trade. The principle of the division of labor is as essential to the understanding of the role and significance of international trade as it is essential to the understanding of domestic trade.

The specialization of skills incident in the division of labor widens, of course, the scope of international (or even, more generally, of inter-regional) trade. For not only those goods will be purchased abroad which *cannot* be produced at home, but also goods that *can* be produced at home, albeit only at a cost higher than that at which they may be obtained from foreign countries. The advantage of the foreign producer may be due to more abundant mineral deposits, to greater fertility of soil, to richer forests, to a climate more favorable to certain lines of production. In certain instances, special skills have been cultivated and developed over lengthy periods of time among the inhabitants of some special area. The classical example is that of the Swiss watchmakers. This highly skilled craft has been cultivated for a great many years in certain parts of southwestern Switzerland, e.g., in the hamlets of the Jura Mountains. The watch industries of Geneva, Neuchâtel, Le Locle, etc., all derive their strength from an old tradition of watchmaking among local craftsmen. Certain advantages in production can be derived from the country's size [3] and from the level of its economic development. Thus, in an economically highly developed country like the United States, with a vast home market, industry can apply the cost-reducing methods of mass production to a greater extent than can industries of other countries. Consequently, many industrial articles can be sold in the world market at a competitive price, even though workers engaged in their pro-

[3] This consideration would lose much of its importance, of course, in a completely free-trade world.

duction are paid high wages and enjoy a high standard of living. Advanced industrial skills and productive efficiency based on a large domestic market provide the country with this competitive advantage in international trade.

Division of labor due to the "absolute advantage" that certain countries have over others in the production of particular goods is by no means characteristic of international trade alone. Adam Smith already has pointed out how similar this phenomenon is to one that can be currently observed in the daily life of individual persons:

"It is the maxim of every prudent master of a family, never to attempt to make at home what it will cost him more to make than to buy. . . . What is prudence in the conduct of every private family, can scarce be folly in that of a great kingdom. If a foreign country can supply us with a commodity cheaper than we ourselves can make it, better buy it of them with some part of the produce of our own industry, employed in a way in which we have some advantage. The general industry of the country . . . is certainly not employed to the greatest advantage, when it is . . . directed towards an object which it can buy cheaper than it can make." [4]

The inter-regional and international division of labor, along the lines of "absolute" advantage in costs of production, is a matter of both logic and experience. The division of labor can and does go, however, beyond the limits determined by these "absolute" regional advantages. There can be trade between two countries, one of which has an absolute advantage over the other in all the goods produced (and this even if we assume that both countries produce the same goods). The theory of international trade, from Ricardo onwards, has made a very searching inquiry into that kind of situation, and the *theory of comparative costs* is the outcome. That theory, which has been worked out in great detail by generations of students of international trade, explains, in reality, an important consequence of the division of labor.[5] The following passage from Bastable's *Commerce of Nations* clearly and briefly states the general significance of that conception as well as its application to the trade between nations:

[4] Adam Smith, op. cit., Book IV, Chapter II.

[5] See, in particular, Gottfried Haberler: *Theory of International Trade* (London, 1936) and Jacob Viner: *Studies in the Theory of International Trade* (New York, 1937).

quently, their export market, and both countries will fall below the level of efficiency that would prevail under free-trade conditions. All of this, however, is another part of our story and will be told in a later chapter.

Another objection that might be raised against the doctrine of comparative advantage is this: "Aren't we assuming too much rationality and too much knowledge on the part of both individuals and nations when we say that they will specialize in the pursuits in which they are, relatively speaking, *most* efficient?" This is a fair criticism and we must be on our guard, of course, lest we take too literally the abstractions of pure theory. As in other things of life, so in this also, the process of trial and error has many applications. Some individuals choose a career while they are under misapprehension concerning their real talents and abilities; some change their profession before hitting the one for which they are most suited, some miss it altogether. There are satisfactions other than money-income and these are often sought even at a pecuniary sacrifice. In our world—about the protectionist tendencies in which more will presently be said—there are other objectives of policy than the achievement of the greatest possible amount of welfare. Political and social considerations play an important role and may considerably counteract the movement towards greater and greater specialization. It is when we abstract from the political, social, and, let us add, emotional factors, that we are left with the purely "economic" considerations of absolute and comparative advantage. And in that more circumscribed area, these considerations add a good deal to the understanding of the economic forces that operate in our societies, nationally as well as internationally.

In addition, they afford useful guidance in planning certain economic policies. Many countries today are—or would like to be—on the threshold of new economic developments. Large-scale investment plans are contemplated and are tied up with projected international loans and investments. Now in the making of these plans it is a wise course to pay as much attention as possible to the industrial structures and opportunities of both debtor and creditor countries. The process of economic growth always involves the giving up of the least efficient industries and the expansion of the most productive ones. This applies equally to the more and to the less developed countries. In the course of these developments not only new industries get established and certain other industries get improved and perfected, but there are also "migrations" of industries from region to region and from country to country. Thus, e.g., England specialized more and more during the inter-war years in high-grade textiles, and Switzerland in precision watches and precision instruments, while other countries developed considerably the manufacture of lower grades of textiles and of "cheaper" types of watches. These industrial "migrations" must take place if we are to reap the benefits of economic progress—and other adaptations to changing conditions are required as well. The "doctrine of comparative advantage" provides the intellectual framework against which specific issues can be placed. For, if it be true that nations as well as individuals follow the path of greatest aggregate advantage, changes in conditions affect the nature of the advantage itself and the direction in which it must be sought.

It is quite evident, therefore, that in a changing world we must expect changes in the pattern of the international division of labor and in the structure of international trade. Yet allowances often fail to be made for these changes. Some argue as if the structure of imports and exports had to remain forever what it has been in some past period. They engage in elaborate calculations, based on past statistics, which are supposed to show what this or that country is likely to import or to export in the years to come, but ignore important dynamic factors, thus stultifying the conclusions reached. There are others, on the other hand, who argue that because of technological progress a deathblow has been dealt to international trade: henceforth, with the munificent help of chemistry, there will be no need for imports— everybody will find everything right in his own national backyard! It is of the greatest importance for the development of sound economic policies that the factor of change should be acknowledged and its impact properly interpreted.

4.

The basic motives for which people engage in trade are the same regardless whether it is trade between individuals residing in the same locality, trade between individuals living at a great distance from one another in the same country, or between in-

dividuals inhabiting different countries. In the latter case alone
do we deal with an international transaction and speak in terms
of imports and exports. The political division of the world into
separate units, each with its own currency, with its own economic policies, and its own rules applying to the commercial
and financial transactions across its boundary lines, creates new
problems and, let us say right away, new difficulties for persons
engaged in international trade. Whereas, speaking of purely domestic transactions, it is quite well understood that both the
buyer and the seller of commodities and services derive a benefit
from the transaction—otherwise they would refrain from entering into it—this is much less clearly understood with respect to
international trade, where questions are often raised as to which
is more beneficial, imports or exports. In the field of domestic
transactions it is well understood that benefits of trade do not depend on whether someone has, during a given period of time,
sold goods (or services) for a greater or smaller amount of
money than the amount which he has spent on his purchases,
thus either increasing or reducing his holdings of cash. In the
matter of international trade a doctrine prevailed in the age of
mercantilism (sixteenth to eighteenth centuries) that an export
surplus is to be striven for because it results in an increase of a
nation's holdings of precious metals (the well-established means
of settling international accounts). When that doctrine became
—at least temporarily—discredited,[8] the emphasis tended to
swing to the other extreme: what matters in international trade,
it was said, are imports; exports are merely a means of paying
for imports. Imports add to the quantity of goods available for
the consumption of the nation; exports reduce that quantity.

In the United States the wholesome reaction against over-
estimating exports and underestimating imports (as was customary for many years past, and still is in many circles) has
resulted in reversing the over- and under-emphasis, while maintaining a lop-sided approach to problems of international trade.
Thus in an important publication of the Department of Commerce we read that "In the final analysis exports are important
principally as a means of obtaining imports."[9] Making that

---

[8] It reappeared, in a different form, in our own days; see Chapter V.
[9] August Maffry and Hal B. Lary: *Foreign Trade after the War* (Washington: Bureau
of Foreign and Domestic Commerce, Department of Commerce; October 1943), p. 2.

point of view his own, Mr. Stuart Chase, in a recent popular book on international trade, flatly (and mistakenly) asserts: "Imports first." [10] Now it may be suggested that in expressing this opinion he stops far short of the final stages of the analysis. In pursuing that analysis further, we should find that imports and exports *both* come first—because *both* are essential features of the international division of labor, and because *both* are closely interwoven with the operation of the "domestic" economy.

The crux of the problem lies in the fact of the international division of labor, from which arises the need for imports as well as for exports. The former is due to the fact that there exists in the public an effective demand for goods which, as we have seen, cannot be produced at all at home or cannot be produced as advantageously as they can be secured abroad. The latter is due to the fact that the specialization incident in the division of labor involves production not only for the home market but also for the world market. Individual concerns produce for domestic consumption as well as for export, and the foreign market is as important to them as the domestic market: the loss of demand in either market means a decline of sales and may lead to a distressing use of red ink in bookkeeping operations. For producers of cotton in the United States, who in 1929 exported over fifty per cent of their output, or for producers of office appliances who exported between thirty and forty per cent of their output, or even for producers of industrial machinery who exported between ten and fifteen per cent [11] the purpose of exports was *not* to pay for imports of tin, rubber, and other commodities, but simply to engage in profitable trade. *The foreign market is merely an extension of the domestic market.* Were it not for the above-mentioned implications of the political divisions of the world into separate states, there would be no noticeable difference at all between domestic and foreign commerce.

If we take a national economy as a whole, the picture undergoes a subtle change. Leaving aside international credit transactions, about which much will be said in the next chapter, as well as movements of gold and silver (to be discussed in Chapter III), imports and exports must be equal in money value. It is pos-

[10] Stuart Chase: *Tomorrow's Trade* (New York, 1945), p. 15.
[11] See page 226 for more complete data about the importance of foreign markets to many American industries.

sible, therefore, to say that exports provide the country with the means of paying for imports. In relations between state-monopolies of foreign trade this is the way plans are most likely to be made. According to Stuart Chase,[12] "the first major question" is this: "What do we need to import as a community?" And, since imports have to be paid for, "the second major question arises automatically: What can we ship in exchange for what we need?" And Mr. Chase goes on to say: "Here we have the theory of foreign commerce in its simplest aspect. Observe especially the order of the questions: *Imports first.*" All of which is, broadly speaking, correct—but only for a totalitarian country, the whole economic life of which is ruled by decisions of a governmental planning agency. In a free-market economy, this is not "the theory of foreign commerce in its simplest aspect," not by a long stretch. In a free-market economy exports and imports originate spontaneously in the operation of many markets and in independent decisions of thousands and millions of individuals. There is no sharp dividing line between foreign and domestic commerce (even though tariffs and other regulations make trade across boundary lines more difficult than trade conducted within the national boundaries). All trade reflects division of labor, specialization, and the fact that people work mostly not to supply their own needs directly, but to sell their output in a market—domestic or foreign, as the case may be.

5.

Primitive trade often took the form of "swap" or barter; the scope of which was necessarily very limited—even if, as is likely, it was barter not between individuals but between tribes. Eventually, money of one kind or another made its appearance, and trade changed its character. The introduction of a "means of payment" replaces barter by *two* operations: purchase and sale, which can be separated in space and in time. The seller may keep the money he gets for his commodities and spend it at his convenience on goods and services that he requires. These may come from more distant parts, and there may elapse a more or less extended time between the original sale and the new purchase. Indeed, the seller may not buy anything but lend the

12 Op. cit., p. 15.

money to someone else who will spend it in his own way. All of this creates a great deal of flexibility and adaptability in the processes of trade and is much more suitable than barter to the life of a growing, individualistic community. It is perhaps not an accident that the reappearance of barter-trade (between governments) coincides in the modern world with the resurgence of collectivism.

The "indirect exchange" which superseded barter was what is often called *multilateral trade*. The term applies to international trade, but the type of transaction it denotes is typical of *all* trade. In most general terms, barter involves a "balance of trade" between any two partners on any transaction they enter into. In the case of multilateral trade, there is no such immediate balance. In the long run and provided people do not choose to keep the proceeds of their sales in form of cash, a "balance of trade" tends to develop for every individual, but it is a balance in his relations with the whole outside world—and not with any particular partner. The baker may deliver bread to the doctor and yet, enjoying excellent health, have no need for the doctor's ministrations; yet he may buy clothing for a value greater than that of the bread sold to the tailor. He will use the *surplus* obtained in his dealings with the doctor to pay up the *deficit* incurred in his transactions with the tailor, and so forth.

Under barter transactions are limited by the fact that there must be established a *bilateral* balance between any two trading partners. Under the multilateral system the balance exists between one partner and *all* of the others, meaning that each partner remains solvent (normally, at least) but that he rarely buys from anyone the exact equivalent—in money terms—of what he sells to him.

The term "multilateral" applied to this "all-round" settlement is rather clumsy and it might not be difficult to replace it by a better one; since, however, the expression is widely accepted and often used we shall not confuse the issue by new semantic inventions. The origin of the term is this: since the deficit incurred by Country A in its dealings with Country B is paid by means of a surplus achieved in its trade with Country C, the balancing of A's accounts involves a "triangular" settlement—and the same is true of B and C. Hence a "triangular" settlement, in contrast to a "bilateral" settlement or barter. By broadening the notion to cover a situation where there are many (*multum*) partners, the term "multilateral" was coined to designate this more comprehensive and more complex mode of settlement. To be quite correct, we should speak of *multilateral settlements* rather than of *multilateral trade*. Settlements result, of course, not only from commercial but also from financial transactions; we shall make allowances for these in the next two chapters, arriving ultimately at a complete picture of the network of international settlements.

Multilateral trade exists when trade between Country A and the rest of the world is balanced,[13] but not necessarily the trade between Country A and each of the Countries B, C, D, and so forth. Bilateralism, on the contrary, is the name of a system in which the balance of trade is achieved between couples of countries: A and B; A and C; A and D; etc. This can only be realized in practice under a system of strict government controls. Bilaterally balanced trade between states comes close to the primitive inter-tribal barter and, in our time, represents a striking economic retrogression. Multilateral international trade, which flourished in the nineteenth and early twentieth centuries, and the re-establishment of which is one of the objectives of American foreign economic policy, is an extension to the world at large of a system which is so beneficial in the domestic affairs of a free-market economy.[14] It favors the international division of labor, facilitates trade, and, when extended to financial transactions as well, results in a world-wide system of multilateral settlements.

If not interfered with by governmental controls, international trade develops spontaneously along multilateral lines. "Bilateralism," on the other hand, represents a sort of strait jacket into which trade may be pressed by state regulations, but from which it escapes as soon as these regulations are abandoned. It is important to realize very clearly the difference between multilateral trade and barter (or bilateral trade). To be sure, the aim of trade is to exchange certain goods for other goods; barter and multilateral trade are merely different ways of achieving that ob-

---

[13] Leaving aside, for the moment, the question of capital movements.

[14] For a detailed statistical study of multilateral world trade, see: *The Network of World Trade*, prepared by the Economic Intelligence Service of the League of Nations and published by the League in 1942 (distributed by Columbia University Press). See also the article by Folke Hilgerdt: "The Case for Multilateral Trade," *American Economic Review*, Supplement, March 1943.

jective. We have seen how, domestically, the introduction of money added scope and flexibility to trade and made the division of labor and the specialization of skills more likely to be achieved. Internationally, barter can only be practiced by governments of countries and constitutes a long step towards state socialism; in addition, barter interferes with the international division of labor, reduces the volume of trade, and interferes with its adaptability and flexibility. Yet we find in current literature a good deal of confusion between barter and the more advanced forms of trade which involve monetary instruments and the operations of free markets. This is due, in large part, to mistaking the final results of the process for its mechanics.

The nineteenth century and the first thirty years of the twentieth were the age of undisputed multilateral trade. But when in 1931 the mechanism of multilateral settlements broke down under the strains of an acute financial crisis, bilateralism was resorted to as a method of alleviating the difficulties experienced by certain countries. The crisis has failed to be met by an effective international action, the emergency became chronic, and bilateral settlements became more and more frequent. It was then discovered, primarily by the ingenious Dr. Schacht, that there were advantages to be derived by an economically strong country when using bilateral trading methods in relations with weaker countries. It was also discovered that bilateralism presented very concrete advantages for a country preparing for war. And so it happened that all through the thirties bilateralism grew in importance. It found its admirers and apologists. Advocates of economic collectivism saw in it a wedge through which state control could be introduced into an otherwise free-enterprise economy. The argument that "after all the purpose of trade is to swap goods for goods," was often heard —and often misleadingly used. Then came World War II. And now that we are emerging from the war years, we find ourselves in the need of building a new world economy—after the havoc that two world wars and one great depression have played with the system on which we used to depend. In many countries collectivism and nationalism may prove a favorable climate for the survival and further growth of the bilateralist pattern of foreign trade. Other countries, like the United States, are striving for the reconstruction of a system of multilateral settlements.

Still others, like Great Britain, are divided on that issue but likely to choose the multilateral pattern provided they have confidence in its workability. Only the United States can provide to the world an assurance that the system will work, by adopting a bold, imaginative, and consistent foreign economic policy, backed by an informed and enlightened public opinion.

6.

Within the confines of one and the same country, trade encounters no obstacles other than those due to physical impediments such as mountains, deserts, non-navigable waters—and distance itself. Left to its own devices trade develops along the lines indicated above, and division of labor, specialization, and a multilateral network of settlements grow spontaneously. The operations of a free market and of the price mechanism govern the distribution of resources and direct production and commerce. If the world were one single state, this would be, in its broad outline, the whole story of trade, and we could move to the next chapters dealing with credit and with money. But the world, as we know it, is divided into many separate states and reference has already been made to the interferences with and restrictions upon trade which are frequently introduced by the various national governments.

That governments can and do interfere with trade is an old story. Much less old is the idea that they might abstain from so doing and that *free trade* between nations might be of great advantage to all of them. While several earlier writers have referred to the desirability of free international trade, it was Adam Smith who most forcefully advocated such a radical departure from prevalent restrictions and controls, and who presented a most compelling case for freedom of trade as source of national well-being. *The Wealth of Nations,* published in the year of the American War of Independence, has become the intellectual cornerstone of the free-trade doctrine of which, in later years, Richard Cobden was to be the greatest political champion.

The economics of the free-trade position are very simple and consist in the demand that the advantages of the division of labor, of specialization of skills, and—let us add—of multilateral trade be extended beyond the limits of individual countries to the world at large. Intellectually, the case for free trade is very strong indeed. Were this not so, there would be a good case for trade barriers *within* individual countries, and such a case has never been seriously presented. In our days, as in the days of mercantilism, the case for trade barriers is presented in the name of economic as well as political advantages; but, as will presently be shown, the economic arguments are specious and acquire significance only when related to the undercurrent of nationalism, the political creed of their advocates. Since the contemporary collectivist trend greatly strengthens nationalism, trade barriers find today more advocates than ever, while free traders are, more than ever, likened to the dodo and dismissed as Utopians; all of which fails to answer their argument that the wealth of the world is best served by what serves so well the wealth of individual nations, to wit: by a wide and free market open to large and unfettered trade. It may be said at once that the complete free-trade position calls for the freedom of international movements not only of goods, but also of capital (in monetary terms) and of human beings. It also calls for a single unit of economic valuations, i.e., for stable relationships between the monetary units of the various countries.

In saying all this we are making it abundantly clear how far removed the free-trade ideal is from the realities of the present world—this, of course, by itself does not make the ideal unworthy of being striven for. For, after all, the ideal of perpetual peace between free nations seems also very far removed from a world that has just gone through the second devastating world war in thirty years, a world in some parts of which guns are still roaring and people are being killed in battle, a world in which human liberties are still being trampled by despotic or totalitarian regimes. So we must agree to go beyond barren and complacent rationalizations of the present (in the name of what is often called "realism") and seek goals which may appear unattainable . . . until they have actually been reached.

The "Battle of Free Trade" was fought for over sixty years before it was won. It was won in one country alone due to that country's very particular circumstances. Because she was the center of a great and growing commercial empire, England's adoption of free trade exercised, for a time, a liberalizing influence upon the commercial policies of certain other countries, especially of France. The victory did not last. The battle had been waged and won in England alone and this was not sufficient, as the rest of the world practiced—and often preached—economic nationalism. There has never been, to date, a truly international attempt at establishing free trade. Even the establishment of the League of Nations which was to make peace secure was not accompanied by the establishment of a free and open world market. Economically, free trade was nothing else than a demand for a "One World" economy. That demand has remained unfulfilled. The fact that the world has failed to achieve either economic stability or political peace cannot, of course, be blamed upon the failure to establish free trade. Still, the coincidence might give us pause: for, after all, these three failures *might* be related to one another and *may* be the result of common underlying causes.

Free trade, as advocated by Richard Cobden and his friends, was far from being a purely economic objective. It was part of a widely conceived philosophy of international peace. Nothing can express better the political aspects of free trade than the following lines quoted from Cobden's speech delivered at Wrexham, Wales, on November 14th, 1850, at a great meeting held under the auspices of the Peace Society:[15]

"When I advocated Free Trade, do you suppose that I did not see its relation to the present question [of peace], or that I advocated Free Trade merely because it would give us a little more occupation in this or that pursuit? No; I believed Free Trade would have the tendency to unite mankind in the bonds of peace, and it was that, more than any pecuniary consideration, which sustained and actuated me, as my friends know, in that struggle."

The desire "to unite mankind in the bonds of peace" is still with us, more urgently perhaps than ever because of the realization that another war, an atomic war, may lead to the wholesale destruction of our civilization. And is it too rash to hope that this desire might be implemented in terms of economic as well as political policies?

If free trade is a political as well as an economic doctrine, so is protection. Obstacles have been built across the path of international trade under the impact of nationalism, in the quest for

15 Richard Cobden: *Speeches on Questions of Public Policy,* edited by John Bright and James E. Thorold Rogers (London, 1870), vol. II, p. 421.

protection of special interests, in the quest for national power, or to safeguard national economic planning. We shall presently examine in more detail the different reasons for which tariffs have been raised and other controls and restrictions introduced. Here it will suffice to make two additional comments. One is that governmental encouragement of exports is as contrary to the ideals of free trade, as is a governmental restriction of imports. Free trade demands that the world market should become an organic extension of the home market of every single country; it does not urge the growth of trade beyond what would develop spontaneously under the influence of the market processes and of the division of labor. The spread in our times of state-socialism creates a serious obstacle to the achievement of free—or even of freer—trade, inasmuch as imports and exports come to be determined not by market processes but by over-all governmental plans. Indeed, it may be said that the great issue before us is not so much between free trade and protection, as it is between free-enterprise trade and state-regulated trade.

The second comment concerns *private* interferences with international trade carried out through the instrumentality of international *cartels*. Cartels are agreements between private companies for the purpose of limiting competition among them. They are concerned with prices, with quantities sold, with areas in which each member is allowed to operate. International cartels restrict the scope of international competition, interfere with the effectiveness of the international division of labor (by maintaining in operation less efficient industries), and with multilateral trade.[16] Cartels can be sponsored by industries without government support, or they may be promoted by governments themselves. The United States is at present the only country within which cartels are illegal; its policy with respect to international cartels is as yet in a formative state, though, to be entirely consistent, international cartels would have to be as strongly opposed as are domestic cartels. If we consider "restraints to trade" as being damaging and harmful, we must oppose *all* such restraints, regardless of whether they be tariffs,

[16] See Corwin D. Edwards' *Economic and Political Aspects of International Cartels,* a study made for the Subcommittee on War Mobilization of the Committee on Military Affairs, U. S. Senate (Washington: Government Printing Office, 1944); and *A Cartel Policy for the United Nations* by Corwin D. Edwards and others (Columbia University Press, 1945).

cartels, or other devices.[17] All such obstacles will have to be vigorously opposed, and eventually removed, if trade is to follow the lines of greatest economic advantage, if the division of labor is to yield its best results, and if a system of multilateral settlements is to operate smoothly throughout the world.

[17] Such as quotas, restrictions on foreign payments (exchange control), regional "preferences," and so forth. In our days tariffs are the least unsurmountable obstacles to international trade as compared with the other devices.

CHAPTER II

Foreign Investments

FOREIGN INVESTMENTS are investments which the residents or the government of one country make in another country. Governmental investments take the form of loans; private investments fall into one of three categories: loans, equity investments, or direct investments. The reason for private foreign investments is the same as that for all investments: the anticipation of returns. Foreign bonds will be bought by those investors who have confidence in conditions in the particular country in which a company or the government has issued the bonds, and who find the terms more attractive than those of available domestic securities. Stock of a foreign company will be purchased by investors who find that particular company of interest to them as a source of future dividends or as outlet for other entrepreneurial plans. Finally, a group of capitalists may start a brand-new venture abroad by establishing a foreign company, supplying it with funds, and going into business in foreign countries. Or again a company may finance the establishment of a foreign branch or subsidiary. The last-named types of foreign investment are what is called "direct investment"; they have increased considerably during the pre-war decades and are likely to be of great importance in the years ahead.

Some of these foreign investments may be particularly risky and venturesome—those which aim at railroad construction, at the opening up of new mines, and so forth. Many great fortunes have had their origin in such ventures—and much capital has been lost in others. Those particularly "adventurous" and risky investments are usually referred to as "venture capital." They have been instrumental in the development of North America, certain areas of South America, of Africa, and of the Far and Middle East. Under modern conditions the days or private ventures of this kind may well be almost gone, and public investments are likely to take their place. The development of "backward" areas is today a recognized objective of national policy in practically every underdeveloped country of the world; governments are pledged to it and nations expect it, yet it raises serious financial problems, most of them of international scope.

The need for foreign funds appears on a private and public level, individual and national. Individual concerns try to borrow funds abroad if they can obtain them in a foreign capital market more cheaply than in the domestic market; or they may float equity securities abroad if the domestic market is not receptive, due, primarily, to the scarcity of capital in the country. These private transactions may be offset, in part, by other transactions taking place in the opposite direction. This is especially likely to happen in relations between equally developed countries; there are British investments in the United States and American investments in Great Britain. The sum total of investments made in a given country by foreign investors does not necessarily measure the *net* influx of capital into that country. In addition, it must be noted that even if a country makes no investments abroad but merely constitutes an outlet for investments of foreign investors, there arises a current of interest and dividend payments, as well as of repayments of debt from the former country towards the latter ones, so that the *net* influx of capital is again smaller than the volume of new investments made.

On a national level a country needs foreign capital if its import requirements exceed its ability to provide an adequate *quid pro quo* in the form of exports. In a growing country, which needs an increasing amount of equipment, larger and more varied supplies of raw materials, and the services of foreign experts and technicians, and whose resources are not yet adequately developed to produce a volume of exports sufficient to pay for these imports, there will be felt a sustained need for foreign loans and for ownership-investments made by foreign capitalists. This need will be further increased owing to the growth of the national standards of living, because not only will the population consume more of the domestic output, thus restricting the volume of goods available for export, but there will be a gradual growth of imports for purposes of consumption. In addition to machinery and raw materials, an advancing country will start to import, e.g., oranges and bananas, coffee and cocoa, as well as radios, better quality textiles, watches, etc. These are familiar developments in the economic growth of free societies; a totalitarian society, on the other hand, may reduce imports of consumers' goods to a strict minimum, while expanding exports to the greatest possible extent, thus keeping low the national living standards in the interest of the growth of industrial capacity. Of course, even a totalitarian government may find it necessary to allow for a certain growth of standards of living in order to forestall popular discontent. It is important to realize, however, that the sooner standards of living are allowed to grow in an expanding "backward" country, involving a growth of imports of consumers' goods, the larger the volume of foreign capital will be required to achieve a certain level of industrialization.

In order that the economy of an underdeveloped country should successfully be built up, that country's capital imports must be regular and sustained, not occasional and intermittent. The achievement of such stability depends to a large extent upon the economic conditions in capital-exporting countries and the policies of their governments. In the interwar years, the spasmodic and unreliable character of capital movements has been the cause of much mischief, and debtor and creditor nations alike suffered greatly in consequence. How to achieve, in the future, a greater continuity in these transactions is one of the most serious long-range problems that confront the world economy at the present time. In the latter part of the nineteenth century and in the early part of the twentieth, there existed *de facto* a high degree of stability of international capital movements, a result of circumstances rather than of design; in the years ahead such stability as we shall achieve will have to be the outcome of carefully devised and well-executed policies.

Underdeveloped countries require, for their growth, an influx of foreign capital; there is no doubt whatever about it. But how are their needs to be satisfied? Why does capital move towards these areas of the globe? The private investor is often motivated by a desire to obtain raw materials; more generally, he is attracted by the anticipation of higher returns on his foreign investments than are obtainable in the domestic market. The more advantageous the conditions in the capital-importing country, the more eagerly private capital will come in. Governments of these countries can, by special measures, encourage foreign capitalists to move in, or again, by other measures, they can discourage their investments. In the past many special privileges were given to foreign investors and businessmen in countries which occupied a low level of economic development,

often without sufficient regard for the welfare of the local population. The "profit motive" was driven hard, leaving a legacy of
resentment and ill will. It would be wrong to say that this
"colonial" type of investment did no good to the countries into
which capital was imported; indeed, the groundwork was often
laid for their future growth. But the fact of paying inadequate
attention to the needs and living standards of the population, the
excessive "exploitation" by foreign capitalists brought forth a
reaction in the form of intense nationalism. In more recent years
many frictions developed and many discriminations came to be
practiced against foreign investors. Outbursts, such as the virtual
expropriation in Mexico of certain American oil interests or the
reaction in Poland against certain French investors, were, in the
thirties, an indication of the need for some "code of fair practices" applicable to foreign investments. During the last war,
the United States and Great Britain gave up the special privileges
("concessions") enjoyed by their businessmen in China. The
trend is now definitely away from "colonial exploitation." The
danger is that the pendulum may swing too far in the other direction and that nationalistic governments may practice discriminations against foreign nationals engaged in business—or
investing capital—in their country. A sound, but not entirely
adequate, principle, recently proclaimed by the China-America
Council of Commerce and Industry, is that "foreign private capital should be on the same basis as domestic private capital." [1]

A particular hazard to international investments arises from
the fact that governments can restrict the freedom of outgoing
movements of funds by the establishment of "exchange control." If a foreign capitalist invests money in Country X, he wants
to be free to use the income earned on that investment in any
way he likes. He may wish to re-invest it in Country X, or he may
want to spend or invest it in his own country or anywhere else
in the wide world. And the same applies to the proceeds of the
repayment (if the investment is made in the form of a loan), or
the liquidation or sale of the investment. Here the principle of
"equality of treatment," as formulated above, does not suffice.
Indeed, the fact that the residents of Country X cannot freely
transfer their funds abroad is no excuse for applying such re-

[1] *New Horizons for China Trade,* Annual Report of the China-America Council of
Commerce and Industry, Inc., for the fiscal year 1944–45 (New York, 1945), p. 43.

strictions on foreign payments to a foreign investor. A country which practices restrictions on foreign payments becomes therefore a doubtful outlet for the investments of foreign capitalists, and if, nevertheless, its government wants to attract capital from abroad, it must enter into special agreements by which the rights of the investor are safeguarded. This, too, is an area in which much work remains to be accomplished—unless, of course, we should witness in the future the restoration of a full freedom of international payments.

2.

In the past private capital has been the predominant source of foreign investments, and it is likely, in the future, to become again a very important factor in international financial operations. During the war years its role has been very small due to the magnitude of the amounts involved and of risks incurred, and this is carried over into the period of reconstruction. The International Bank for Reconstruction and Development is intended to provide a bridge between public and private investments through the instrumentality of loans given or guaranteed by this newly founded inter-governmental credit institute. It is conceivable that governmental guarantees given to private investments will be practiced also outside the Bank, thus helping the revival of private international capital movements. Only when the world is restored to a more settled economic and political life will large-scale private investments become possible without any public guarantee whatever. This will happen in some parts of the world earlier than in others; in a very few instances it is happening already. Countries that adopt full-fledged state-socialism or collectivism will remain, presumably, for good and all outside the orbit of private investments; with the spread of collectivism the scope of inter-governmental loans is correspondingly and permanently increased.

Private investment funds are derived from accumulated savings and from the operations of modern banking. Governments have two sources from which they can obtain means of extending foreign loans: taxation and borrowing. In practice the former method is not likely to be used. As to borrowing, we could distinguish between two further possibilities, one of which is again not likely to occur in practice: the government of Country A, in order to extend a loan to Country B, can either borrow from the inhabitants of B or from the government (or inhabitants) of another country, C. The second course would be adopted only under very particular circumstances. Normally, a government finances its foreign lending operations with funds borrowed in the domestic capital market. Hence, an increase of governmental foreign lending will generally be associated with a corresponding growth of the *domestic* public debt of the creditor country.

Unlike private investments, inter-governmental loans cannot be explained in terms of the "profit motive." Governments do not extend loans to one another for the sake of income. Other, very weighty considerations are the reasons for these loans (or for governmental guarantees given to privately issued loans); among them, the following are of particular importance:

1. The desire to assist a friendly country in its economic reconstruction (after a war or a natural cataclysm) and in its economic development. The motive may be entirely political, as in the case of loans given for the purpose of developing the military equipment or defenses of the borrowing country, or it may be a combination of political and economic considerations. The latter leads us to the next order of considerations.

2. The desire to create a foreign market for the production of the creditor country's industries. This may lead to the "tying" of the loan to commodity exports by the creditor country, i.e., the loan contract may include a provision which commits the debtor country to spending the proceeds of the loan within the creditor country. The economic significance of "tied loans" will be discussed later on; what needs stressing in the present context is the fact that such loans are given for the express purpose of stimulating exports. This is a factor of considerable practical importance in the discussions that are currently taking place in the United States on the subject of foreign investments.

3. The desire to promote in the world higher levels of economic activity and a larger volume of international trade. While the creditor country has every right to expect that under such circumstances its own exports will increase, its objectives are broader than merely to promote exports in the short run. A stable and growing world economy with a growing division of labor and an expanding volume of trade is an objective the at-

tainment of which can be greatly facilitated through a steady flow of capital from more advanced to less advanced areas of the world.[2] It is to be hoped that this consideration will exercise a great deal of influence on lending decisions of governments in the decades to come.

3.

Let us now trace the course of economic developments incident in international capital movements. Borrowers in Country A obtain funds in Country B from investors who buy bonds of companies of A issued in B, or lend money in some other form. The first thing that happens is that borrowers from A come into possession of bank balances in B, whereas B-investors acquire claims against individuals or corporations in A. The same happens if the loan takes place between governments. Still the same happens if there is no loan but an equity investment or a partnership investment or a "direct" investment. Of the three last-mentioned cases, one results in B-capitalists acquiring stock in A-companies, whilst these companies acquire balances in B-banks; the second in a B-capitalist becoming partner in a business located in A, that business acquiring funds in a B-bank; and the third in the establishment in Country A of a company (or branch office) owned and financed by B-capitalists with funds obtained and located in B.

In case the above should sound too abstract, let us assume that a Brazilian industrial concern borrows funds in the United States by issuing bonds through a New York house of investment bankers. The issue is sold to the American public and the Brazilian firm becomes owner of a hundred-thousand-dollar bank balance in one of the commercial banks of New York. All that happened so far is that American investors have acquired Brazilian industrial bonds and that the Brazilian concern who issued the bonds has acquired, from these American investors, a bank balance. The transaction results, first of all, in a change of ownership of the bank balances involved. What will the Brazilians do with their U. S. dollars? They can do one of three things—or all three of them:

---

2 Cf. Eugene Staley: *World Economic Development* (Montreal: International Labour Office, 1944).

1. They can buy equipment, etc., in the United States and ship it to Brazil. This will result in a further change of ownership of the bank balances—back into American hands—and in a movement of goods from the United States to Brazil. The capital transaction, in monetary terms, will thus give rise to a series of commercial transactions between the two countries.

2. They can buy other currencies with the dollars they own and spend the proceeds in other countries. Consequently, there will be a movement of goods from one or more countries outside the United States to Brazil. Since these foreign currencies will have been bought with U. S. dollars, the dollar balances in New York banks will have passed from Brazilian ownership to that of British, Swiss, or French capitalists. These can either use the dollars to buy goods in the United States, or they can sell them to importers of American goods, or they can hold on to them. If they hold the dollars they will, in effect, have extended to the United States a short-term loan,[3] and thus "cancel" the corresponding outflow of capital from the United States. To the extent to which the dollars *originally* borrowed by the Brazilian concern are *eventually* spent on goods, American exports will correspondingly increase.

3. They can sell the dollars to the central bank of Brazil or to other Brazilian businessmen and use the proceeds to buy goods and services in the Brazilian market. In that case there will be no immediate effect of the loan upon international trade. But, unless Brazilians hold on to dollar balances (thus extending, as it were, a short-term credit to the United States), the dollars will eventually either be spent by Brazilian importers of United States goods, or sold against other currencies as in the preceding case.

To sum up, the extension of a foreign loan will lead to one of three developments:

1. A corresponding increase of exports by the creditor country to the debtor country;

2. A corresponding increase of imports by the debtor country from the rest of the world, and an increase of exports by the creditor country to the rest of the world—the actual pattern of

---

[3] Actually, the dollar balances may be sold to central banks of the respective countries, and these banks will either hold them or sell them to importers or to persons who have other reasons to make payments in the United States.

these imports and exports being determined by a variety of circumstances. (If some foreign capitalists or central banks decide to hold increased balances of the creditor country's currency, there will be a correspondingly smaller increase in that country's exports.)

3. The proceeds of the loan may be sold to co-nationals of the borrowers or to the central bank of their country and may be kept idle in bank accounts.

The first of these possibilities increases bilateral trade between the creditor and the debtor country; the second increases multilateral world trade; the third amounts to a cancellation of the "capital movement" and leads to no commercial transactions. This last case has an important monetary significance because it results in increasing the foreign exchange reserves of the debtor country; some international loans are made for that purpose alone.[4]

When the loan contract obligates the borrower to spend the proceeds of the loan in the creditor country, we say that the loan is *tied*. "Tied loans" are the financial expression of "bilateralism" and form a part of the same system which includes bilaterally balanced barter-trade to which reference was made in the preceding chapter. The second of the three cases listed above, however, represents the financial counterpart of multilateral trade. In order to realize that case in practice, international payments must be free, i.e., balances must be freely convertible from one currency into another. In addition, in order to avoid frictions and losses, it is important that the exchange rates between the various national currencies, i.e., the ratios at which they exchange for one another, should be stable over a period of time. These two requirements, of free international payments and of stable exchange rates, can be satisfied by appropriate devices and policies the nature of which will be explored in the next chapter.

The foregoing analysis applies to all capital movements, whether they are the result of credit operations, of ownership-investments, or even of gifts. It follows from that analysis that capital movements, in the financial sense, unless reversed by

---

[4] It should be noted, however, that increasing foreign-exchange reserves of the central bank can lead to a monetary expansion in the debtor country thus increasing prices, and, in a roundabout way, to an increase of imports.

credit transactions in the opposite direction, become, sooner or later, translated into movements of goods between countries. We call this "translation" the *transfer* of international payments; it constitutes the economic consummation of the financial transactions—involving primarily changes in the ownership of bank deposits, accomplished under varying legal circumstances—which are generally known under the name of "capital movements." In the words of David Ricardo: "Our foreign expenditure is neither paid with gold nor with bill of exchange . . . it must eventually be discharged with the produce of the labour and industry of our people." [5] Attention should be called, in this quotation, to the word "eventually"; the process of transferring capital movements is neither automatic nor is it necessarily rapid, and in our times it frequently encounters difficulties on account of tariffs and other restrictions on international trade. When the system of multilateral settlements works smoothly, capital movements get transferred fairly easily; but when abuses of economic nationalism precipitated, in the thirties, the breakdown of that system, transfer became well-nigh impossible. "Bilateralism" was occasionally resorted to in order to break the deadlock.

4.

One of the most delicate international economic issues is that of the *repayment* of foreign loans. The wave of defaults that swept the world in the decade between the outbreak of the Great Depression in 1929 and the outbreak of World War II, has left bitter memories and has resulted in a rather excessive pessimism regarding international solvency. The view is frequently advanced that international loans are simply camouflaged gifts. This view, however, is very misleading. It is true that international loans have sometimes been defaulted on because they were unsound; but so have been some domestic loans. Or they have occasioned losses to the creditors because of business failures incident to a depression; but so have also many domestic loans. Or, finally, they have not been paid because of the breakdown of the system of multilateral settlements. This last point

5 "A Reply to Mr. Bosanquet's Observations on the Report of the Bullion Committee," 1811, para. 46 (Reprinted in *Economic Essays of David Ricardo*, edited by E. C. K. Gonner, London, 1926).

represents a characteristic risk of international investments. Reference was made before to the importance of free international payments and of stable currency relationships—these issues do not arise within a single country [6] and would not arise within a fully unified, free-trade world economy endowed with a single monetary system. In this sense—but in this sense alone—can Professor Buchanan's pessimistic query be justified: "Is it not possible that the process of capital accumulation with the help of foreign loans is inevitably tenuous by its very nature? . . . One wonders if there is not something in the very nature of capital accumulation with the assistance of foreign borrowing, something more fundamental, which tends to make large-scale defaults highly probable." [7]

In Professor Buchanan's opinion, international loans given for the purpose of industrial development are likely to end in defaults because they are too large compared with the export surplus which the debtor country might eventually be able to achieve. And, of course, the *final* repayment, the transfer in reverse, as distinct from payments made with the proceeds of new loans, can only be accomplished by means of export surpluses. "The game," Professor Buchanan goes on to say, "can continue to be played as long as new loans cloak the difficulty. But this is only another way of saying that debtors need never default as long as creditors are willing to advance them new loans to meet maturing obligations." [8] It would appear from the context that Dr. Buchanan has in mind the liquidation of indebtedness rather than the payment of interest charges. If he means the latter, the statement would be of very limited validity; in the former sense, however, it is very challenging, deserves careful consideration, and takes us straight into the heart of the problem of debt repayment.

Long-term loans can be paid off either with newly secured capital (borrowed or obtained on an ownership basis) or with the proceeds of the debtor's income-bearing operations. This is

---

[6] At least not in a free economy. In the totalitarian economies we have witnessed a suppression of monetary uniformity and of the freedom of payments within one and the same country. The case of Germany in the thirties is especially enlightening.

[7] Norman S. Buchanan: *International Investment and Domestic Welfare* (New York, 1945), pp. 115–6. This book is an important contribution to the understanding of the economics of international investment.

[8] Buchanan, op. cit., p. 116.

true of domestic loans as well as of international ones, though in case of the latter there also arises the before-mentioned transfer problem. If a concern reduces the scope of its "normal" operations,[9] it can reduce its capital without great difficulties. Apart from that case, however, a net reduction of a company's capital must lead to a liquidation of some of its assets and may easily end in default. The real difficulty referred to by Dr. Buchanan is due to the fact of financing capital investments through loans rather than on an ownership basis. The stock of a company is not repayable unless the company goes into liquidation; bonds are repayable—and if they have to be paid off net, this must be done by liquidating some assets, i.e., destroying the health of the company. Such liquidations are more likely to arise in international relations on account of political and psychological factors, but they can happen within the domestic economy as well. If they are to be avoided, new capital must be brought into the enterprise to take the place of the repaid loan. The continuity of the operations demands this maintenance of capital, and there surely need be nothing in it to either surprise or shock us.

So far we have been discussing the problem in terms of individual businesses, whereas Professor Buchanan treats it in terms of national units. Our argument must therefore be re-examined and supplemented. The maintenance of capital in a business financed by foreign funds does not necessarily require new *foreign* capital to take the place of repaid debts. From the point of view of an individual firm it is immaterial whether the new bondholders or stockholders are residents of the country or are foreigners; what matters alone is the terms on which the new funds are obtained. Not so, however, from the national point of view. If foreign loans are paid off with funds accumulated at home, there still remains a problem of foreign payments to be faced. As we have seen before, a *net* foreign payment can only be executed (i.e., transferred) by means of additional exports, or, more precisely, by an appropriate export surplus which can be obtained either by expanding exports or by contracting imports. Additional exports must be made available by domestic production and must be absorbed in foreign markets. In a system of multilateral settlements, this leads to world-wide commercial transactions, the final result of which is to increase the exports

[9] I.e., leaving aside the contraction of business during a depression.

of the country which makes the payments and to increase the imports of the country that receives them. Now if the transfers involved are very large as compared to the volume of "normal" trade of these countries, they may encounter great difficulties, leading to monetary breakdowns and to defaults. This is, presumably, what Dr. Buchanan has in mind when he writes that "perhaps what happens when countries pass through investment booms heavily financed by foreign borrowings is that the contributions to net exports almost inevitably tend to be too small relative to the remittances for which the country becomes obligated through its foreign borrowings. As a consequence default becomes inescapable." [10] If he speaks of interest payments, there is no necessity for the default if both creditor and debtor countries "play the game" properly; we shall revert to that point presently. But if what he has in mind is the repayment of the principal, then the whole foregoing chain of reasoning must be brought into the picture. A repayment of the principal is by no means necessary if dealing with countries as a whole, even though each individual loan must be repaid. It becomes necessary, however, when the continuity in foreign investments is broken and a sudden cessation of new lending occurs. Hence the importance of that continuity. The following statement by Dr. Rosenstein-Rodan is worthy of attention in this context:

"One point . . . may be mentioned where the economist frequently comes into conflict with the banker or 'finance man,' who does not think in terms of a country as a whole and who expects not only a yield on capital but also repayment of the capital. *The economist affirms that repayment of capital is utterly unnecessary.* Even if it could be arranged, it would constitute considerable waste. . . . The economic system does not permit a country to repay vast amounts of capital. . . . What really matters about a good investment is that it should pay a good dividend. Individual shareholders can, of course, sell their shares if somebody else acquires them. In the same way those countries which 'repaid' loans in the nineteenth century did so simply by getting new loans out of which the old ones were paid. When planning international investment we have only to ensure a guaranteed yield on capital invested, and need not worry about the repayment of capital." [11]

10 Buchanan, op. cit., p. 115.
11 P. N. Rosenstein-Rodan: "The International Development of Economically Backward Areas," London: *International Affairs*, vol. XX, No. 2 (April 1944), p. 162. (Italics added).

The italicized sentence considerably overstates the case by using the term, "utterly unnecessary," where all that need be said is that net repayment may result in great difficulties and that it may, therefore, be undesirable. Similarly, it is much too easy to say that we "need not worry about the repayment of capital": the lender of capital will always, most naturally, worry about that very matter! Dr. Rosenstein-Rodan's history of the repayment of loans should not stop with the end of the nineteenth century but continue into the twentieth: for in the past thirty years or so, as by-product, to be sure, of two wars, great amounts of indebtedness were paid off by the United States, Canada, India, etc.—and paid off with goods, not with proceeds of new loans.

Finally, and this is a very important point, the passage quoted mixes up loans with equity investments, interest with dividends. Interest can be guaranteed, dividends cannot. Equity investors do not expect repayment, bondholders do. If we want investors to drop the idea of capital repayment, we must urge them to buy stocks or to become partners in new or going businesses, and we must urge them also *not* to buy bonds and not to *lend* money in any form whatever. A loan contract provides for repayment; if we want to get rid of the *avoidable* perplexities and difficulties inherent in the repayment of capital, we must promote direct investment and equity investment instead of bonded and other debt.

That is the upshot of our argument—and it is a crucial conclusion. It must be regretted that the growth of state-socialistic economies and of inter-governmental credit transactions makes it very likely that these lessons of economic analysis, supported by practical experience, will probably be ignored in the years to come.

One further comment to complete the picture. Reference has been made before to loans made for political, rather than economic, reasons. Such loans evidently cannot be repaid without more or less serious difficulties. Mostly, they do not promote the economic growth of the debtor country, nor do they lead to an increase of its capacity to export; hence even the payment of interest on such loans may encounter considerable difficulties. It might therefore be suggested that outright *gifts* are generally preferable to purely political loans.

5.

Creditor and debtor countries must, as we said before, "play the game" properly. What this means is simply that the former countries must adopt policies favorable to a growth of imports, the latter—policies favorable to the development of exports. In the case of creditor countries (which means countries which have *net* foreign investments) this "rule" must be translated into the terms of tariff policy, etc. If the transfer of interest and dividend payments resulting from foreign investments is to be carried out without friction, the creditor country must be willing to accept more goods and services, including expenditures of its nationals traveling abroad, than it provides to the rest of the world.

As for the debtor countries, attention must be paid as to what kind of investment is financed with foreign capital. The best outlet for foreign capital is investment in production and communications which leads to a growth of exports from the debtor country. Nineteenth century investors were more aware of this than our contemporaries, and their investments led to a greater expansion of the debtor country's exports than did the investments made in the 1920's. When investments are purely private, it is up to the investor to watch the situation and to refuse loans for the unsound kind of ventures. Actually, there are ventures which are entirely appropriate from a domestic investment point of view, yet would not be fitting objects for the investment of foreign capital: e.g., residential building. On the other hand the opening up of mines, the improvement of roads leading to plantations of exportable produce, *certain* power developments, railroads, etc., all of these are appropriate objects for foreign investment because they increase the ability of the country to produce, trade, and export. These may be long-term ventures; what matters are exports which will be possible once the "backward" areas have grown and developed. There are many export articles which cannot be planned for, of course, but others can be anticipated and promoted. In our day, when government planning has acquired a growing importance in this field of economic development, government plans must take the commercial counterpart of financial transactions very seriously into consideration. There is no international SEC to protect the investors-to-be from unsound schemes; it may be that some such agency will have to be eventually devised. We have recently acquired, however, with the establishment of the International Bank for Reconstruction and Development, an institution which can afford, in the years to come, a good deal of guidance on the subject of international investment outlets.

It is highly desirable that some future world economic conference should deal with the question of formulating an international convention in which the broad policy obligations of debtor and creditor nations alike would be set out. Such a convention, along with one concerning trade practices and one dealing with the conduct of monetary relations, would establish the groundwork for a smoothly operating world economy.

The International Bank for Reconstruction and Development, first proposed by the United States in November 1943,[12] was brought to the blueprint stage at the Bretton Woods Conference of July 1944 and came formally into being at the end of December 1945. The reasons for its establishment were set out in the following terms in the preamble of the U. S. Treasury proposals:

"The provision of foreign capital will be one of the important international economic and financial problems of the post-war period. Many countries will require capital for reconstruction, for the conversion of their industries to peace-time needs, and for the development of their productive resources. . . . Even in the early post-war years it may be hoped that a considerable part of the capital for international investment will be provided through private investment channels. It will undoubtedly be necessary, however, to encourage private investment by assuming some of the risks that will be especially large immediately after the war and to supplement private investment with capital provided through international co-operation." While the proposal stemmed from the concern over post-war reconstruction, the Bank[13] was proposed "as a permanent institution to encourage and facilitate investments for sound and productive purposes."

The Bank is an entirely new departure in the field of international finance, a co-operative scheme for mutual credit-aid

[12] *Preliminary Draft Outline of a Proposal for a Bank for Reconstruction and Development of the United and Associated Nations,* U. S. Treasury Department, November 24, 1943.

[13] We shall henceforth refer to the International Bank for Reconstruction and Development as "the Bank."

and credit-guarantee of its members. It is, in part, a long-term credit institute, in part an agency to guarantee the interest and amortization payments on loans issued with the Bank's approval in the free capital markets. Its charter is incorporated in the agreements reached at the Bretton Woods Conference.[14] The capital of the Bank has been set at ten billion dollars of which 9.1 billion has been allocated to governments of countries represented at the conference. Twenty per cent of the Bank's capital is to be paid in;[15] the remaining eighty per cent is to serve as a guarantee fund and will be called only when the Bank has to fulfill obligations resulting from its guarantees. As an institution dealing in a great many currencies, the Bank requires a high degree of international monetary stability; its membership has therefore been restricted to countries which belong to the International Monetary Fund.[16] The Bank is an inter-governmental institution and is going to transact its business through the treasuries, central banks, and other such public bodies of the member-states.

We need not enter here into the purely technical and administrative aspects of the Bank.[17] Its purpose is to facilitate the access to investment funds for war-torn and underdeveloped countries. The Bank is not going to provide "venture capital" for the financing of very risky projects; it is likely to be cautious in its decisions. The following excerpt from Article I of its charter gives a clear idea of the scope of its future operations. Besides other, more general objectives, it is the Bank's purpose:[18]

"To promote private foreign investment by means of guarantees or participations in loans and other investments made by private investors; and when private capital is not available on reasonable terms, to supplement private investment by providing, on suitable conditions, finance for productive purposes out of its own capital, funds raised by it, and other resources."

[14] Cf. United Nations Monetary and Financial Conference, Bretton Woods, N. H., July 1 to July 22, 1944, *Final Act and Related Documents*. Washington: Department of State Publication 2187, pp. 68–97.

[15] Two per cent is to be paid in within sixty days of the beginning of the Bank's operations in gold or U. S. dollars; eighteen per cent is to be called later and will be payable in the currency of the member states.

[16] See Chapter III, section 7.

[17] See M. A. Heilperin: *International Monetary Reconstruction: the Bretton Woods Agreements* (New York: American Enterprise Association, 1945), pp. 54–61.

[18] *Articles of Agreement on the International Bank for Reconstruction and Development*, Article I (ii). Cf. "Final Act and Related Documents," op. cit.

The phrase "when private capital is not available on *reasonable* terms" and, later, the words "on *suitable* conditions" open a very interesting line of speculation. The management of the Bank will have the right to determine which terms available in the private capital market are "reasonable" and what are "suitable" terms to be offered by the Bank itself. If it proceeds wisely and advisedly, it will be able to normalize capital-market conditions and to discourage certain past abuses. It will also make it easier for less economically developed countries to obtain access to capital on terms comparable to those at which it is available, in the free market, to borrowers in more advanced countries (whose credit standing is better established). The Bank can finance projects both private and public, but the former must have the approval of the respective national governments.

Among the Bank's operations, guaranteeing of loans approved by the Bank but issued in the free market will initially be secondary to the extension of loans with its own funds or with funds borrowed by the Bank in the open market and re-lent by it. If a default should occur on a loan guaranteed by the Bank, the debt service will be carried out by that institution until the debtor resumes payments. All member-states will participate in these payments made by the Bank in proportion to their holdings of the Bank's shares. Thus the risks of the investors are spread among all the members of the Bank. For the United States this is a very important point, since, for years to come, the American public will be by far the largest body of investors in the world. This mutual guarantee system is the greatest innovation the Bank has brought into the field of international finance. The scope of that institution is, of course, rather limited, compared to the volume of international investment in prosperous periods of the past decades; if the Bank proves to be successful, however, its scope may be expanded.

The fact that loans made under the Bank's auspices will only be granted after very careful study of the project and after getting the best available expert advice will do more than safeguard these particular investments. It will, most likely, create a precedent and establish standards that will exercise a great deal of influence on international loans granted outside of the Bank, improving their economic soundness.

CHAPTER III

Monetary Relations between Nations

INTERNATIONAL MONETARY RELATIONS parallel, in part, relations that exist within one country. As in the case of trade, inter-regional relations have much in common with international ones; indeed, the latter are a special case of the former. Day in and day out, many transactions take place which involve payments from one part of the United States to another. As a result of these payments, the geographical distribution of money changes all the time. Owing to the fact that each locality has incoming as well as outgoing payments, only the *net* balance needs to be actually paid—and elaborate clearing arrangements reduce the actual payments to these *net* balances. The total amount of money in circulation is regulated by the Federal Reserve authorities (or, in other countries by the central banks), and, in part, by the Treasury. Normally, there is a uniform monetary circulation in a country, and money can move freely from place to place and from bank account to bank account.

The money supply of every single locality increases or decreases according to the *net* result of all the transactions carried out by its residents with people living somewhere else. Bank statistics and statistics of privately held notes and coin could reveal how, on each day, the monetary situation of that community has changed. But such statistics are never compiled for single towns or cities and hardly ever for single states. Actually, they are of no particular interest except to the student; the geographical distribution of money follows the changing pattern of business and is a passive, not an active, element in the situation. This is so because the country has a uniform monetary system as well as national agencies responsible for the shaping of monetary policies and for the maintenance of smoothly operating facilities for inter-regional payments. It also ties in with the existence within the country of freedom of trade, of an advanced division of labor, and of what we called in Chapter I a system of multilateral settlements.

As we move from inter-regional to international payments the factor of political boundaries acquires very much importance. There would be no scope for the discussions that follow if the world were organized into one single state, nor, indeed, if the various political entities into which our planet is divided entertained no commercial or financial relations with one another. Since, however, the realities of the world lie in between these two extreme conditions, we must now explore the mechanism of international payments, that is to say payments which involve more than one country and more than one currency.

The first thing to emphasize in that connection is that modern means of payment—notes and demand deposits in banks—are usually acceptable only in the country of their origin. Dollar notes and dollar deposits can, under normal circumstances, buy goods and services only in the United States; French francs, notes, and deposits can only be so used in France, etc. It is true that notes of a certain country may enjoy so much confidence among the population of another country that they will be accepted as a means of payment *de facto,* even though they are not the legal currency of that country. This happens at times of monetary inflations when the population loses confidence in its national currency. But these are exceptional cases; we note their existence but will concentrate on the more typical situation.

In the most general case—that of each country having its own national currency unrelated to currencies of other countries—payments between countries will lead to the purchase of one currency in terms of another. Each currency (notes and bank deposits transferable by check) can buy goods and pay debts only in its own country of origin. Therefore people in Country A will only acquire the amounts of Country B's money which they need to execute their payments in B. These payments are the result of all the commercial and financial transactions taking place between the residents and governments of these countries. Each country—and for simplicity's sake we shall assume, to begin with, that there are only two countries in existence—has its own monetary unit. We call *rate of exchange* the price of one unit of one currency expressed in terms of the other currency. Thus if you have to pay *four* B francs for *one* A dollar, the rate of exchange is four to one for the dollar, or, reciprocally, one quarter to one for the franc. The rate of exchange, as every other price, is determined by supply and demand conditions in foreign exchange markets, and these, in turn, result from the scope of commercial and financial operations between countries.

Whenever all the outgoing payments of a country exceed its incoming payments, there will be a relative superabundance of its currency in foreign exchange markets, and its "price" will fall. In the contrary case, there will be a relative scarcity of that currency and its "price" will go up. When incoming and outgoing payments balance, the rate of exchange remains stable. Any program aiming at exchange stability must therefore provide a means of keeping incoming and outgoing payments of the various countries balanced, which can be accomplished in different ways. Without a stabilizing "mechanism," exchange rates between currencies would be subject to more or less considerable day-to-day fluctuations since, in practice, the payments of a country are never balanced on any one day. There might be large seasonal fluctuations, if a country's exports take place only during certain parts of the year, while her imports are spread more evenly (or the other way around). If prices are moving up in one country and not in the other, the rate of exchange of the first country in terms of the second will decline, and it will go up in the contrary case. The reason for it is simple: were the rate to remain stable for a time, in spite of divergent price movements in the two countries, exports of A would decline because, due to the rise of prices in A, they would become more and more expensive to buyers in B. On the other hand, buyers in A would find B products increasingly attractive (because prices in B are assumed to be stable or even declining). A's imports would therefore increase. As a result A's payments *to* B would increase and its receipts *from* B would decline, and under these circumstances exchange stability cannot be maintained. So long as domestic prices in A and B move in different directions, the rates at which their currencies barter for one another will be continuously altered. This will happen even if they move in the same direction but with varying intensity, when, for example, there is a mild price increase in one country and a considerable increase in the other. Leaving aside both small price fluctuations, which in practice would not matter very much, and very large inflations (due, e.g., to war), we find that the large-scale, sustained price movements are a feature of the so-called "business cycle." Without entering here into an extended technical discussion, let us emphasize the fact, borne out by experience and accounted for by theory, that the maintenance of long-run stability in foreign exchange rates depends upon the existence in the various countries of a similar pattern of business cycle developments. We speak then of a "synchronization" or "co-ordination" of business cycles. Within one and the same country this is accomplished inter-regionally by the effect of a single monetary system, of free trade, and free payments. Internationally, the problem presents serious difficulties and its solution is among the major items on the postwar agenda of world economic organization.

2.

If we allow for exchange-rate fluctuations, a country's foreign payments are always in balance through the simple expedient of exchange-rate adjustments. Should it be desired, however, to maintain stable exchange rates between the various national currencies, then there must be in existence an internationally acceptable instrument of payments by means of which the country having a "deficit" can settle her accounts. The most widely used instrument of that kind has always consisted of precious metals, especially of gold. Monetary mechanisms, which will presently be described, facilitate these settlements of international accounts; once the "deficit" is paid, accounts balance. A country having a "deficit" in her foreign payments can resort, of course, to various policies aiming at the restoration of equilibrium. These are policies aiming at an expansion of exports or a reduction of imports; policies aimed at attracting foreign short-term funds and policies favoring the inflow of foreign (long-term) capital. If the payments deficit is purely temporary, short-term credits obtained abroad may be sufficient to bridge the gap. An increase of rates of interest in the deficitary country, when conditions of confidence are favorable, will be sufficient to attract such funds; or another way of securing them may be designed, such as the International Monetary Fund which came into being at the end of 1945. If the deficit is due to a "chronic" import surplus connected with the economic development of the country, the situation can best be helped by an influx of foreign capital, along the lines presented in Chapter II. Finally, if the deficit is the result of lasting changes in the economic environment (such as the loss of certain export markets due to new inventions replacing the previously exported product) or lasting changes in the international flow of investment funds, a change in the structure of foreign trade will provide the only means of restoring equilibrium in the country's balance of payments.

In the last-named case, a country may seek an expansionist or a restrictionist solution, the former involving a growth of exports, the latter a decline in imports. The availability of the expansionist solution depends upon the commercial policies of other countries; in a free-trade world that solution would be by far the most frequently used, while in a tariff-ridden world it often remains beyond the realm of practical policy. The policy of restricting imports can, of course, be controlled by the country itself; and the "protection" of the balance-of-payments equilibrium is the real or alleged reason for many import restrictions and limitations of foreign payments. Exchange control, a powerful weapon of modern economic nationalism, is usually first introduced to "protect" the balance of payments.

In this connection a most important cause of disequilibrium in international payments enters the picture. It is the so-called "flight of capital" or "hot money." It may happen that a crisis of confidence develops with respect to the currency of some country, due to political or social developments, or to economic difficulties. Protracted payment difficulties or a progressive depreciation of the foreign-exchange value of the currency may also end in a crisis of confidence. When this happens, there is a widespread desire to sell large amounts of that currency against foreign currencies enjoying a higher degree of confidence. The result is a large supply of the "distrusted" currency at a time when the demand for it is limited by the volume of regular payments foreigners have to make in the country undergoing the crisis. Clearly, this leads to a most serious disturbance of the balance-of-payments equilibrium. There arises a great temptation to check the crisis by restricting the freedom of exchange transactions so that people who wish to sell the currency they no longer trust should be unable to do so. This involves a prohibition on the export of notes, and a licensing system for the purchase of foreign exchange, along with the centralization of all such dealing under the authority of a government agency. Whenever *exchange control* is thus established, it tends to be applied to all foreign payments, not only to the above mentioned transactions.

The term "capital flight" is, of course, a misnomer. Money does not actually leave the country, except for minor transfers of notes. It remains on deposit accounts with domestic banks. What does happen, however, is a wave of transfers of ownership; the deposits change hands. And, as this involves transfers of domestic balances to new owners residing abroad, against payment in the form of foreign balances, the foreign-exchange market gets into the picture and exchange rates are affected, often, as we know, in a very serious manner. When, for example, New Yorkers sell their balances in New York banks against balances in San Francisco banks, nothing further happens (except for a possible movement of bank reserves from the one city to the other) because the United States has a single monetary system. But if New York and California had different monetary units and separate monetary systems, such a wave of transfers of property rights would result in depreciation of the New York dollar as against the dollar of California. Internationally, this phenomenon has played a disastrous role in the thirties and represents a major source of concern for the future. The new international monetary arrangements agreed upon at Bretton Woods include measures to deal with such emergencies.

"Capital flights" (as we shall go on calling them, this usage being too generally accepted to be subject to change) are fed, in part, by the activities of speculators. Whenever foreign-exchange stability breaks down, speculators step into the picture and their operations aggravate the crisis. This is one of the main arguments to be advanced against the schemes of "flexible" or freely fluctuating rates of exchange as have been advocated by certain writers [1] as a method of maintaining equilibrium in balances of payments. An *assured* stability of exchange rates, safeguarded by institutional arrangements and appropriate policies, is the most effective way of discouraging this kind of speculation; more generally, it makes capital flights less likely to happen by strengthening the confidence of the public in the currency. Stability of exchange rates is a very fundamental factor in the establishment

[1] See Charles R. Whittlesey: *International Monetary Issues* (New York, 1937).

of an environment favorable to the steady growth of multilateral trade between nations and of foreign investments. International agreements on monetary policy implemented by appropriate institutional arrangements create monetary unity where otherwise diversity reigns supreme; by that means they go a long way towards overcoming the monetary consequences of the division of the world into politically "sovereign" states and bring us as close to a unified world currency as we can get under prevailing conditions.

3.

The incoming and outgoing payments of a country are—in a free economy—the result of thousands of individual transactions and decisions. They hardly ever balance from day to day, but, as we have seen, they must of necessity balance over longer periods of time. "Of necessity," because, as we have seen, equilibrium is always eventually reached through exchange-rate adjustments, through other "corrective" transactions, or through movements of precious metals which are internationally acceptable as means of settling accounts. The unbalancing and balancing of a country's foreign payments take place continuously, day after day.[2] Because, however, balance-of-payments difficulties affect monetary stability and thereby influence the country's foreign trade and finance, it is useful to get as much information as possible about the country's foreign transactions. In consequence of collecting that information, annual summaries are being drawn up which present at a glance the incoming and outgoing payments of the country during a past calendar year. The assumption is made that during such a span of time payments get into balance; an assumption which is not unreasonable since the balancing process is continuous. To illustrate the argument of this chapter, we quote below the principal balance-of-payments figures for the United States for the years 1928, the year preceding the outbreak of the great depression, and 1938, the year preceding the outbreak in Europe of World War II.

[2] Except in an economy in which all foreign transactions are strictly controlled by the State and are often carefully planned ahead of time. This generally goes hand in hand with "bilateral" settlements of accounts.

This table is based on material prepared in the Bureau of Foreign and Domestic Commerce of the Department of Commerce.

BALANCE OF PAYMENTS OF THE UNITED STATES, 1928 AND 1938

(in millions of dollars)

	1928		1938	
I Current trade transactions		+707		+942
Merchandise trade (net)	+1,037		+1,134	
Service items (a) (net)	—330		—192	
II Long-term capital movements		—546		+328
Net movements of principal	—847		+97	
Net interest and dividend payments (b)	+647		+384	
Personal and institutional remittances (b)	—346		—153	
III Short-term credit transactions (net)		—348		+344
IV Gold and silver movements (net)		+291		—1,863
Gold	+272		—1,657	
Silver (b)	+19		—206	
V Unexplained items		—104		+249
		0		0

(a) Including: shipping and freight, travel expenditures, government expenditures.

(b) These items are classified by the Department of Commerce in Category I together with "service items," under the general heading of "Other Current Transactions."

Source: Hal B. Lary: *The United States in the World Economy,* Washington: U. S. Department of Commerce, 1943.

Several comments on the above are indicated. Group V, called "unexplained items," is a balancing item included in order to allow for all the unrecorded payments and for all the errors in estimates, on the assumption, explained above, that the balance of payments actually *balances.* A certain amount of short-term credit operations often escapes the recorder's eye and the same is true of certain tourist expenditures.

It will be noted that gold and silver movements are the prime factor in keeping accounts balanced when exchange rates are stable (as is here the case). The reader will discover, no doubt, that incoming payments are marked with a "plus" sign and outgoing payments with a "minus" sign. Thus a country's imports are a "minus" item, and exports a "plus" item—by which no value judgment is intended, mercantilists old and new notwithstanding! Since incoming gold is an import item and outgoing gold an export item, they are designated respectively with a "minus" and a "plus" sign; this is entirely logical but it may at first surprise the reader who may be thinking of gold as money and not as merchandise. Thus in 1928 payments were kept in balance with the help of an outflow of gold and silver amounting to nearly three hundred million dollars, while in 1938 the United States accepted in excess of eighteen hundred million dollars worth of precious metals, having securely bolted her door to increased merchandise imports.

As we are concerned in the present context with international payments, we have provided in the table data relating to *net* payments resulting from each of the main groups of transactions. In both years the United States had an export surplus of merchandise and an import surplus of services. In 1928 this country was an *exporter* of capital, on long-term and on short-term account, to the tune of close to nine hundred million dollars. In 1938 there was a net *influx* into the United States of funds amounting to nearly seven hundred million dollars. It is the change, between 1928 and 1938, in the short-term credit transactions which is particularly striking; it was due very largely to the "flight of capital" from Europe, i.e., the acquisition by foreigners of balances in American banks, and to the influx of gold into America's "safe-keeping."

Short-term credit transactions fall into three main categories which unfortunately, cannot be the object of precise statistical estimates: (a) credit transactions which are a corollary of trade and investment operations (commercial credits, unspent proceeds of new loans, etc.); (b) credit transactions induced by increases in the rate of interest for the purpose of bringing the balance of payments into equilibrium; and (c) "hot money" or the proceeds of capital flights. Whereas the first two groups are economically very beneficial, the third group is, as we know, very disturbing and undesirable. Future arrangements with respect to monetary relations between nations will have to encourage the first two brands of short-term credit transactions, while discouraging the third kind.

4.

Exchange-rate stability is important, as has been emphasized above, from the point of view of both international trade and international finance. That importance is greatest, contrary to popular opinion, from the long-run point of view. In the short-run it is possible to make certain safeguarding arrangements. An importer can buy the foreign currencies he will eventually need to pay for the imported merchandise at the time of placing the order; he may buy them in a "forward" market, i.e., for future delivery, thus saving himself the need of an immediate outlay on his part. A borrower abroad on short-term may also use the "forward" market as a means of safeguarding himself (or "hedging") against an increase in the exchange value of the currency he will eventually need to settle his debt.

In the long run, however, such "hedging" is of no avail. As regards current trade, this is a short-term transaction and therefore fairly immune to exchange fluctuations. But the international division of labor and the regional (and national) specialization of production is a long-run proposition. Changes in technology, new discoveries, rising standards of living, new needs, and changes in tastes, all of these affect the channels of trade and the structure of production in individual areas and countries. Such changes represent modifications in the *basic* conditions among which economic life operates and to which it must always adapt itself. Indeed, the resistance to such adaptation, "insensitiveness to the necessity for structural adjustment," as Professor Allan G. B. Fisher calls it,[3] can be the source of considerable economic disturbances and produce, all by itself, "quite a tidy series of depressions."[4]

Now this need for adaptation and the resistance to adaptation are difficult enough to cope with in practical economic policy without aggravating the problem through monetary instability. Fundamentally, changes in the structure of production and in

---

[3] Allan G. B. Fisher: *Economic Progress and Social Security* (London, 1945), p. 239.
[4] Ibid., p. 240. This has been, according to Professor Fisher, an important factor in the grave economic disturbances of the inter-war period. See below, Chapter IX.

the currents of trade are made necessary by the changes in costs and prices which result from the previously mentioned circumstances. But a change in ratio at which one currency exchanges for another, when this change is durable or cumulative rather than to be a mere momentary oscillation, modifies cost and price relations between the two economic territories. Some product produced in Country A may be sold in B at a competitive price when one A dollar sells for four B francs; when the B currency depreciates, however, and one A dollar now costs eight B francs but prices in B have not risen in the same proportion, the product previously exported from A to B becomes too expensive for B residents and cannot be sold there in the former quantities. Or again, after the depreciation of its currency, B's exporters may be able to greatly expand their sales in A of some particular commodity, thus leading to the growth, in B, of the corresponding industry. Note that in either case nothing has changed in the basic economic conditions—only the rates of exchange have changed—and yet the structure of industries in the two countries and the structure of trade between them have been altered. This alteration may not last—exchange rates may, after a time, move in the opposite direction. But the harm would have been done: the destruction of an industry in one country, the expansion of an industry in the other country, both in response to ephemeral changes in exchange rates, not to changes in basic economic conditions.

Advocates of "flexible" exchanges answer the foregoing argument by indicating that the exchange-rate fluctuations are themselves due to changes in basic economic conditions, that they are merely corrective measures. This *may* be the case, but experience shows that it is *not always* the case. An alteration of long-range exchange rates between currencies, or in *parities,*[5] is necessary, broadly speaking, in two cases: (1) when there are some fundamental changes in the economic situation of one or both of these countries due to technological factors, to cataclysmic wars, etc.; and (2) when these countries practice divergent price policies and dissynchronize their business-cycle developments. Now the first case is not very frequent in peace times and can be dealt with, whenever it arises, with the help of international agencies; as we shall see presently, the recently established International

---

[5] Leaving aside short-term oscillations around a parity.

Monetary Fund provides an excellent instrument of handling such emergencies. As for the second case, it raises a very serious issue, that of economic nationalism and internationalism. Exchange stability, based as it is on an international co-ordination of business-cycle policies and on an international integration of business-cycle developments, is a postulate of economic internationalism. Exchange "flexibility," on the other hand, going hand in hand with the "insulation" of a country's domestic economic developments from those of other countries, is the expression, in the monetary field, of economic nationalism. And, as will be shown later, whenever economic nationalism turns to stable exchanges, it seeks that stability not by means of international mechanisms and agreements, but by means of independently planned national exchange controls.

The lack of stability in exchange relations between national currencies, of which we have seen the disturbing effect on the international division of labor and on currents of international trade, exercises an equally disturbing influence upon capital movements. The existence of a common monetary unit is a factor of greatest importance in the financial contracts within a country; internationally the nearest approximation to it is a system of stable exchange rates. In the absence of such stability, short-term credit transactions expand, to be sure, by the effect of speculation and "capital flights": the more uncertainty and instability there is, the "hotter" money becomes. But, at the same time, long-term investments decline because of new factors of risk connected with exchange instability. Even a threat of depreciation acts as a deterrent to the bona fide investor in foreign securities; what is needed in order to create the necessary confidence is the establishment of trusted agencies for the maintenance of international monetary stability. As we have seen in the preceding chapter, the foreign investor is interested, in addition, in the freedom of international payments. Capital is loath to move into a country which is made through payments' restrictions into a "capital trap." Hence exchange stability obtained by means of exchange control is inadequate to meet the requirements of foreign investment.[6]

The reasons why the foreign investor requires long-term ex-

---

[6] At least of *private* foreign investment: it may not interfere with inter-government loans, especially if given for political reasons.

change stability are almost too evident to require a detailed explanation, but it may be well to note that such stability is also very important from the point of view of the debtor. What is important for the creditor, is the maintenance of value of his investment (and of the income derived from it) in terms of his currency; the debtor is interested, on the other hand, in the amount of the commitment in terms of *his* currency. Whenever the relationship between the two currencies changes, one or the other of the two parties is likely to suffer a loss. For the creditor it would be a straight loss, for the debtor an increase of the financial burden in terms of his own currency.

The balance of this chapter will be devoted to a discussion of three methods of securing exchange stability: the internationalist gold standard, the nationally planned exchange control, and the new system worked out at Bretton Woods, which represents a move in the direction of internationalism made in the environment of a highly nationalistic world.

5.

To give an adequate account of the origins, functioning, and disintegration of the gold standard would require several substantial volumes.[7] In the framework of the present inquiry it will be sufficient, however, to indicate broadly the main features of that monetary system, once so unquestioningly accepted, later—and now—so bitterly controverted. The gold standard is of interest to us here as a method of keeping international balances of payments in equilibrium and, thereby, maintaining the stability of foreign-exchange rates. It came into being quite spontaneously, was developed and safeguarded by design, and crumbled under the impact of World War I, never to be fully revived again. Two principal conditions made the existence of the gold standard possible: 1) the growth of world trade and of foreign investments within the framework of free markets, the prevalence of multilateral settlements of international accounts,

[7] The reader may find the following books of interest: Sir T. E. Gregory: *The Gold Standard and Its Future* (London, 1934); E. W. Kemmerer: *Gold and the Gold Standard* (New York, 1945); Leo Pasvolsky: *The Necessity for a Stable International Monetary Standard* (Paris: International Chamber of Commerce, 1933); W. A. Brown, Jr.: *The International Gold Standard Reinterpreted, 1914–1934*, 2 vols. (New York, 1940).

and the steady confidence existing throughout the largest part of the world; 2) the fact that the national monetary systems of most economically advanced countries were linked to gold.

The development of banking methods in the eighteenth and nineteenth centuries reduced the role of metallic currency as compared to paper currency; later on, bank deposits (transferable by check) became, in some of the countries, the leading means of payment. Still, the unfortunate experiences with nonconvertible money during and after the Napoleonic Wars led to the restoration of a link between precious metals (gold and silver) and bank notes and deposits. London was in the nineteenth and early twentieth centuries the leading financial center of the world and England was on the gold standard. This no doubt contributed to the spread of the system. England was then a great import market for raw materials and other goods, an important supplier of manufactured goods and of shipping, banking, and insurance services, a leader in the free-trade movement, and a great investor of capital throughout the world. All of this was of great importance in the development of the international gold standard.

A country has a gold-standard currency if the "gold contents" of its monetary unit is defined by law and if there is a free gold market in which gold can be bought and sold against national currency. The former is the basic feature of the system, and it means that the price of gold is fixed by law and kept stable through the operations of the central bank or treasury. The free market for gold (i.e., the free convertibility of currency into gold and of gold into currency at the stated price) is a method of keeping the price of gold stable. From an international point of view what matters most is the freedom of gold imports and gold exports and the unrestricted access to gold for export purposes. Now, if the price of an ounce of gold is legally fixed in terms of each of several currencies and if gold can move freely from one country to another, there develops a very neat and useful method for setting the exchange rates between the various currencies. Since an ounce of gold costs, say, twenty-five dollars in Country A and one hundred francs in Country B, it follows that twenty-five dollars of A equals one hundred francs of B. This gives us the rate of four francs to one dollar as the mint *par* or *parity* between the two currencies. It will now be shown that so long as both countries remain on the gold standard and maintain their statutory price for gold, actual rates of exchange will remain in the close neighborhood of the parity.

Let us assume that there is a temporary deficit in the balance of payments of Country B. If nothing else happens, the rate of exchange will fall and it will become necessary to pay for one hundred dollars not four hundred francs but, say, four hundred and twenty francs. If both countries are on the gold standard, however, it will be possible for persons in B who have payments to make in A to buy and ship gold instead of buying balances of A-currency at their increased price. Now to ship gold from place to place costs freight and insurance charges; these will be different between any two points on the globe. Let us assume that in our case the cost involved amounts to one per cent of the value of gold shipped. To pay one hundred dollars in form of gold will then cost four hundred and four francs. This is more than the parity of four hundred but less than the four hundred and twenty francs, which would have had to be paid if there were no means of payment common to both countries. It might happen that it is A which has a deficit in her balance of payment; the cost of shipping gold from A to B being again one per cent, residents of A will have to pay one hundred and one dollars for four hundred francs (which corresponds to *about* three hundred and ninety-six francs for one hundred dollars).

As long as fluctuations in exchange rates remain within the limits of 3.96 to 4.04 francs to the dollar, payments will be made by means of foreign notes or bank balances. Once these limits are reached, gold movements will start instead. Thus the rate of 4.20 referred to before could not be actually quoted because there would be no quotation higher than 4.04. That rate will be quoted throughout the whole period of gold outflow from B to A. When the deficit in the balance of payments disappears (because of expanded exports, reduced imports, or financial operations), the rate of exchange will fall below 4.04 and the outflow of gold will stop. Let us assume that the improvement is so considerable that it is now A that has to pay more money to B than it receives. Then the rate of exchange will fall to 4.0 and below, until it reaches the level of about 3.96. At that moment a gold inflow from A to B will start, and while it lasts, the rate will remain at the 3.96 level. We call these two "critical" rates the *gold points;* the higher one is the *gold export point,* the lower, the *gold import point;* they represent the limits of admissible fluctuations in rates of exchange and the extent of achieved stability.[8]

Under the international gold standard, movements of gold have two principal functions: one is to serve notice of a balance-of-payments disequilibrium; the other is to keep exchanges stable for the time being, pending the correction of that disequilibrium. It may be that the unbalance is simply due to the fact that receipts and payments are not synchronized, so that at certain times there appears a deficit, at other times a surplus. This is the most frequent source of exchange fluctuations, and the existence of an internationally acceptable means of payment—gold—[9] makes it possible to keep exchanges stable in spite of this lack of synchronization between a country's receipts and its payments. A second corrective factor—and a very important one—consists of short-term credit transactions. Under the unwritten "rules" of the gold standard, the central bank of a country steadily losing gold would increase its discount rate, which would be followed by an increase of the rate of interest paid by commercial banks on demand deposits. A lowering of rates would take place in countries steadily receiving gold. These "differential" movements of interest rates would—under conditions of general confidence—lead to the acquisition of balances in the gold-losing country by foreigners eager to obtain a better yield on their funds. Many of these transactions would take place between banks and might involve considerable amounts. These credit operations would, of course, reduce the required volume of gold movements. Adequate statistical studies are still lacking, but it is more than likely that these international "movements" of short-term balances played a very important (and frequently underrated) role in the functioning of the gold standard.

A much more publicized and much less important feature of the gold standard mechanism consists of domestic price move-

[8] We are using, as an example, the case of only *two* countries, but the argument can be easily generalized to *many* countries. Under conditions of multilateral settlement, what must balance is not payments between A and B, but between A and the rest of the world.

[9] Or, more generally, of *international reserves,* of which gold is a particular instance. As we shall see later, there can be various kinds of such reserves.

ments taking place in response to the outflow and inflow of gold. The theoretical argument concerning these price movements runs along the following lines: the central bank of the gold-losing country increases its discount rate and restricts its note circulation;[10] this contraction of money in circulation, accentuated through the operations of the banking system, results in a price deflation; this in turn stimulates exports and restricts imports of the gold-losing country; and so, in the end, the balance is not only restored, but receipts exceed payments and gold pours back into the country. The opposite course of events is supposed to take place in the country receiving gold.

This argument, which we have stripped of its many elaborations and refinements, is at the basis of the widely held view that the operation of the gold standard required periodic deflations and inflations in the countries belonging to that system. This view, which as we shall see later serves to buttress the doctrines of economic nationalists, fails to be supported by adequate factual evidence. It is true that the maintenance of a common monetary standard synchronizes business fluctuations and leads to a spread of booms and depressions, but it is far from proven that the *operation* of the gold standard has ever brought about a depression that would not have otherwise taken place. The depressed condition of the British economy after the return to the gold standard in 1925 was due to the level at which the pound sterling was stabilized as well as to many other factors. Contrary to the often-voiced opinion, it was *not* the result of the operating characteristics of the gold standard itself.

Reference has been made to an important aspect of the gold standard, namely the co-ordination of business-cycle developments of the member countries, which is a consequence (as well as a prerequisite) of this system. The system, as it existed prior to 1914, was a *voluntary* one; there were no agreements and no commitments attached to it—but a country that would pursue an independent course of price deflation would find itself the outlet for a gold inflow that would check and reverse the deflation; while a country that would pursue an autonomous course of inflation would lose its gold and drop out of the "system," either adopting exchange control or allowing its currency to

[10] In order to protect the "gold cover" of its note circulation, i.e., the ratio between its gold reserves and the note circulation.

depreciate. It is true, therefore, that a country on the gold standard would participate in wide international upward and downward movements of business activity. It is also true that these movements would be largely influenced by what happens in the large economic units, the United States, Great Britain, etc. One can derive from that certain requirements with respect to the responsibilities of the large economic units as members of an international system; this is a matter which we shall encounter again as our inquiry unfolds.[11] All that needs to be emphasized in the present context is the fact that *international monetary stability* (i.e., stability of exchange relations between national currencies) *must be associated with an international solidarity and discipline on the part of the various countries.* We cannot build an integrated world economy if the individual countries maintain a full autonomy in matters of economic policy instead of working together towards common goals. This conclusion, incidentally, applies to *all* monetary systems, not only to the gold standard.

The gold standard was the monetary system of an essentially peaceful world, where confidence reigned, trade was reasonably free, capital movements between countries regular. This monetary system grew organically out of the conditions of the world economy; it was not the product of a deliberately conceived plan. It was a system based on voluntary participation of countries that domestically had defined their monetary unit in terms of gold; there had been between them no convention or agreement whatever about the "rules" of their economic behavior. Spontaneous, empirical, and free, the gold standard worked well as long as circumstances were favorable to its operations; and it fell hard when they became adverse. That World War I destroyed it is no wonder: no international monetary system could survive the breaking up of the world economy and the stresses and strains of world-wide warfare. That it was neither fully restored nor successfully operated after 1919 was a corollary of the general failure of the makers of the "lost peace" to rebuild an integrated and well-knit world economy.

Its critics have often called the gold standard a "fair-weather system": it certainly provided no mechanism to cope with mas-

[11] Cf. Ragnar Nurkse: "Conditions of International Monetary Equilibrium," *Essays in International Finance,* No. 4 (Princeton University, 1945).

sive "capital flights" or with sudden stoppages in the international flow of investment funds. Its equilibrating mechanism, described above, presupposed the existence of steady confidence so that short-term funds would "move" from country to country in response to relatively small differential changes in interest rates. It was also predicated upon the existence of parallel price movements (or business-cycle developments) in the various countries, and upon the easy adaptability of international trade to changes in the volume and direction of capital movements. These conditions have never been fully realized since August 1914, and in their absence the gold standard could not work.

The reconstruction of the twenties did not lead to the establishment of enduring international monetary arrangements. Trade became less flexible, owing to the growth of protective tariffs; capital movements were less regular; confidence, injured by the war, remained brittle. To complicate matters, there developed a feeling that the available gold reserves might become inadequate to meet the requirements of an international monetary system, on account of the rise in prices and an anticipated decline in the world output of new gold. In consequence, various devices were introduced to "save" on the monetary use of gold, and these devices, like the *gold-exchange standard* made the monetary arrangements still more vulnerable. A simple and effective way of increasing the value of gold reserves was disregarded, namely, the increase of the price of gold. This could have been done by reducing simultaneously and in the same proportions the gold content of all the national currencies, without affecting thereby the parities between the currencies. At the same time, the increase of the price of gold would have stimulated its output, as it did, indeed, after 1931. But the unwritten "rules" of the gold standard were silent on the subject of the price of gold and habit—regardless of reason—made the stability of price inviolable. It was not until the Bretton Woods Agreements of 1944 that the matter was dealt with constructively.

There was no consistent method, under the gold standard, of handling major balance-of-payments disturbances. Even though every country had the right to change the gold parity of its currency at will, this was not being done and there developed a widespread—but erroneous—impression that gold-standard countries were pledged to the maintenance of the "gold content" of their monetary unit under all circumstances. Yet, at times, changes in the economic conditions of a country make it very advisable to alter the foreign-exchange value of its currency by modifying its parity; it is most important, however, that such changes should be made not unilaterally but by agreement with other countries. It is interesting to note that prior to the Bretton Woods Agreements no international machinery had ever been established for dealing co-operatively with the question of parity adjustments.

6.

Exchange-rate stability between the various national currencies can be sought by means of an elaborate system operating through the medium of free markets and multilateral commercial and financial transactions, linking all the countries into one single co-ordinated network, or it may be sought by means of direct control exercised by individual governments over the incoming and outgoing payments of the country. The latter method, which involves the centralization of all foreign exchange transactions in the offices of a governmental agency, is called *exchange control*. The state (through its treasury or another agency) becomes the sole buyer and seller of foreign exchange at rates which it has the sole authority to determine. From a market price, the rate of exchange becomes an imposed price, and supply and demand of foreign exchange are henceforth matched not by the market process but by express planning.

Flights of capital afford the most frequent occasion for the establishment of exchange control. Their disruptive effect upon balances of payments is very well known. They are the result of crises of confidence, and the best safeguard against their recurrence is the removal of the causes of these crises. However, political reasons sometimes militate against this logical course, and, even if the course is adopted, it may take a long time before the causes of trouble are completely removed. Meanwhile, if the flight of capital were to go on unchecked, the situation would deteriorate more and more and the cure would be more and more difficult.

Now the most effective way to check a flight of capital is to

establish exchange control and authorize only those payments
which are the outgrowth of "legitimate" commercial and financial transactions. Thus, if someone wants to acquire a balance in
foreign currency, he must apply for a permission to the agency
administering exchange control and indicate the reason why he
needs that balance. If the reason is the payment for imported
goods, or the payment of a foreign debt which is falling due,
or a remittance to an ailing relative, he will obtain the license;
but if he wants to get away from the local currency or to speculate in foreign exchange markets, a license would be withheld.
Administered wisely and with moderation, exchange control
may prevent capital flights without interfering in any other way
with international payments.

However, experience shows us that exchange control, once
introduced, may tend to be perpetuated. It may become the regular way of keeping the balance of payments in equilibrium without being subject to the international "discipline" of the gold
standard (or another such system). Should this happen, the situation will gradually be altered and the scope of controls will expand. Exchange control can be side-stepped by various more or
less elaborate and clever moves. This matters relatively little if
the control is intended to be a short-lived emergency measure;
it matters a good deal if it is to be a permanent and efficient system of balancing the country's foreign payments. In order to
close the loopholes, the government must adopt more and more
stringent controls and inflict increasingly drastic penalties upon
violators of its regulations.

Among the essential features of an extended exchange control is the concentration in the hands of the government of the
ownership of all foreign balances resulting from foreign transactions and, eventually, of all foreign assets previously owned by
the residents of the country. All these balances and assets are
paid for by the government in local currency and become a pool
out of which foreign exchange is provided for government-ap-
proved foreign payments. The allocation of the balances made
available for payments abroad presents many difficult problems.
The control authorities must set up a plan for the over-all structure of the country's foreign payments, month by month. Quotas
must be set for imports, for financial transactions, tourist expenditures, etc. This requires elaborate blueprints and im-

portant policy decisions which reach far outside the field of monetary relations. Commercial and financial relations between the country and the rest of the world are affected by the way in which exchange control operates. Imports can not only be curtailed, but their structure can be influenced by the way in which foreign exchange is allocated. And this, in turn, reacts upon the structure of production and consumption at home. Thus, step by step, we are led deeper and deeper into a system of state planning of the national economy. It is well known that state socialism requires the use of exchange control; what is less clearly understood is the fact that by introducing exchange control into a free-market economy, we may easily start a chain of events, the eventual outcome of which is a substantial degree of state socialism.

The story does not end here. The allocation of foreign exchange between different foreign countries gives much scope to manifold discriminations and even to political pressures. Exchange control and bilateral settlement generally go hand in hand. Exchange control is a "direct" method of securing a balance-of-payments equilibrium; and it is more direct than ever when applied to the balance of payments with each foreign country separately. As a rule, this leads to a restriction of foreign transactions. At the same time, discriminations result in international frictions and ill will. International capital movements are discouraged, and if exchange control checks "undesirable" capital flights, it also checks the very desirable influx of investment capital from abroad.

We have come a long way from the initial purpose of exchange control, that of forestalling the disruptive effects of "hot money." Exchange control is not merely an emergency measure; it can also be a deliberate instrument for insulating a country's economy from the rest of the world without giving up exchange stability, and for placing the country's foreign economic relations under strict governmental control. It is an efficient instrument of both economic nationalism and of state socialism.

As an emergency measure, exchange control should be of as short duration as possible, lest it degenerate into a permanent system with a great capacity for growth in the described directions. But in order to remove exchange control, it is necessary to cure the emergency. And this involves many economic and political measures, domestic as well as international, and often requires much courage, wisdom, and determination. Since the condition of the balance of payments of every individual country is, in the final analysis, the outcome not only of the domestic situation and of national policies, but of the whole network of international relations as well, the help and co-operation of foreign countries may be needed in order to bring quick and effective remedy to a serious disturbance. This kind of emergency would seem to offer great scope for organized international collaboration. With the establishment of the International Monetary Fund the world has acquired a new agency which is likely to play a very significant role in the years to come in giving assistance to countries which are in the throes of balance-of-payments difficulties.

7.

The International Monetary Fund [12] has been agreed upon by representatives of forty-four countries at the Bretton Woods Conference of July 1944 [13] and has become legally established by the end of December 1945 after a sufficient number of ratifications had come forth. The establishment of the Fund has been preceded by comprehensive investigations centering on proposals for an "International Stabilization Fund of the United and Associated Nations" prepared by Dr. Harry D. White and his associates of the U. S. Treasury Department, and the proposals for an "International Clearing Union" worked out by Lord Keynes for the British Treasury.[14] The successive elaborations of the proposal were the object of far-flung technical discussions, and there developed a heated public debate both before and after the Bretton Woods Conference. Some day a very interesting book could be written about the "Bretton Woods Debate," that controversy having had technical, political, and even emotional

[12] Cf. George N. Halm: *International Monetary Cooperation* (Chapel Hill, N. C., 1945); M. A. Heilperin: *International Monetary Reconstruction: the Bretton Woods Agreements,* op. cit.; John H. Williams: *Postwar Monetary Plans and Other Essays,* 2nd ed. (New York, 1945).

[13] Cf. United Nations Financial and Monetary Conference, *Final Act and Related Documents,* op. cit., Annex A: Articles of Agreement of the International Monetary Fund, pp. 28–67.

[14] The reader will find it of interest to refer to the article by Professor Jacob Viner, "Two Plans for International Monetary Stabilization," *Yale Review,* Autumn 1943.

aspects which make it into one of the great monetary debates of modern times. After the experiences of the inter-war years, the gold standard has become the center of stormy and conflicting emotions. One school of thought erected it into a rampart not only of monetary stability but even of moral righteousness; the other made it the epitome of all economic mistakes, a worn-out shibboleth of the past, a symbol of obscurantism and reaction. The modern believers in the "Golden (gold standard) Calf" as well as the denouncers of the "Golden (gold standard) Scapegoat," all decried the new proposals. One group viewed with misgivings any divergencies from the gold standard; the other group viewed with alarm any resemblances to the gold standard. More deeply rooted was the feeling of the ones that the new system represented too great a departure from monetary internationalism, and the feeling of the others that too large departures have been conceded from their postulate of a full freedom of national monetary and economic action. On the technical plane many important questions and objections were raised by serious students of monetary questions, and answered by others. Experience alone can settle some of these issues.

What, then, is the setup of the new international monetary system? In describing it, a lengthy passage will be quoted from *The Stakes of Bretton Woods*, a statement issued in April 1945 by the Committee on International Policy of the National Planning Association. In view of the controversy referred to above, it will be to the reader's advantage to offer a summary statement of the Fund's organization and operations that is not the work of one man but has been perfected, discussed, and approved by a representative group of economists. The account that follows leaves out all secondary and detailed technical matters, but includes all of the basic features of the new system.[15]

"The International Monetary Fund is the outgrowth of the experiments made in the 'thirties with stabilization funds, and of the desire to devise a monetary system more flexible than the gold standard and better able to cope with the instabilities and emergencies of the postwar world. While one of the Fund's purposes is to 'facilitate the expansion and balanced growth of international trade,' it is primarily

[15] Cf. *The Stakes of Bretton Woods:* A Statement by the Committee on International Policy of the National Planning Association, Washington, D. C., 1945, pp. 7–8. The present writer served as *rapporteur* of that group.

conceived as a *cooperative international scheme* to supply its members with the working balances of foreign exchange necessary to meet temporary variations in their international balances of payments and thus to promote the revival of free international payments.

"As part of the cooperative effort, each member contributes to the Fund a pre-determined amount of gold and of its national currency and accepts specified limitations on its freedom of action with respect to exchange restrictions and changes in parities. In return, each member of the Fund is assured of help in case it faces temporary disequilibrium in its balance-of-payments. Under the Fund's system, every country obtains a 'line of credit' equal in size to its contribution to the Fund's resources. It can use, every year, 25 percent of that 'line of credit' to obtain from the Fund foreign exchange against its national currency. In that way, a member's own monetary resources can be supplemented by the Fund, thus helping that member to meet its obligations resulting from a deficit in its balance-of-payments.

"Should a member suffer from a major and continuing economic disequilibrium, a change in its monetary parity may be desirable. The member has under these circumstances the right to make minor changes in the parity of its currency aggregating 10 percent, after consulting with the Fund but without necessarily securing its concurrence. The Fund's concurrence must be secured, however, for parity changes aggregating more than 10 percent. This provides an orderly procedure for parity adjustments, leaving to members a limited freedom of action without approval of the Fund.

"It is true that the Fund is obligated to concur in changes of parity made necessary by 'fundamental disequilibria.' This term, however, is undefined. It will be a matter for agreement between the management of the Fund and the member concerned as to whether or not a disequilibrium is fundamental, and how large a parity adjustment is necessary to meet the situation. The management has considerable discretionary powers in determining whether the member has used the Fund in the spirit of that institution or in violation of that spirit. In the latter case, the member may be disqualified from further use of the Fund's resources. While the management of the Fund, when making decisions, is not allowed to object to a proposed change in par values 'because of the domestic, social, or political policies of the member proposing the change,' members obligate themselves to collaborate with the Fund to help it to maintain exchange stability.

"With respect to exchange controls, members are allowed to keep them during a five-year transitional period from war to peace but are expected, though not obliged, to liquidate them gradually in consultation with the Fund. After three years the Fund shall make a report on the controls then in force. The only kinds of exchange control which are sanctioned for an unspecified period are those relating to capital movements and those resulting from the rationing by the Fund of scarce currencies. The latter may not, however, be 'more restrictive than is necessary to limit the demand for the scarce currency to the supply held by, or accruing, to the member,' and must be removed as soon as the scarcity is ended.

"As regards the long-term operations of the Fund, members are instructed to introduce exchange restrictions rather than to use the Fund whenever they are faced with a flight of capital; but they are prohibited from imposing any restrictions on current payments resulting from commercial transactions, interest payments on loans, moderate payments for amortization of loans, and moderate remittances for family living expenses, etc. In brief, while the proposals do not eliminate exchange controls altogether, they limit their scope and place them under international supervision.

"It must be noted that members of the Fund undertake to abstain from engaging in competitive currency depreciation, and are prohibited from engaging in multiple-currency practices or discriminatory arrangements except as authorized under the Agreement and approved by the Fund. The Agreement on the Fund is not explicit concerning the right of members to organize regional currency groupings, but it is contrary to the spirit of the Fund to continue such groupings after the end of the transition period. Provision for a transition period was inevitable because Britain, for example, could not possibly give up the protection of the sterling area until she had an opportunity to deal with blocked sterling which represents her external war debt and until the revival of international trade provided her with a degree of security with respect to current transactions.

"Reference often is made to the 'scarce currency' problem. The Fund has provisions not only to help countries overcome temporary deficits in their balances of payments, but also to deal with the consequences of a country's chronically selling more than it is willing to buy or to invest, thereby keeping other nations continually indebted to it on current account. Such a situation would result in the currency of that country becoming scarce in comparison to the current demand for it, and there would be danger that the Fund's holdings of that currency might become exhausted. To forestall that, various provisions have been introduced into the Agreement, the most drastic of which would require the rationing of the scarce currency by the Fund. In immediate prospect, and in the foreseeable future, the United States dollar is probably the only currency which might be affected by this provision. The best way to avoid the development of a dollar scarcity, is for the United States to adjust its commercial and financial policies to its position in the world.

"It is not intended that the Fund should be used to any appreciable extent by countries which have abundant monetary reserves of their own. There are provisions which make it necessary for countries to use their reserves to the same extent to which they resort to the Fund, and to re-purchase gradually from the Fund their currencies held by it in excess of their quotas as their monetary positions improve. Graduated charges on the use of the Fund's resources serve as some deterrent to an excessive use of the Fund's facilities, while other provisions permit the management to intervene should a country use its credit facilities for programs not permitted by the Fund.

"Article V, Section 3 of the Fund Agreement gives the legal right to any member (whose currency has not been declared by the Fund to be 'scarce') to buy annually foreign exchange from the Fund within the limits of 25 percent of its quota until its quota is exhausted, but only for purposes which lie within the defined scope of the Fund's activities. Section 5 of Article V gives the right to the Fund's management to determine whether a member is using the Fund in a manner contrary to its purposes and to prevent such misuse. Each member is under obligation to maintain the gold value of the Fund's holdings of its currency, and the Fund has a right to demand that the currency be made available for purchases in the country of its origin.

"The total size of the Fund is to be $8,800,000,000, of which the United States is to contribute $2,750,000,000. It is estimated that the total gold subscription to the Fund will amount to $1,643,000,000 and that its gold and dollar resources will be equal to about $3,700,000,000. The voting power of the United States, proportionate to its subscription in the Fund, is to be 28 percent of the total votes.

"It should be noted that capital needs incident to relief, reconstruction, and development are not supposed to be met out of the Fund's resources. The Fund, therefore, has a strictly limited objective which is monetary rather than financial. While the sales by the Fund of foreign exchange to members in effect are extensions of short-term credits, these credit extensions should be incident to the main purpose of the Fund which is to normalize and, broadly speaking, to stabilize international monetary relations."

The new system departs from the gold standard in several major respects: 1) it provides a machinery for parity adjustments by international consent and opens the doors to a co-operative approach to the solution of balance-of-payments problems of member countries; 2) it introduces legal commitments for members with respect to specified policies, whereas there were no actual commitments under the gold standard; 3) it uses gold but creates, in addition, a supplementary fund of monetary reserves consisting of currencies of all the member countries; 4) it recognizes the obligations both of countries with a balance-of-payments deficit and of countries with a surplus, but without formulating any precise "rules of the game" comparable to the unwritten but rather clear rules of the gold standard; 5) it allows for the use of exchange control to check capital flights and to ration "scarce currencies" (in addition to those controls that are authorized during the transition period).

In the light of the discussion in earlier parts of this chapter, the first three changes must certainly be welcomed. It is a pity, however, that no "rules of the game" have been formulated concerning the behavior of "deficitary" and "surplus" countries,[16] and the provisions concerning exchange control can give rise to justified apprehensions. It is earnestly to be hoped that once economic order and stability are restored in the world, it may become possible to re-establish fully the principle and the practice of free international payments.

[16] There is much truth, on the other hand, in the views expressed on that subject in the Macmillan Report: "It is difficult to define in precise terms what is implied by the 'rules of the game.' The management of an international standard is an art and not a science, and no one would suggest that it is possible to draw up a formal code of action, admitting of no exceptions and qualifications, adherence to which is obligatory on peril of wrecking the whole structure. Much must necessarily be left to time and circumstances." (*Committee on Finance and Industry Report,* His Majesty's Stationery Office, Cmd. 3897, London, 1931, paragraph 47.)

BOOK TWO

Economic Nationalism

CHAPTER IV

"Old-Fashioned" Protectionism

THE MOST WIDESPREAD interference with international trade takes the form of *customs duties* collected by the authorities of the importing country on merchandise coming from abroad. (In certain instances there are also export duties.) The total list of duties in effect in a given country at a given time is called "tariff." [1] The effect of import duties is to increase the price that the population of the importing country must pay for the foreign article. Several consequences follow: 1) Domestic producers are better able to compete with foreign producers because, instead of meeting the foreign price (inclusive of transportation costs), they now have to meet the foreign price *increased* by amount of the duty; 2) the volume of imports falls if the demand for the taxed commodity is adversely affected by the rise in price due to the import duty;[2] 3) Public revenue increases by the amount of duties levied. Furthermore, as result of the first point, domestic production is encouraged in fields in which, without the tariff, the national demand would be satisfied by means of imported merchandise. Since this encouragement is obtained at the cost of higher prices paid by the domestic consumer, the effect is comparable to a *subsidy* paid to producers of the tariff-protected commodities. Actually, from the point of view of the international division of labor, tariffs and subsidies are entirely comparable. It will be noted that the cost of the tariff to the public is concealed and its incidence is often difficult to ascertain, whereas the cost and the incidence of subsidies are much clearer.

Tariffs are assimilated into the price structure through raising the price of dutiable articles; exporting countries may overcome, to a certain extent at least, the effects of the tariff in the importing

---

[1] The following definitions are quoted from *The Tariff and Its History* (United States Tariff Commission, Washington, 1934), p. 1: "As related to customs duties, the word tariff has the following meanings: (1) A list or schedule of articles of merchandise with the rate of duty to be paid to the Government for their importation or exportation. (2) A duty levied according to such schedule, or such duties collectively, especially on one class of articles; impost; as the *tariff* on silk. (3) The law in which a schedule of duties is fixed and imposed; also, the principle in general, governing the imposition of duties."

[2] In technical language, if the *elasticity of demand* is greater than unity. This is the most frequent occurrence; if the import duty is small, however, the volume of imports may remain unaffected by its imposition.

countries by lowering their selling price. This can happen in one
of three principal ways: by lowering costs of production at home;
by accepting lower profits; by charging a lower price to foreign
buyers than is paid by domestic buyers. The last method takes
us into the field of so-called *dumping*. Dumping violates the
principle of uniform, non-discriminatory price. It is often coun-
tered by tariff increases in the importing country, but it must be
noted that it receives its principal encouragement from the fact
of existing tariffs.[3]

What are the reasons for the imposition of import duties?
Leaving aside the concern with employment (about which more
will be said later), imports are subjected to customs duties for
two principal reasons: in order to provide a source of revenue
for the government of the importing country; and in order to
protect a domestic industry against foreign competition. The
two objectives are in part, mutually exclusive: in order that
the import duty should provide revenue, it must not result
in any significant curtailment of the volume of imported
merchandise and therefore be unable to afford "protection"
to domestic industry; whereas the more effective the protection and the smaller the volume of imports, the lesser is the
public revenue obtained from the levy.[4]

The revenue aspect of the tariff is not to be neglected. It played
an important role in the United States in the nineteenth century,
in Switzerland up to World War I, as well as in many other
countries. Even after Great Britain adopted free trade, a few
revenue duties were maintained. But the other reasons for tariffs
are far more important and it is upon these that we shall concentrate our attention. Broadly speaking, protective tariffs stem from
two main considerations: one is the pursuit of certain *national*
objectives; the other is the desire of particular interests to limit
competitions.

[3] In order to make dumping possible, the country practicing it must have a tariff
against re-importation of that particular commodity; otherwise the differential between
domestic prices and export prices could not be maintained.

[4] It is interesting to note that when Lord Keynes advocated in 1931 the adoption by
Great Britain of a general tariff, he argued his case on the grounds both of revenue and
of protection. The contradiction was more apparent than real because what Keynes
argued for was a *general* tariff: industries producing goods for which demand was
highly "elastic" would thus be protected because imports would fall as result of the
duty; whereas less "elastic" imports would provide an increase in revenue for the
public exchequer.

2.

Among *national* reasons for tariffs, the following are the most important:

(1) Protection of industries necessary for national defense;

(2) Protection of young but promising industries, which, once established, would need protection no longer;

(3) The desire to influence the basic economic and social structure of the country;

(4) Protection of domestic production and employment in emergency situations.

Let us examine briefly these four groups of arguments:

(1) *Protection of industries necessary for national defense.* Even Adam Smith admitted that "defense . . . is of much more importance than opulence," [5] thus acknowledging that welfare is not the sole criterion regulating economic policy. The protection of "key industries" became, during World War I and after its end, the spearhead of increasing economic nationalism. It extends, of course, not only to the manufacturing industry but also to power and to agriculture. As outcome of his comprehensive studies about the reasons of the failure to liberalize international trade after the end of World War I, Professor William E. Rappard reaches the following conclusion highlighting the importance of the national defense argument for tariffs:[6]

"It is essentially because Europe and the world have not really been at peace since 1914 that all efforts at promoting and at liberating international trade have been so signally unsuccessful. Mindful of the oft-quoted saying of the father of economic liberalism to the effect that 'defense is much more important than opulence,' contemporary statesmanship, even when sincerely convinced of the material benefits of freer trade, has more or less deliberately sacrificed them to considerations of national security. That is the real solution of our riddle."

It is hardly necessary to say that this argument has often been used by special interests urging the introduction of new tariffs

[5] *The Wealth of Nations,* op. cit., Book IV, Chapter II.

[6] William E. Rappard: *Post-War Efforts for Freer Trade* (Cobden Lectures delivered at the London School of Economics, February, 1938), Geneva Studies, Vol. IX, No. 2 (Geneva Research Center, Geneva, 1938), p. 64.

or opposing the reduction of existing duties, regardless of whether the tariff was *really* indispensable for national defense or not. Thus we find, in recent Congressional hearings, the following statement made by Mr. C. W. Carlson on behalf of the American Glassware Association and the National Association of Manufacturers of Pressed and Blown Glassware:[7]

". . . Glass working is an art that should be developed and encouraged. Glass working is vital to our national defense. What would our own military have done during the war without skilled glass workers?"

Opposing any future tariff reductions, Mr. Carlson went on to say:

"Shall we permit the industry to die because of its inability to compete with low foreign wages? Shall we discontinue the training of skilled workmen? Shall we discontinue technological research which has been of such great value to our Army and Navy?"

Note the introduction of the "low wage" argument about which a good deal will have to be said later. Note also the failure to draw any distinction between the manufacture of optical and similar glassware needed for war purposes, and the manufacture of glassware for everyday use and for decorative and artistic purposes. This is a clear case of an exaggerated and emotional appeal to the national security argument. During these hearings, the same was done by spokesmen for a variety of industries. Let us quote, for example, Mr. Walter W. Cenerazzo, National President of the American Watch Workers' Union:[8]

". . . by the exhibits and facts which I will present to you today I trust you will have a clearer picture of the absolute necessity of the American watch industry to the United States. . . . I shall prove to you that the American watch industry is as vital to national defense as are the generals of our Army, the admirals of our Navy, the G.I.s, chemicals, guns, shells, planes, tanks, and ships."

This somewhat "hyperbolic" statement contains, of course, an element of truth, but its application should have been limited to

---

[7] House of Representatives, Committee on Ways and Means, Hearings on the *1945 Extension of Reciprocal Trade Agreements Act* (H.R. 3240), vol. I, p. 1479.

[8] Ibid., p. 1105.

military requirements and not extended to the whole industry. Mr. Cenerazzo went on to say that:[9]

"The emergency arrived in 1941. The American watch and clock industry was understaffed because Swiss competition had thrown out of employment thousands of capable workers." (No data were supplied to bear out this contention.)

Strangely enough, a few pages later Mr. Cenerazzo quotes, without challenging it, a statement by Roland Gsell, retiring president of the American Watch Assemblers' Association, to the effect that:[10] "It is always a source of amazement that, throughout World War II, we have been able to import from Switzerland," showing that complete self-sufficiency in watches is by no means necessary for the United States. The effectiveness of the whole statement is greatly impaired, too, by its abusive complaints against the competition of the "Swiss watch monopoly." Would it be that Mr. Cenerazzo simply resents foreign competition?

Enough about glass and watches! The moral of these quotations is that, important though the argument of national defense is, it lends itself to widespread abuse.

(2) *Protection of the so-called "infant industries."* This argument is, historically, almost as venerable as the preceding one; it goes back to Alexander Hamilton's *Report on Manufactures* of 1791, and was later adopted by the German economist Friedrich List whose *National System of Political Economy* (1841) exercised a profound influence upon the protectionist doctrines of the second half of the nineteenth century. The argument is plausible: it is beneficial for a country to develop a diversity of production which is justified by its natural conditions but has not been attained so far due to the backwardness of its national economy. These new productions might, however, never come into being due to the competition of foreign producers who have the advantage of well-established techniques and of large markets. Once the experimental stage is over, once markets are developed, the "new" country might find itself in possession of a highly efficient industry, fully capable to stand on its own feet and to keep its own, *without protection,* in competitive world markets. This reasoning is not only plausible—it is also essentially cor-

9 Ibid., p. 1108.
10 Ibid., p. 1113.

rect. Yet experience shows that this argument, too, is likely to be abused. The "infant" industries never seem to grow up to the point where tariff protection could be removed. "Incubator babies" turn into "iron-lung adults."

The explanation is simple. In the first place, in every industry there are more and less efficient firms; the more efficient ones could do without protection, the others would go under without it (as, indeed, they should!). Since domestic prices, which keep alive the least efficient producers, result in higher profits for the more productive ones, the sentiment of the industry as a whole tends to favor the maintenance of the existing import duties. Imperceptibly, the protection of young industries turns into the protection of invested capital, of "vested interests." In order that the "infant industries" argument should be scrupulously applied, protection should be granted only after careful study and only for a limited duration; and it should be ruthlessly withdrawn when the time is up. Whether that would be *politically* possible is, of course, an entirely different matter!

(3) *Desire to influence the basic economic and social structure of the country.* This reason for tariffs really goes beyond the scope of "old-fashioned" protectionism, but it may be convenient to include it in the present account. It may be considered that economic diversification is desirable beyond the limits provided by the "infant industries" argument. Or it may be considered desirable to maintain and protect agricultural production, in spite of its high costs, in order to keep in existence the social group of farmers, often viewed as the bulwark of stability. This group of protectionist arguments dovetails in part with the protection of "new" industries and partly with the protection of "key" industries required for national defense; the essential motivation here is, however, purely social.

(4) *Emergency measures.* There are situations in which protective tariffs can be excused on the grounds of short-term expediency, of the urgent need to meet disturbing situations. Anti-dumping duties and duties imposed to counteract foreign currency depreciations belong to that category. One cannot emphasize too strongly the need of adapting a country's industrial structure to enduring changes in basic economic conditions; but there can be no reason whatever why a country should allow an

established industry to get into serious difficulties simply because another country resorts temporarily to dumping or to exchange depreciation. It is, of course, always advantageous for a population to obtain goods at the lowest possible price—a fact usually disregarded by protectionists!—but if a short-lived advantage is to be paid for by the destruction of an industry, the net outcome is detrimental and should be forestalled—even at the price of *temporarily* imposed customs duties. Actually, when an international agreement concerning rules of "fair play" in international economic relations is reached some day, dumping and unilateral currency depreciations are likely to be outlawed [11] and that particular reason for tariffs will disappear.

In a nationalistic world there remains another group of emergencies which arise in times of depression and call for special protective measures. In the absence of a sufficient degree of international collaboration, the difficulties brought about by a depression are dealt with by national and nationalistic methods. Nothing affords as much justification for nationalism as the lack of international co-operation; and the greater the growth of nationalism, the more difficult it is to achieve the required co-operation. It is a vicious circle, very vicious and very destructive. Once caught in it, mankind must hammer its way out with heavy, determined blows. And this requires a measure of courage and of wisdom such as is only too rarely found among leaders of men. We shall see, in the next chapter, how the nationalistic disintegration, rationalized into the doctrine of "autarky," became the dominant creed of the day; and in a later section of this inquiry we shall discuss the nature of policies that might prevent our falling again into the "vicious circle" of the thirties.

3.

The principal reason for "old-fashioned" protectionism lies in the fear of competition and the reluctance to make adjustments to changing conditions. Both of these are very characteristic and widely encountered attitudes of people who, *in theory,* favor free enterprise and believe in progress. Yet free enterprise implies, indeed postulates, competition, while progress implies change!

---

[11] As far as currency depreciations are concerned, the matter is already dealt with in the statute of the International Monetary Fund.

So, of course, the arguments actually used in advocating tariffs are nicely dressed up and given a "respectable" appearance. Thus, Mr. Carlson, whose remarks before the House Ways and Means Committee were referred to before, was careful to assure the committee that:[12]

"United States manufacturers of hand-made glassware are fully cognizant of the necessity of stimulating foreign trade. They are not interested in creating tariff barriers merely for the purpose of eliminating competition. All they are seeking is the equal opportunity of selling wares made by American workmen at American labor rates that is given foreign manufacturers using labor at low foreign wage rates."

At the same hearings, Mr. Emil Rieve, General President of the Textile Workers' Union of America, C.I.O., made a strong plea for the renewal of the Trade Agreements Act and for further reductions of tariff rates in the course of future negotiations between the American government and foreign governments. His testimony was all in favor of freer trade until the textile industry was reached; then Mr. Rieve went on as follows:[13]

"The reciprocal trade agreements program is, to date, properly not subjecting the textile industry to full international competition particularly because of war conditions. . . .

"The American national interests and those of other countries developing their standard of living demand the continuance of the American textile industry.

"On an over-all basis, it appears that further reductions in tariff rates for textile products are not seriously feasible. . . .

"The American textile industry must be considered by the government agencies as being justly entitled to the protection from foreign competition which it has enjoyed. . . ."

It is very easy to pay lip service to freer trade while insisting on protection for one's particular industry! Easy and illogical and unconstructive. And it is done by business spokesmen and labor spokesmen and agricultural spokesmen. There is always a neat verbal way to present the case—and a helpful Congressman to support it. The hearings held in April and May 1945 before the Committee on Ways and Means of the House of Representatives

[12] *1945 Extension of the Reciprocal Trade Agreements Act,* op. cit., Vol. I, p. 1477.
[13] Ibid., Vol. II, pp. 2384, 2387, 2389.

over the extension of the Reciprocal Trade Agreements Act, are a veritable mine of information, and a perusal of the two fat volumes containing their transcript (three thousand pages in all) is a very rewarding experience.[14]

Labor has been very instrumental in promoting high-tariff policies on the grounds of cheap-labor competition,[15] although this argument is also often used by business. Actually, in the United States this is the most frequently voiced protectionist argument. It is interesting to find it denounced and refuted by several enlightened labor spokesmen. In the above quoted *Hearings on the 1945 Extension of the Reciprocal Trade Agreements Act,* Mr. Jacob S. Potofsky, Secretary-Treasurer of the Amalgamated Clothing Workers, after asserting that: "The two-way trade agreement deal, reducing barriers both ways, is . . . entirely sound," went on to say:[16]

"Some people say the standard of living of the American worker will be reduced if tariffs are cut down. We do not hold this view. We think that high wages result from high productivity, imaginative and progressive managerial leadership, and good union organization— and not from tariffs. . . . The only effective protection the American worker has against so-called foreign competition is not a tariff barrier against foreign goods but efficient production at home and a decent standard of living abroad. . . . Real competition is not between wage rates but in unit cost of production."

In the course of the same hearings, similar views were advanced by Mr. James B. Carey, Secretary-Treasurer of the C.I.O. "Trade," he said, "is a two-way street. We cannot achieve full employment and full production in the United States by expanding our exports without expecting to import foreign goods." He then continued as follows:[17]

"There are those who contend that the American standard of living would be lowered by admitting foreign goods into this country; that American workers would be thrown out of jobs and that we could not compete with low-priced foreign goods produced under low-wage

[14] See also: *Post-war Economic Policy and Planning,* Hearings before the Subcommittee on Foreign Trade and Shipping. Special Committee on Post-war Policy and Planning, House of Representatives, Part 4, September, 1944–January, 1945.

[15] Cf. Margaret Hardy: *The Influence of Organized Labor on the Foreign Policy of the United States* (Geneva, 1936).

[16] Op. cit., Vol. II, p. 2225.

[17] Ibid., pp. 2378–9. Italics added.

conditions. Here are the facts: The principal industries affected by imports are textiles, wood, paper and pulp industries, fishing, mining and glass manufacture. Only a relatively small proportion of American workers is in these industries, and of these only a limited number is directly affected by imports. . . .

"The maximum number of workers employed in industries whose goods compete with similar goods produced abroad is little more than 2,000,000. *American workers are thus affected to a very limited extent by tariffs whereas all workers as consumers are injured by high tariffs.* . . .

"We [i.e, the C.I.O.] wish it to be understood that we are in no sense advocating a policy of free trade. We are advocating a friendly spirit of international give and take so that tariff adjustments will be made which will be of the greatest benefit to the American people as a whole."

These are sound and wise views. Low wages are mostly the *result* of low productivity and go up as productivity grows. It is only when authoritarian political rule prevents wages and living standards to follow rising productive efficiency [18] that unsound and unstable competitive conditions result—and then tariffs or other forms of import restriction may be advisable. The aim of these is then twofold: on the one hand to avoid upsetting the economy of the importing country over artificial and unstable conditions abroad; and on the other to exercise pressure on the country whose population suffers from authoritarian rule. Apart from that kind of situation, it is perfectly absurd to levy import duties against the produce of cheap labor. To do so is to prevent the less developed countries from taking part in the international division of labor and, therefore, from improving their economic condition and the living standards of their population.

It is interesting to note that the American fear of foreign "cheap labor" competition is matched by the fear, often voiced abroad, of the competition of American "high efficiency" output. Actually the world needs all that can be produced and the sole problem is whether the international division of labor is to be allowed to direct human energies into most advantageous channels or not. Competition means alertness—it also means adaptability to change. And these, as we have already pointed out, meet in our societies with a strange amount of resistance.

[18] Such was the case in Japan before the war and in Germany since 1933.

4.

Attempts to limit competition are by no means restricted to the field of international trade. In the United States interstate commerce encounters a variety of obstacles, in spite of the work of the Interstate Commerce Commission. And, of course, there are many attempts at monopolistic combines against which the anti-trust legislation is directed, enforced by a special division of the Department of Justice. The issue of *international* cartels is still open, however, and ways of dealing with them must yet be devised.

The resistance to change is noticeable not only in foreign trade but also in domestic relations. Technological progress entails the growth of new industries and the decline of certain old ones. This involves liquidations of investments with incident losses of capital, and movements of labor from industry to industry with incident discomforts and "technological" unemployment. The latter can be mitigated through public facilities for retraining and through subsidies for moving into a new location. When such changes occur, there develops a tendency, on the part of capital and on the part of labor alike, to hang on to the declining industry even at the cost of discomfort and loss to the community as a whole. A good example, mainly domestic but having an interesting bearing upon foreign trade problems, is offered by the activities of Mr. James C. Petrillo on behalf of the American Federation of Musicians, of which he is president.

The development of the phonograph and of the radio, and especially the combination of the two, has reduced, in recent years, the demand for the services of bands. It would be natural to expect, in consequence, a decline in the number of new aspiring musicians and, without the interference of the Federation, this is what would have happened. However, by the use of ruthless pressures, the account of which exceeds the scope of the present study, Mr. Petrillo was able to enforce a much wider employment of musicians than would otherwise be the case. The result is that more men go into an intrinsically declining profession than would normally find employment in it—and the cost of it is borne by the public, directly or indirectly. But, on the other hand, the membership in the Federation of Musicians is

maintained, and so are the resources and the power of that organization—and the power of its leader.

Now, Mr. Petrillo's Federation enjoys, practically, a monopoly status within the United States (without being subjected to
anti-trust laws). And nothing is more dangerous to a monopoly
than imports from abroad which bring into the picture an element of competition beyond the control of the national monopolist. Hence, the monopolist's natural impulse is to press for tariff
protection. The anti-monopoly effects of free trade would be
quite significant, if only we could bring ourselves to make such
a radical departure in commercial policy. But, going back to Mr.
Petrillo, how can one impose a tariff on music? Well, one can
prevent foreign musicians from entering the country otherwise
than on conditions prescribed by the Federation—and this has
actually been done. There remained, however, one important
loophole: the radio. And so Mr. Petrillo decided to *rule* that radio
stations in the United States must henceforth ban programs
originating abroad, except in Canada. Here are his arguments:[19]

"There's the tariff. The manufacturers lobby to keep cheap material
out of the country. There's the immigration law. The Government,
everybody, protects themselves against [cheap?] labor. Why . . .
should we be exempt? You know what happened to Swiss watches.
They stopped some from coming into this country. We're trying to
see that foreign musicians, in person or by air, don't get our jobs."

Thus, like a cancerous growth, trade restrictions tend to spread
more and more widely. If they remain unchecked, they strike at
the very existence of good international relations. It is the general public that foots the bill, while special interests collect the
pecuniary benefits. But since the "public" is everybody, it is un-
organized and amorphous, unable to fight against powerful
groups and lobbies, each with its own ax to grind. Yet it is in
the interest of the great majority of people that technological advance and other basic changes should be allowed to become translated into appropriate changes in the industrial structure of the
various countries.

[19] Cf. The *New York Times,* December 26, 1945. Mr. Petrillo presented his views
at the annual party of Local 10 (blind musicians) and Local 208 (colored musicians)
held in Chicago on December 25, 1945.

5.

Interferences with international trade are not limited to the imposition of import duties. There are other and very much more effective forms of trade restrictions: import quotas, exchange control, import prohibitions, all the so-called quantitative trade controls about which more will be said in Chapter VI. While customs duties work through the price mechanism and are assimilated into it without otherwise interfering with the individual's freedom of choice and decision, these other instruments of trade restriction interfere with the price mechanism and with the operations of a free enterprise economy.

Other interferences with the international flow of goods directly affect exports. Export duties have been practiced at various times and places in the past and can be encountered in our days as well. Even more disturbing to the steadiness of international trade are export subsidies.

Unlike the "new" economic nationalism which leans toward bilateralism, the "old-fashioned" protectionism favored the multilateral system of trade and of payments. This found its fullest expression in the principle of non-discrimination and in the so-called *Most-Favored-Nation clause.* It has become the general rule in the course of the nineteenth and early twentieth century that the trade regulations adopted by one country should grant equality of treatment to all the foreign countries rather than to discriminate in favor (or against) one or some of them. That principle—challenged today in many quarters but staunchly supported by the American government—has important economic and political consequences. Economically, it protects sound international division of labor and removes an invidious source of arbitrary decisions about the orientation of currents of trade. Politically, it removes a source of frictions and misunderstandings as well as an instrument of pressure by stronger upon weaker nations. In the thirties, when this principle was largely discarded, its value was demonstrated by default as it were.

Commercial treaties between nations have been customary since ancient times. The modern treaties began in the twelfth century and were mostly developed by the Italian city-states. Commercial treaties regulate conditions of import and export trade, the admission of ships to harbors, coastal trade, and a great many other matters relative to commercial and financial transactions between the two countries and to movements of people between them. Tariff agreements form, of course, the most important part of commercial treaties and, since the treaties are usually bilateral, discrepancies and discriminations might easily (and often did) develop. The desire to reach international uniformity in spite of the bilateral character of treaties, and to eliminate discrimination, gave birth to the Most-Favored-Nation clause (thereafter referred to as the "M. F. N. clause").[20] The name of this provision is misleading at first glance: its actual purpose is precisely to avoid that any country should be treated with more favor than any other. What the name actually means is that the treatment granted to the country most favorably treated is extended to all countries which are at the benefit of the M. F. N. clause. Thus if Countries A and B conclude a new trade treaty which provides for a lower tariff rate on the importation of motor cars from A into B, this lower rate will be *automatically* applied to cars imported from any country whose treaty with B includes the M. F. N. clause. There are various forms of the M. F. N. clause; the most common—and that which is endorsed by the American government—is the *unconditional* and *reciprocal* clause. That means that Country A will grant the M. F. N. treatment to Country B without any special conditions, provided only that B grants the M. F. N. treatment to A.

The *unconditional M. F. N. clause* has the great advantage of generalizing every tariff concession and eliminating discrimination as far as the group of countries that adopt that clause in their commercial treaties is concerned. It has been rightly said that this treatment has also certain disadvantages, namely:[21]

(1) It diminishes the value of every concession because the area to which it is applied is extended;

(2) It hinders a concession to one treaty state, because this would subsequently benefit automatically a stronger competitor;

(3) By adapting the concession to the special conditions of

---

[20] Cf. T. E. Gregory: *Tariffs: A Study in Method* (London, 1921); Jacob Viner: "The Most-Favored-Nation Clause in American Commercial Treaties," *Journal of Political Economy*, Vol. XXXII, February–December, 1924; N. Ito, *La Clause de la Nation la plus Favorisée* (Paris, 1930).

[21] Quoted from the article on "Commercial Treaties" in the *Encyclopædia Britannica* (1943 edition).

the treaty state, its extension to the other most favored countries can in practice be excluded.

Everything considered, the M. F. N. treatment is a most useful device for counteracting protectionist and forestalling discriminatory tendencies in international commercial relations. It is desirable that it should be successfully rescued from its current eclipse by the efforts of American negotiators.

6.

The freedom of international trade can be restricted by private as well as public measures. Individually, of course, importers and exporters cannot influence the broad currents of trade—but monopolistic organizations of producers can interfere with trade as effectively, and even more effectively, than governments. These organizations are called *cartels,* and if they include companies belonging to various countries they are called *international cartels.*[22]

"The word cartels, though centuries old, was first used in the year 1879 to designate private market-control mechanisms of entrepreneurs. . . . The term cartel has been used in the United States in public discussions and scientific publications in the traditional sense to mean collective market controls of private entrepreneurs."[23] A good deal of emotion has come to be attached to this term, partly because all monopolistic arrangements are in ill-repute in this country, partly because of the ambiguous role certain cartels played during the war. Objectively, we must look upon international cartels as organizations which are formed for the purpose of seeking special benefits for their members by disrupting and reorganizing channels of international trade, by limiting or eliminating competition, fixing prices, reducing the scope of the spontaneous forces of the market, and reducing opportunities for the international division of labor. We shall briefly survey the various methods of action of international cartels; in doing so we shall draw heavily upon the

[22] See: Dr. Corwin D. Edwards: *Economic and Political Aspects of International Cartels,* a study prepared for and published under the auspices of the Subcommittee on War Mobilization of the Committee on Military Affairs, U. S. Senate, Washington, 1944; Erwin Hexner: *International Cartels* (Chapel Hill, N. C., 1945).

[23] Erwin Hexner: op. cit., pp. 3, 7.

study prepared by Professor Corwin D. Edwards when he was chairman of the Policy Board, Antitrust Division, Department of Justice. First, concerning cartels as devices to control markets.[24]

"(1) *Control over prices.* The central purpose of cartels is to maintain prices at levels higher than would otherwise obtain. Sometimes this result is sought by direct price-fixing arrangements, but more frequently by controls of production and allocations of markets. . . . The level of prices established by cartels after their control of the market is assured differs from case to case in accordance with what the traffic will bear. . . . The degree of stability established by cartel prices also differs in accord with surrounding circumstances. . . . In some industries in which control by the cartel is incomplete or intermittent, periods of high prices have repeatedly induced an increase of productive capacity sufficient to break the cartel and bring about a precipitous price decline. The price fluctuations of such cartelized products as rubber, though infrequent, have been extreme and disastrous. In spite of such variations, *the typical purpose and effect of cartelization is to set prices higher than would prevail under competition, to reduce them as seldom as possible, and to raise them further whenever opportunity permits.* . . .

"(2) *Impairment of quality.* Though cartels seldom concern themselves directly with the quality of cartelized goods, a necessary effect of their monopolistic character is to diminish incentives to improve quality and to limit opportunities for the buyer to protect himself against low quality. . . .

"(3) *Allocation of trade territories.* One of the most prevalent cartel methods is allocation of territories to individual concerns or groups. Each participant undertakes not to sell in territory assigned exclusively to others, and often agrees also not to sell to customers who are likely to export to such territory. The effect of such undertakings is to restrict investments abroad, to restrict exports not only by cartel members but by their customers, and to deprive consumers of imported commodities. . . . *The purpose of such agreements is to acquire a monopolistic position in markets which are regarded as peculiarly valuable.* . . . *Cartel arrangements made in this spirit have often been inconsistent with the development of international trade. They have limited some or all of the participating concerns to sale in their home markets or in nearby territory.* . . .

"(4) *Restrictions of supply.* Restrictions of available supply are prominent among the methods by which cartels undertake to maintain prices. In some cases cartel restrictions take the form of absolute

24 Op. cit., pp. 10–12, 15, 19–20, 23–4, 25. Italics added.

limits upon the amount which may be produced, sold, or exported. This form of restriction obviously subordinates the consumers' demand for additional quantities to the industry's desire for additional profits. . . .

"(5) *Allocation of production and of industrial fields.* Closely associated with industry-wide programs for the restriction of output are arrangements which set limits upon the amount or nature of production by certain particular concerns. . . ."

The conclusions which follow from the above account are hardly favorable to international cartels. The fear of competition which leads to the imposition of import duties is also at the bottom of cartel arrangements. A further motive is, obviously, the desire for monopoly profits and a third—and by no means the least important—is the quest for economic and even political power. The British cartel movement stems predominantly perhaps from timidity about competition; the German cartels, greatly encouraged and later controlled by the state, became the handmaiden of power politics. American companies have frequently entered into international cartel agreements, while public policy in that respect is not as yet clearly determined.

CHAPTER V

Forward to the Past — The New
Economic Nationalism

THE ECONOMIC DOCTRINES of the nineteenth century (including the latter years of the eighteenth) stand in strong contrast and violent reaction to the state controls over economic life and to the extreme economic nationalism of the mercantilist era—an era which lasted for two to three hundred years, nearly till the end of the eighteenth century. We have seen that in the nineteenth century even economic nationalism took the relatively mild forms of "old-fashioned protectionism," accepting the main tenets of a liberal society and of *laissez-faire* capitalism. The political and social thinkers of that period were emphatic in their devotion to free institutions at home and—mostly—to free trade among nations. We have seen that Cobden had a passionate craving for peace—as well as for welfare—and considered free trade as a highway leading to both of these aims.

In opposition to their mercantilist predecessors, the liberals of the nineteenth century believed in an underlying solidarity of national interests (a belief for which they were to be greatly derided by their twentieth-century critics!) and were looking forward to the growth of a well-knit community of nations. They opposed alike the power of the state vis-à-vis its citizens and the power of the state vis-à-vis other states. Favorable, in domestic matters, to a limitation of the powers of the government, they favored, internationally, the limitation of national sovereignty. That these two limitations of the power of the state tend to go together should be clear—though it is often lost sight of in our own days. A state that has very considerable powers at home is prone to affirm its independence and power in international councils; while a state which insists on its full sovereignty in international relations finds it necessary to an increasing extent to organize the country internally with a view to building up its strength, its independence, its freedom of action.

The doctrines and policies of the nineteenth-century liberalism have been increasingly challenged in the last decades of that century. The story of how this happened and an analysis of the factors leading to the resurgence of extreme economic nationalism and to the expansion of state powers urgently need to be written. The "liberal" trends, however challenged, prevailed, by and large, until the outbreak of World War I. They were greatly weakened by the war and in many cases reversed. Since 1914 international peace has never been secure, and, as Professor Rappard indicated in a passage previously quoted, this insecurity was the principal reason why the postwar movement towards freer international trade failed in the twenties. It is also one of the factors which account for the growth of the "new" economic nationalism.

Writing just after the end of World War I, Professor E. S. Furniss made the following interesting comments:[1]

"It is essential to nationalism, as modern nations have learned from the harsh experience of war, that the economic energy of a country be subjected to the control of a central intelligence 'in whose prudence and disposition it is to improve, manage, and fashion it to more or less advantage.' The diffused control which a laissez-faire policy places in the hands of those who possess the purchasing power can be relied upon to devote the labor energy of the nation to the production of goods and services having at the moment the greatest utility to individual consumers. But there is, and can be, no assurance that individual values will coincide with national values, and that the economic goods produced at the command of those who are willing and able to buy them will take a form applicable to national aims and purposes. This truth, whose rediscovery was an incident of the strenuous times through which the world has recently passed, was a commonplace of Mercantilist reasoning accepted without argument by the social writers of the eighteenth century."

National insecurity and nationalist aspirations, on the one hand, economic collectivism, on the other, are the parents of the troublesome offspring, that fashionable "young man about town" in the world of contemporary politics and economics (and how like his mercantilist grandfather he looks!), the "new economic nationalism."

[1] E. S. Furniss: *The Position of the Laborer in a System of Nationalism (A Study of the Later Theories of the Later English Mercantilists)* (Boston and New York, 1920), pp. 39–40. This important study should be required reading for everyone interested in mercantilism or dealing today with the problem of full employment.

"Great economic and social forces," wrote Lord Morley in his *Life of Richard Cobden*,[2] "flow with a tidal sweep over communities which are only half conscious of that which is befalling them. Wise statesmen are those who foresee what time is thus bringing, and endeavor to shape institutions and to mould men's thought and purpose in accordance with the change that is silently surrounding them. To this type Cobden by his character and his influence belonged."

Half a century later, a countryman of both Cobden and Morley started a great and successful campaign again to "mould men's thought and purpose in accordance with the change" that was surrounding them, not silently this time, but amidst the intermittent din of war and the rising rumble of depression-born discontent. John Maynard (later Lord) Keynes came out in favor of national self-sufficiency in an article published in 1933 in the *Yale Review* and three years later again took a determined stand in favor of economic nationalism in his *General Theory of Employment, Interest and Money*. Easily the most influential volume on economics that appeared in the past thirty years, it includes an eloquent vindication of mercantilism and is the principal source of intellectual inspiration for the modern generation of economic nationalists. The (now streamlined) car of social change had got into motion again; impressed by its speed and by its modern trimmings, did we but realize that it was moving in reverse gear?

2.

"In England between the years 1660 and 1775, dominant nationalism produced an intricate system of foreign and domestic policy, correlated with a structure of doctrine and theory which in many respects bore a fundamental likeness to that to which we have been growing accustomed in recent years"—wrote Professor Furniss in 1920,[3] thereby giving proof of an exceptionally keen insight into the fundamental social currents of the day. It was not until ten or fifteen years later that this insight became more general. With the appearance of Keynes's *General Theory*, mercantilism became once again academically respectable—one

---

2 American edition (Boston, 1881), p. 636.
3 E. S. Furniss: op. cit., p. 3.

hundred and sixty years after Adam Smith delivered his devastating attack upon it.

Mercantilism—what was it actually? It was a body of doctrines developed in England, France, and other western European countries from the sixteenth to the eighteenth centuries and concerned with economic policies of the state. It was not a uniform body of theory but rather a collection of many separate strands converging upon the central theme of state control of the nation's economy and of its trade with the outside world. Mercantilists were concerned with welfare and with power—and they considered strict governmental regulation of economic life as being indispensable for the attainment of either. They were greatly influenced by the political rise of the national state, by the prevalence of war and conflict, and by their concern over increasing both national production and the national stock of precious metals in which they saw a "treasure chest" in times of war and an expression of wealth at all times. The mercantilist policies were essentially nationalistic, often directed *against* the outside world. Their interest in foreign trade revolved around its net outcome in terms of inflow and outflow of precious metals; the principal aim of foreign trade was to obtain additional quantities of them. In the pursuit of increasing production, mercantilists urged a strict state supervision of both industry and labor, as well as the regulation of domestic consumption.

To give an example, here is a policy prescription which appeared in 1673 in *The Grand Concern of England Explained:*[4]

"As for the loss of Foreign Trade we had, and the want of the Consumption that used to be of our Manufactures in Foreign parts, no other reason can be given, but that Foreigners are able to make their work cheaper than we do, and thereby are able to undersell us where-ever we come. . . ."

The author goes on

". . . to enjoyn all English men not to wear anything but what is of our own Growth and Manufactures; which will increase Consumption at home, and set those at work who now live idle, and by giving them full work, would bring down their wages; so that then we having our Wool and Leather cheaper than Foreigners have, and be-

4 *The Grand Concern of England Explained* . . . (London, 1673), pp. 54–5 (quoted in Philip W. Buck's *The Politics of Mercantilism* (New York, 1942), p. 47.

ing able to manufacture them at as easy rates as they do, it will then necessarily follow, that we may undersell them in foreign markets. . . ."

As regards the international scene, mercantilists "saw a group of national states, organized domestically to develop their full economic strength and appealing to their subjects to contribute their utmost to that end, competing with each other for a limited amount of trade [5] and treasure,[6] hoping always to sell and never to buy, and continually willing to use force to achieve their greatness." [7]

Neo-mercantilists share the belief of their spiritual ancestors that trade means conflict and reject Cobden's idea that trade and peace go hand in hand. To the extent, therefore, that they desire peace, they advocate self-sufficiency—which, incidentally, tallies with their interest in planning autonomously the economic life of the country, in "insulation" from outside influences. This brings us back to Lord Keynes's article on "National Self-sufficiency" from which the following passages are well worth quoting:[8]

". . . it does not now seem obvious that a great concentration of national effort on the capture of foreign trade, that the penetration of a country's economic structure by the resources and the influence of foreign capitalists, and that a close dependence of our own economic life on the fluctuating economic policies of foreign countries are safeguards and assurances of international peace. It is easier in the light of experience and foresight to argue quite the contrary. . . .

"I sympathize . . . with those who would minimize, rather than with those who would maximize economic entanglements among nations. Ideas, knowledge, science, hospitality, travel—these are the things which should of their nature be international. But let goods be homespun whenever it is reasonably and conveniently possible, and, above all, let finance be primarily national.

". . . I am inclined to the belief that, after the transition is accomplished, a greater measure of national self-sufficiency and economic isolation among countries than existed in 1914 may tend to serve the cause of peace rather than otherwise. . . .

---

[5] One of the mercantilist fallacies which, to judge by its prevalence today, seems to be imperishable.

[6] Gold and silver.

[7] Buck: op. cit., p. 113.

[8] John Maynard Keynes: "National Self-sufficiency," *Yale Review,* Vol. XXII, Summer, 1933, pp. 757, 758, 760.

"National self-sufficiency . . . though it costs something, may be becoming a luxury which we can afford, if we happen to want it. . . .

"We each have our own fancy . . . we each should like to have a try at working out our own salvation. We do not wish, therefore, to be at the mercy of world forces working out, or trying to work out, some uniform equilibrium according to the ideal principles, if they can be called such, of *laissez-faire* capitalism. . . . We wish . . . to be our own masters, and to be as free as we can make ourselves from the interferences of the outside world." [9]

These views are controverted in the following observations by Professor Lionel Robbins who, in later years, became Keynes's closest associate in the promotion of international economic collaboration: [10]

"The idea is plain. To secure peace, some sacrifice . . . of the wealth which comes from international division of labor is desirable. But unfortunately it seems to rest upon a delusion. We will not pause to inquire how long 'ideas, knowledge, science, hospitality, travel' are likely to remain free when goods are 'as far as is reasonably and conveniently possible' homespun. . . . But we must recognize that this policy is incapable of being generalized. Mr. Keynes . . . may be right in supposing that, within the Empire, it would be possible at some sacrifice to reach greater self-sufficiency than in the past . . . There are certain other national groups in a similar position. But it is really ridiculous to suppose that such a policy is possible for the majority, given their present national boundaries. Given the present political divisions of the world, to recommend autarky as a general policy is to recommend war as an instrument for making autarky possible. No doubt Mr. Keynes would repudiate this. . . . It would be absurd to depict Mr. Keynes in any way as a war-monger. But . . . it is not absurd at all to depict war-mongering as the eventual consequence of policies which, in a fit of premature discouragement at the absence of quick success of his earlier internationalism, he has been led, half desperately, half frivolously, to adopt."

After the outbreak of World War II, events brought Lord Keynes much closer again to his "earlier internationalism," but many of his followers continued moving inexorably ahead on the path of extreme nationalism, economic and otherwise.

[9] See also: Keynes: *General Theory of Employment, Interest and Money* (London and New York, 1936), pp. 381–3.

[10] Lionel Robbins: *Economic Planning and International Order* (London, 1937), pp. 320–1.

Keynes's activities during the last years of his life,[11]—as author of the proposals for an "International Clearing Union," as one of the principal architects of the Bretton Woods system of "new monetary internationalism," as negotiator (in the fall of 1945) and chief defender in England of the American loan to Britain and of the economic agreements that accompany the loan—made him one of Britain's leading spokesmen for international collaboration and for multilateral trade. Some of his once ardent followers turned against him, in consequence, with often undisguised rancor.[12]

Having laid the intellectual groundwork under the modern resurgence of mercantilist nationalism and provided an academic rationalization for the ideological "tidal sweep" which resulted from war, insecurity, and collectivism, Lord Keynes would have been the first to denounce the extremist applications of his teachings. Keynes was, fundamentally, a liberal, a peace-lover, and a man of the world, while a great many of his followers were rabid nationalists and viewed state socialism with favor. There can be no doubt that his writings and teachings of the thirties did much to attract such a following. More recently, Keynes found himself in the position of that character from the fable who has been described by Goethe in verse and by Dukas in music! It would seem that towards the end of his career Keynes was no longer a "Keynesian" in good standing. Having long been known and admired for his courage not only to promote non-conformist ideas, but also to change his ideas and openly admit that fact, Keynes, but for his untimely death, might have given up his neo-mercantilism of the thirties and reverted to the internationalism of his earlier days. Instead, his last important works written in the thirties will now remain an inspiration to economic nationalists for years to come.

3.

The central preoccupation of the "new economic nationalists" is with employment. Like mercantilists, they are looking upon the national economy as an entity which must be managed and

---

[11] He died on April 21, 1946.
[12] For instance Paul Einzig in *The Banker,* London, January 1946, p. 17. Another "Keynesian," Thomas Balogh, attacked Keynes in a letter to the London *Economist* of January 5, 1946. Such instances could be multiplied.

controlled by the state; and they consider that the problem of employment ought to be settled on a national basis and by means of public policy. They do not trust, on the whole, the operations of the market system; instead they are favorably disposed towards collectivism. They consider that economic depressions that originate at home can be brought under control by means of appropriate national policies; but they view with concern depressions that originate abroad. They consider that appropriate measures of "insulation" can keep such disturbing influences away from a country's economy, thus making it possible to carry out the national plans and programs from which a stable prosperity is expected to result.

Politically, the new economic nationalism fits very well into the contemporary trend towards increasing the scope of economic planning by national governments and their agencies. The protagonists of that trend take it more or less for granted that by adopting specific plans and by carrying them out through appropriate systems of control, the government can promote, achieve, and maintain national full employment. The main emphasis is currently placed in these discussions on employment rather than on productivity—a point of view that is not without serious influence upon the international aspects of the problem, leading as it does to an insufficient recognition of the advantages of the international division of labor.

The propensity to plan economic developments through the agencies of the central government leads, in turn, in the direction of nationalism: generally, the powers of a government extend only to the limits of the national boundaries of the state; beyond these limits agreements and compromises must be reached with the governments of other states, and foreign economic conditions must be taken into consideration. Hence, the efficiency of planning and of control is the greatest within the country and declines when international considerations come into the picture. Therefore, advocates of centralized planning are inclined to seek their objectives through purely national measures. They are frequently impatient with international "interferences" and "complications" and are tempted to keep international economic relations at a minimum.[13]

---

[13] Cf. Lord Keynes: *General Theory of Employment, Interest and Money*, op. cit. Chapter XXIV; Sir William H. Beveridge: *Full Employment in a Free Society* (London

Historically, the new economic nationalism came of age at a time when the importance of developing business-cycle policies came to be generally acknowledged while, at the same time, there was not enough international economic collaboration in the world to make possible a world-wide attack on the problem. In the absence of an organized international approach, the pressing problems incident in the "great depression" of the 1930's had to be dealt with independently in the various countries. The lack of collaboration intensified nationalism. The nationalist solutions were mostly far from successful, but this failed to check the growth of the new nationalist doctrines. The "new" nationalists claimed that the world of 1930 was largely inherited from a preceding era of widespread economic internationalism; if only they could fashion it in the future in accordance with their own preferences, how much more successful would their policies be in practice! Hence, the advocacy of "insulation," the tendency to minimize the importance of foreign trade, the strong emphasis on the need for comprehensive national planning. Similar in that respect to the mercantilists of old, the "new" economic nationalists favor government regulation of production, trade, consumption, and employment. Their central objective and most successful slogan is *Full Employment*. Therefore, let us inquire into the meaning of that term.

4.

"Full employment" is one of those economic terms that are apt to arouse strong emotions rather than convey clear meanings. Such terms are apt to become the politician's weapon and the demagogue's delight; and, in retrospect, one is likely to find that a semantic innovation of doubtful value has been acquired at a heavy social cost. The reasons for the emotional appeal of the term "full employment" can easily be discovered: a generation that has gone through the hardships of the "Great Depression" and has experienced the hopelessness and misery of protracted mass-unemployment cannot fail to enthusiastically endorse a program—or even a slogan—which promises everybody a steady

---

and New York, 1945), especially Part VI; T. Balogh: *The International Aspects of Full Employment* in *The Economics of Full Employment* (Oxford, 1944); Henry A. Wallace, *Sixty Million Jobs* (New York, 1945).

job. As a political slogan, the term "full employment" is an attractive and a promising invention and is being worked hard on both sides of the Atlantic. It is only when we subject its meaning to a searching analysis that doubts and perplexities appear. More perplexities follow once we inquire into methods of action, into policies and institutions which lead to the proposed goal.

Those who speak of "full employment" have in mind not the employment of natural resources or of industrial plants, but the employment of available manpower. This notion, in spite of its apparent simplicity, gives rise to important queries. What is the employable population of a country? Shall it be defined as consisting of all men and women between the ages of X and Y who are physically and mentally fit for work? How are the age limits and the standards of fitness to be determined? Are all the employable persons to be guaranteed jobs? Are they all going to be obliged to work? If not, how can we determine in advance the number of those who will want jobs? Or we may simply mean that every employable person who wishes to work is to be guaranteed a job and be given one by the state if unable to find it without such assistance; this would mean "full employment of all those who are employable and wish to have a job." That notion is far from rigorous but it is, at least, operationally acceptable.

Let us go a step further. If the government assumes responsibility for full employment,[14] can it oblige a man or a woman to accept any job assigned him by the competent government agency? How about the right of an individual to choose, leave, and change a job? If the individual retains these rights (and in a democratic society it is essential that he should keep them), the task of the government to guarantee a job to everybody all the time becomes a very hazardous undertaking. So perhaps "full employment" does *not* mean that every employable person is to be assured of a job all the time? If that is the correct interpretation, the notion becomes unclear again. Actually, the term "full employment of manpower" can have two clear meanings and a good many hazy ones. The two *clear* meanings are the following:

[14] In the British White Paper on "Employment Policy" (May, 1944, Cmd. 6527) the opening sentence reads: "The Government accepts as one of their primary aims and responsibilities the maintenance of a high and stable level of employment after the war."

(1) Compulsory work for everybody whom the government considers fit to work. An individual has then almost no freedom to choose his job, to leave it or to change it. The government guarantees a job to everybody and plans the whole economic life accordingly; but everybody becomes liable to carry out the tasks that are assigned to him. This is—in essence—the formula of state socialism. It is applied, to a larger or lesser extent, in a war economy, though for different reasons. It can be applied rigorously or be attenuated. Its general principle is clear and consistent, but is neither liberal nor democratic. Besides adopting this system consciously, it is not impossible to drift into it gradually, having once accepted the general principle of a governmental guarantee of jobs.

(2) Avoidance of protracted mass-unemployment by appropriate business-cycle policies. This means forestalling booms and attenuating depressions, and is likely to fall short of "full employment" in the literal sense of the word. Minor cyclical unemployment would remain as well as structural unemployment due to changes in technology and in consumers' tastes. Being more flexible, this conception of "full employment" leaves to people their rights with respect to choosing and leaving a job, or, indeed, not working at all. It is also compatible to the maintenance of a free-enterprise economy. This approach calls for a variety of public policies, monetary, fiscal, etc. Much further study will be necessary before an adequate program of policy can be devised. In countries that wish to maintain their free-enterprise economy, especially in the United States, such studies are urgently needed.[15]

The term *full employment,* as used in the writings of economists, in political statements, and in current arguments and discussions, is rarely defined in a way which would make it clear which of the above-described meanings is intended. The omission is regrettable and may even be dangerous. Under certain circumstances the government might move in the direction of "full employment one" whereas the public might expect the realization of "full employment two"; or again, a sequence of

15 Cf. *Towards More Production, More Jobs, and More Freedom,* A Statement on National Policy by the Research Committee of the Committee for Economic Development (New York, 1945).

events may take place leading gradually from "two" to "one." Sir William H. Beveridge's recommendations, included in his *Full Employment in a Free Society,* provide, for example, for six main areas of state control: (1) a long-term program of planned public expenditures, including the regulation of private business investments, subsidies to consumers, etc.; (2) state control of all banking; (3) control over the location of industry, which "must be exercised ultimately by a central authority making a national plan for the whole country" (p. 170); (4) organized mobility of labor, involving a compulsory use of employment exchanges for all young people under eighteen;(5)permanent control over prices of selected goods; (6) state control of foreign trade. Should all these controls be well-established, the national economy would be subjected, in effect, to a centralized state control!

Full employment of the first type can only be sought by a national policy operating in an insulated economy; this involves, eventually, a full governmental control over the national economy and, of course, over all the dealings with foreign countries. An intensification of economic nationalism inevitably follows.

By contrast, full employment of the second type can be sought either by a national policy operating in insulation from the rest of the world, or by a national policy co-ordinated and integrated with the national policies of other countries. We shall presently examine these two alternatives more closely. First of all, however, we must deal with another important point: is "full employment" of man power a *sufficient* criterion of economic policy? Is it correct to proclaim it, as is so often done, to be *the* aim of economic policy, or are there other criteria to be considered? And if there are other criteria, are these supplementary to or conflicting with that of "full employment"?

Until the advent of the depression of the thirties, economists were less interested in employment than in national income. The "maximization of national income" is the objective with which the economic theory of the nineteenth and early twentieth centuries primarily concerned itself. And, in terms of that theory, economic equilibrium was not fully reached till all the factors of production, including labor, were completely employed, *and till each of them was employed in the most productive way possible.* More recently, a change of emphasis was brought about by the deep and protracted depression, a climax of ten years of economic developments, which, following the end of World War I, were full of uncertainties, difficulties, and contradictions. In England, these ten years were only semi-prosperous, with a hard core of chronic unemployment; in the United States, the ill-founded belief in a "permanent prosperity" gave way to an equally ill-supported doctrine of "secular stagnation." The chronic unemployment in England during the twenties, and the protracted large-scale unemployment all over the world in the thirties brought to the fore the issue of employment. In 1936 Lord Keynes presented a theory which was to acquire a great deal of importance and in terms of which a national economy could maintain a stable equilibrium even while having a large body of unemployed. Special policies were advocated to prevent this from happening. In the new doctrine, the emphasis was shifted from productivity to employment. *Employment at any cost* was deemed preferable to unemployment.

Aside from exceptionally serious depressions, the real choice does not lie, however, between employment at any cost, on the one side, and unemployment on the other. Actually, it lies between the various ways of securing employment and between the various settings in which the economic system can be made to function. The pre-Keynesian criteria of economic worthwhileness still hold good, even though at times they must be amended and brought up to date. We cannot rely any longer on automatism alone; we must supplement it by policy. We cannot expect unemployment to be always self-liquidating. The complex problems inherent in business cycles must be solved by carefully thought-out policies. But anti-depression policies must not be concerned with employment alone; they must embrace all the component elements of a well-working economy. If the economy functions smoothly, there is no chronic mass unemployment; if it is conducted with due regard for productivity and yield, standards of living go up; if it maintains trade relations with the rest of the world, there follow all the advantages accruing from an international division of labor.

5.

Let us now examine the impact of the "new" economic nationalism upon the question of business cycles and of international
trade. We have seen that economic stability may be sought within
the narrow confines of the national boundaries of an "insulated"
country, or within the broad expanse of the world economy. The
choice depends to some extent upon the interpretation given to
the phenomenon of business cycles: do we have a world-wide
business cycle with different regional manifestations or are there
as many national cycles as there are countries? This question is
not mere logical hair-splitting: according to how it is answered,
we are led to business-cycle policies devised by international
agreement or to policies based on purely national considerations.
Needless to say, internationally-minded economists give the first
answer; economic nationalists give the second.

The fact that the world is divided into separate states, each
with its own economic policies and political institutions and controls, each collecting its own statistics in its own particular way,[16]
makes it seem plausible that *national* business cycles do exist.
But is this not a mere statistical illusion? Is it not misleading to
believe that an economic movement so pervasive and so deeply
rooted as the cyclical alternation of prosperities and depressions is
based on the historical accident of political boundaries? The
world's resources are unevenly distributed both on the surface
of the planet and underneath it, and international trade and finance continuously redistribute them among people living in
various parts of the globe. If trade is free, prices of staple commodities tend to get equalized throughout the world (except for
costs of transportation), and other prices tend to be more or less
indirectly related to each other. Regional specialization of production tends to grow with expanding trade and transcends
national boundaries. The international division of labor increases,
as we know, the efficiency of individual countries in particular
branches of production; the specialized industries acquire a productive capacity geared to the world market at large, not to the

[16] The international conference on economic statistics which met in Geneva in 1928
under the aegis of the League of Nations sought a unification of statistical methods
but failed to reach any significant agreements.

domestic market alone. Thus, countries need export markets and they also need imports from abroad. The various national economies are parts of a complex entity, the world economy, and their individual economic destinies are interrelated and intertwined.

It cannot be emphasized too often or too strongly that the underlying physical realities of the planet call for its economic integration. There are, to be sure, great regional diversities in the patterns of economic life, even in one and the same country. This is abundantly illustrated by domestic experiences of the United States. We should expect more and greater divergencies to exist between various parts of the world economy. When trade and capital movements are not free between countries, these discrepancies become greatly amplified. The more restrictions the national governments impose upon economic relations with foreign countries, the more justification there seems to be for the claim that every national economy is a separate entity with its own business cycles, and that each must look for economic stabilization in its own national way. The practice of "old-fashioned" protectionism thus paves the way for the spread of the "new" economic nationalism. An idea, originally fallacious, if acted upon, may in the end create an appearance of its own justification. Economic nationalism brings about the disintegration of the world economy into an aggregate of national economies, loosely linked together; this condition of the world then serves as an argument in favor of applying some more nationalistic and disintegrating policies in order to "insulate" the national economy against "disturbing" foreign influences. The origins of this concept of "insulation" can be found in the controversy over which of the following two objectives of policy is more important: the stability of domestic prices or the stability of foreign exchange rates? Lord Keynes who was among the first to lay much emphasis on that dilemma, presented the issue as follows:[17]

"Since . . . the rate of exchange of a country's currency with the currency of the rest of the world . . . depends on the relation between the internal price-level and the external price-level, it follows that the exchange cannot be stable unless *both* internal *and* external price-levels remain stable. If, therefore, the external price-level lies outside our control, we must submit either to our own internal price-level or to our exchange being pulled about by external influences. If the

[17] J. M. Keynes: *A Tract on Monetary Reform* (London, 1923), pp. 154–5.

external price-level is unstable, we cannot keep *both* our own price-level *and* our exchanges stable. And we are compelled to choose."

In actual reality the dilemma is usually much less sharply defined. As Professor John H. Williams rightly points out:[18]

"Under more normal conditions . . . it will probably be found that the dilemma between the aims of external and internal monetary stability is more apparent than real, and that it arises very largely out of a too literal acceptance of the abstractions of gold-standard theory."

There is no reason for a conflict between the stability of domestic prices and that of exchange rates, unless the various countries adopt widely divergent business-cycle policies. If, e.g., in the face of a depression, one country should adopt an expansionist monetary policy and another country a policy of deflation, as did happen several times during the thirties, a breakdown of the stability of exchange rates is inevitable.

In the above-quoted *Tract on Monetary Reform,* Lord Keynes expressed a preference for national price-level stability as against the stability of exchange rates. In his later writings he continued to favor the independence of national economic action as against international limitations resulting, for example, from the rules of the gold standard. Thus, in the *Treatise on Money,*[19] he argued that exchange stability might lead to economic instability in individual countries on account of the influence that, under the gold standard, is exercised by gold movements upon the rate of interest. The rate might have to be fixed at a level which would preclude the achievement of a domestic investment equilibrium, and thus lead to unemployment. A detailed examination of this argument shows that it is by no means convincing. The rate of interest affected by the gold movements is the short-term discount rate of the central bank whereas the rate that affects investments is the long-term rate on loans made in the capital market. The two are only very vaguely connected, and the latter is much more stable over time than the former. Hence, here also the conflict between domestic and international stability is "more apparent than real."

As we have seen before, the maintenance of stable rates of ex-

---

[18] John H. Williams: *The World Monetary Dilemma* (New York, 1934), reprinted in *Postwar Monetary Plans and Other Essays* (New York, 1944), p. 195.
[19] London, 1930.

change requires an international co-ordination of business-cycle policies. Monetary nationalists would surrender exchange stability as the price of a full freedom of national action in matters of economic policy. But in reality the price is higher than that: without stable exchange rates, the world economy tends to become more and more disintegrated, while the "protection" of the national economy against outside interference calls for various additional restrictions and controls. Since no one desires wildly fluctuating rates of exchange, however, exchange control eventually comes into the picture, along with other restrictions and regulations.

In the thirties policies of "insulation" were very much *en vogue*. It is true that in those years no setup for international economic collaboration was available. Nevertheless, it is noteworthy that the nationalistic course of policy was viewed by many writers not with regret but with approval, as being a wise, modern conception of economic policy. Combined with preoccupations with full employment this nationalistic bias has brought forth a very startling revival of mercantilist views on foreign trade. One could quote many examples of the "new" doctrines on foreign trade, but the following passage from an article published in the *Economist* of London will be sufficient to indicate the tenor of the argument.[20]

"The existence of a negative, or unfavorable, balance of payments is a hindrance to the attainment of full employment. This can be explained either in crude practical terms or in the formulæ of the theoretical economist. To the man in the street exports 'give employment' and imports 'take away employment'—and the man in the street is, in this case, quite right. From the employment point of view the process of trading is that of substituting one type of employment—that 'given' by exports—for another—that 'taken away' by imports—with the object of deriving from the substitution a net increase in productive efficiency. But, clearly, if the trade is unbalanced, if imports exceed exports, the process of exchange takes away more employment than it provides and there is a net deduction from the total of employment."

This is a very odd statement, yet a very characteristic one too. It is the old mercantilist viewpoint dressed up in modern termi-

[20] "Trade and Employment," the *Economist*, London, January 15, 1944. This is one of the *Economist's* widely discussed series of articles entitled "The Principles of Trade."

nology and leaving aside, somehow, the accomplishments of economic research and the experiences of economic practice of the past hundred and fifty years. The attempt at representing advantages from trade in terms of employment is very peculiar if we consider that the "balance" or "unbalance" of trade is calculated in monetary terms, not in terms of man-hours. The effect of given exports or given imports on employment is most difficult to establish, especially if we make allowances for all the indirect effects. And how about the historic experience? How about Britain's systematic import surplus associated for many decades with great prosperity? After all history did not start in 1920! And how about the great unemployment in the United States in the thirties associated with an export surplus? And what can be said, in the light of the quoted statement, about the fact that Great Britain is facing immense post-war difficulties owing to the fact that she can no longer afford as large an import surplus as she used to have in the years past?

All this would perhaps matter but little were it not that the *Economist* voices widely held views. They are presented, in a much more elaborate way, in a number of current publications, and are a factor in the international situation, the practical importance of which must not be underestimated. They represent a striking throwback to mercantilism and might be summed up in the following series of statements:

(a) Imports interfere with full employment; should therefore be kept at a minimum.

(b) Exports are favorable to full employment; should therefore be stimulated.

(c) However, a pressure of exports, linked with a restriction of imports, breeds international conflicts.

(d) While, if exports and imports balance, the effect on full employment is nil.

(e) Hence, foreign trade is, on the whole, unimportant from the point of view of full employment.

(f) And hence also it is essential that full employment should be secured by domestic policy.

Which brings us back to national economic planning within an insulated economy.

CHAPTER VI

State-Controlled Foreign Trade

THE EMERGENCE of state-controlled and state-conducted foreign trade is undoubtedly the most important international economic phenomenon of the twentieth century. This development represents, as we have seen in the preceding chapter, a reversion to mercantilist conceptions—but it far exceeds anything experienced in the sixteenth, seventeenth, and eighteenth centuries. The modern growth of the powers of the state has brought them to a level never before attained.

In Soviet Russia the control by the state of all production and trade involves, of necessity, a state monopoly of foreign commerce. There can be no private foreign trade when there is no private economic activity. In Fascist Italy and Nazi Germany there remained the outward appearances of private enterprise, but all economic activity was controlled (if not operated) by the state—and so were all economic dealings with foreign countries. During the war years all countries, including the United States, subjected their foreign trade to state control in order better to marshal resources for the needs of war. The great economic difficulties faced by Great Britain, France, and other countries as a result of the war and in connection with reconstruction also call for over-all national plans of imports and exports. Now as in the thirties, there is advocacy of state control over foreign trade and foreign payments as corollary of the welfare planning for "full employment." And, finally, the insecurities of the postwar world, in which hostilities are over but peace is not yet firmly established, lead to continued planning for national security, which cannot fail to effect the course and the structure of foreign trade.

In brief, there are *four* main reasons for the growth of international state trading and of state control over private international trading:

(1) The growth of state socialism and collectivism, leading to extensive "nationalization" of economic activity and to state monopolies of foreign trade;

[106]

(2) Planning for national security (a variant of this is the planning for aggressive war of which the thirties offer many telling examples);

(3) Planning for "full employment," which we have discussed in the preceding chapter;

(4) Need to meet rapidly emergency situations, due to the war and to reconstruction, and resulting in major disequilibria in national balances of payments. It should be noted that the pursuit of objectives listed under (1) and (2) above can frequently result in chronic balance-of-payments difficulties, thus making the pressure for state control cumulative.

The historic foreign-trade issue of the nineteenth century consisted of the struggle between free trade and protection. In the United States this continues to be the leading issue, on account of the general acceptance of the principles of a private-enterprise economy. But, viewed in a world-wide perspective, the real conflict today is one between free-enterprise foreign trade and state-controlled trade. Policy decisions adopted by the United States in the next few years are likely to influence very considerably the future of free-enterprise foreign trade in the world, which will, in turn, react upon the future of free enterprise within the United States.

2.

There are two principal instruments by means of which the government can control the quantity, value, and structure of imports. One of them is *import quotas,* the other *exchange control.* The first of these instruments determines the maximum quantities of specific commodities that are allowed to enter the country; the other controls all the outgoing payments and, thereby, the value and composition of imports.[1] The problems of allocation and discrimination that arise in the administration of exchange control are also encountered in connection with quotas. Bureaucracy grows by leaps and bounds, and administrative discretion, bordering upon the arbitrary, becomes the source of discriminations, pressures, and abuses. In order to have some system for de-

[1] Cf. League of Nations Publications, II, Economic and Financial, 1943. II. A. 4, Jacob Viner: *Trade Relations between Free-Market and Controlled Economies;* and 1943. II. A. 5, G. Haberler: *Quantitative Trade Controls.*

termining the quantities and values of authorized imports, a more or less explicit national economic plan must be worked out. Quantitative restrictions adopted under the impact of emergency conditions lead, if co-ordinated and systematized, to a considerable amount of national economic planning. The converse is evidently also true; a country that has engaged upon a course of central planning of its economic life will establish quantitative controls of its foreign trade in order to fit it better into the over-all national plan.

Direct government controls can be used not only to regulate imports but also to plan and promote exports. When the government assumes control over foreign trade, it can also introduce export licenses and establish export subsidies. We have in that respect a great deal of mercantilist tradition. Export licenses tie in with exchange control and serve as a useful check on incoming foreign exchange, preventing exporters from keeping their balances abroad instead of selling them to their own central bank. They are also useful in directing the geographical structure of exports, though this is a less customary procedure.

Import and export controls combined are a part of the trading system referred to in Chapter I and called "bilateralism" about which more will presently be said. Export subsidies are the reverse of import duties, in that they make the exported commodity cheaper to the foreign buyer than would be the case without the subsidy. By that means the output of high cost producers may be kept in world markets and compete with more efficient foreign producers. Subsidies are used in government-sponsored "dumping" for the purpose of obtaining additional amounts of foreign exchange.

Now it will be noted that "autonomous" price policies may, by keeping domestic prices (at prevailing rates of exchange) above world prices, result in export difficulties and in a tendency of imports to grow. Export subsidies and quantitative import controls counteract these difficulties and facilitate—in the short run—the maintenance of equilibrium in foreign payments. Such a way of keeping foreign payments balanced is, however, artificial and purely momentary: the basic causes of disequilibrium remain in existence, and more restrictions and more subsidies become necessary. This is an expensive way of running a country's economic relations with the outside world! Sometimes that way is chosen deliberately in the pursuit of some particular objectives of national economic planning; often, however, as in the thirties, it is "the line of least resistance . . . to bolster up the *status quo* by an import restriction instead of carrying out desirable economic adjustments." [2]

Balance-of-payments difficulties may also be due to exceptionally heavy imports occasioned—as in Germany, Italy, and Japan in the thirties—by the building of a powerful war machine, or—as in many countries at the present time—by the requirements of postwar reconstruction. In either case there is a great temptation to export *at all costs* with the help of subsidies, and to regulate both the volume and the structure of imports through quotas and exchange control.

When trade is state-controlled costs of production lose much of their effectiveness as a factor determining the volume and structure of exports. As Robert Boothby, a Conservative member of the British Parliament and a staunch supporter of state-managed trade, wrote a few years ago with reference to postwar conditions and policies: "*Although costs will no longer be the decisive factor in export trade,* it will still be necessary to produce goods of a kind and of a quality that other countries will wish to buy." [3] The italicized part of the statement is the expression of the ultimate consequences of substituting state control for market prices. Economic relationships lose their significance and are replaced by public administration at home and by ruthless strife abroad. For evidently dumping, subsidies, import restrictions, and various discriminations lead to retaliations and countermeasures. [4] A jungle grows amidst the ruins of a free economy.

The following complaint, voiced by the London *Economist* after the acceptance by Parliament of the American loan and of the commercial policy proposals attached to it, [5] is symptomatic of that fear of the competitive market that psychologically underlies much of the scorn for it that is currently voiced by the "new" economic nationalists: [6]

[2] *Quantitative Trade Controls,* op. cit., p. 37.

[3] Robert Boothby: *The New Economy* (London, 1943), p. 86. Italics added.

[4] Exchange depreciation as a means of furthering exports, a device much favored in the early thirties, became so stultified through reprisals and counterdepreciations that today there are but few advocates of that particular policy.

[5] See below, Chapters X and XI.

[6] The *Economist,* London, December 22, 1945; leading article entitled "The Consequences," p. 898.

"It should . . . be remembered that, under the American commercial proposals, very few special methods can be used to assist British exports. The exchange value of the pound sterling cannot be reduced more than ten percent without the consent of our competitors.[7] Export subsidies are not permitted after the first three years, except for 'commodities in surplus supply,' which the United Kingdom, unlike the United States, does not export. Reciprocal bargains for the mutual assurance of markets are very strictly ruled out.[8] Imperial preference is to be reduced—which will hurt British exports—in exchange for tariff reductions elsewhere—which will not help British exports any more than those of any other nation."

The *Economist,* an exponent—in polite and moderate terms—of the "new" economic nationalism, has on other occasions lauched strong attacks, not against the *principle* of multilateral trade, but against its full *application* by Great Britain in the post-war years. Practical applications of principles matter at least as much, however, as the principles themselves. Vocal tributes paid to principles are of small consequence if life is allowed to go on without any regard for them. The postulate of non-discrimination occupies a very central position in this controversy. The *Economist,* while attacking it, does not discard it outright; instead, it proposes a compromise:[9]

". . . there is, or should be, a clear distinction between discrimination which, without increasing the sum total of world trade, merely transfers markets from one supplier to another, and discrimination which creates new trade between the principals without injuring third parties. If the same name and the same condemnation are applied equally to both, then the doctrine of 'non-discrimination' becomes one of the greatest barriers to trade expansion that exist—indeed in present practical circumstances, perhaps the greatest barrier of all."

Well, this *sounds* more reasonable than it is in reality. Not even the *Economist* could produce a good, objective criterion of policy which would distinguish the good "discrimination A" from the bad "discrimination B." In actual practice, discrimination would be just discrimination, a seed of international ill will and a potent economic dissolvent. The last part of the above quotation is com-

[7] This is a reference to the Bretton Woods Agreements; what these require, however, is not the consent of Britain's competitors but of the authorities of the International Monetary Fund—which is not quite the same thing!

[8] That is a neat euphemistic description of "bilateralism."

[9] The *Economist,* January 13, 1945, article on "Peacetime Mutual Aid," p. 36.

pletely at variance with reality. In the past non-discrimination has had a most wholesome influence upon the growth of international trade, while the effect of its absence has always been stifling and disruptive.

The *Economist's* subtle, moderate, and urbane attacks against multilateral, nondiscriminating trade are peculiarly dangerous on account, precisely, of their apparent "reasonableness." The contours of the picture become blurred; the contrasts appear less important than they are in reality; the reader gets off guard and may accept expedients which contradict and stultify very important principles. An acceptance of multilateral trade, subject to crippling reservations, is more dangerous than a frontal attack, such as, for example, Mr. Boothby's blunt assertion that "the unregulated competitive system of international trade is stone dead and will never be revived. A world-wide flux of frontiers, economic systems, social systems, ideas, philosophies, and faiths will confront us after this war; but 'laissez-faire' capitalism and free trade will not be amongst them. That hoary old shibboleth, 'the removal of trade barriers,' can therefore be thrown without a qualm into the dustbin in which it should have been deposited many years ago." [10] The *Economist's* kind of friendship for economic internationalism might prove more dangerous to its survival than Mr. Boothby's hostility. The saying comes to mind, cynical and yet at times so true: "O Lord, save me from my friends; I can myself take care of my enemies!"

3.

Let us now return to the restrictive devices that are adopted when the state actively and directly undertakes to control foreign trade. We have indicated already that they fall into two main groups: quotas and exchange control. Bilateral clearing agreements are a particular outgrowth of these basic methods. Of these devices, quotas are much less devastating than exchange control. In the words of Professor Viner, "the quota system, as compared to a full-fledged exchange control, involves much less of a break with the free-market economy, much less departure from orthodox monetary practices, much less interference with private business,

[10] Robert Boothby, op. cit., pp. 69–70.

a much lighter and simpler administrative burden." [11] Quotas are more likely, therefore, to be adopted in emergency by countries essentially devoted to private enterprise, while countries on the road to state socialism are generally inclined towards exchange control. As has been pointed out before, exchange control represents an important step in the direction of collectivism.

Unlike tariffs, to which price adjustments can be made, quotas rigidly limit the quantity of particular goods that can enter the country. If, at the formerly quoted price, that quantity falls short of market requirements, the price of the affected commodity will go up. This amounts to the establishment of a monopoly situation in the importing country; consequently, an increased monopoly price is charged to the consumer. The monopolist's profit is earned by the importer or by the exporter or is divided among them, as the case may be. Instead of a larger volume of business at a lower price, we have a smaller volume of business at a higher price. As is the case in all trade restrictions, it is the consumer who foots the bill, partly in the form of higher prices paid for the imported article—or for the "protected" home product—and partly (if he cannot afford the higher price) in the loss of enjoyment he might have derived from the commodity in artificial short supply.

Import quotas introduced as emergency measures in countries, otherwise determined to keep a free-market economy, ought to be abandoned as soon as the emergency is over. On the whole, they tend to be less self-perpetuating than exchange control, but, like all economic restrictions, they create vested interests, both in business circles and among the bureaucracy. The most effective way of avoiding their use altogether probably lies in a co-ordinated international attack on economic depressions.

As we know, tariffs interfere with the international division of labor and reduce its advantages without, however, interfering with multilateral trade. Import quotas, international cartel arrangements, and export subsidies interfere much more thoroughly with the division of labor and with the operation of world markets. To the extent to which they lend themselves to discriminations—and they are in their essence discriminatory—they also represent a certain interference with the effective functioning of multilateral trade. Exchange control, on the other hand, inter-

[11] Jacob Viner, in the League of Nations study: *Trade Relations between Free-market and Controlled Economics,* op. cit., p. 63.

feres directly with multilateral settlements and leads straight into 'bilateralism." The completion of that process is the establishment of a state monopoly of foreign trade. Actually the difference between a full-fledged system of exchange control and direct trading by a state monopoly is one of form rather than of substance.[12] In either case it represents a very great challenge to free-enterprise countries and a development dangerous to the peace of the world. By becoming subjected to a full state control, international trade is taken out of the orbit of private life and moved into that of public affairs. It becomes a part of international relations in general, is subject to political influences and pressures, may be a source of political discords and frictions.

In concluding his inquiry into the varied implications of state-controlled trade, Professor Viner writes:

> . . . the substitution of state control for private enterprise in the field of international economic relations would, with a certain degree of inevitability, have a series of undesirable consequences, to wit: the injection of a political element into all major international economic transactions; the conversion of international trade from a predominantly competitive to a predominantly monopolistic basis; a marked increase in the potentiality of business disputes to generate international friction . . ."[13]

In the absence of international law to govern such relations, as they are governed by well-established judicial processes in private commercial relations, diplomacy will be "the best substitute available for nonexistent law or mores," and that diplomacy "will by inherent necessity be such that the possibility of resort to force in case of an unsatisfactory outcome of the diplomatic negotiations will be a trump card in the hands of powerful countries, and . . . weak countries will have to rely for their economic security primarily on their ability to acquire powerful friends, who will probably be acquirable, if at all, only at a heavy political or economic price."[14]

[12] The emphasis here is on "monopoly"; the state can evidently engage in direct commercial operations for its own account without greatly interfering with the operations of a free-market economy. Here we speak only of the situations which arise when *all* (or most) foreign trade is either conducted by government agencies or by private firms acting under specific government licenses.

[13] Jacob Viner: "International Relations between State-Controlled National Economics," *American Economic Review*, Vol. XXXIV, No. 1, Part 2, Supplement, March 1944, p. 320.

[14] Ibid.

There are ample historic illustrations to bear out Viner's contention. The most notorious case of economic power-politics is that of the commercial policies of Nazi Germany. Even though they have often been described in all their lurid details, it may not be superfluous to remind the reader of one or two typical episodes. In doing so we shall draw on the eye-witness account of Douglas Miller who was Commercial Attaché at the American Embassy in Berlin all through the thirties.[15] Germany developed to the full the system of bilateral trading, dividing her foreign trade into separate sectors, each corresponding to one foreign country. Within each sector Germany drew all the advantages (a) from being a strong economic unit, and (b) from being a debtor of her partner. The former consideration was particularly useful in Germany's dealings with weaker countries, each of which was more dependent upon its trade with Germany than Germany was upon her trade with that particular country. In order to make the dependency greater, many ingenious (and often unscrupulous) devices were used by Germany to break up her partner's trade with the rest of the world, to isolate it from the network of multilateral trade into complete dependency on Germany's good will. In addition to these tactics, Dr. Schacht, the principal architect of this system, discovered that a debtor country can wield a great deal of power over its creditors, providing it is a relatively large debtor. This is explained in the following way by Professor Howard S. Ellis:[16]

"If we look back one step to discover the power which enables one country to impose bilateral trade arrangements upon another we find that the most common source has been the threat of a debtor country in current bilateral trade to stop payment unless conditions suitable to its purposes are met . . . It should be sharply emphasized that this power of the current-account debtor in a given bilateral relation cannot be brought to bear upon a particular country *unless* the bilateral trade of the two is separated from the rest of its trade."

In addition, "if a country knows that another is dependent upon it for new loans, it can secure bilateral agreements"[17] from its would-be debtor. This kind of dependency can be artificially

[15] Douglas Miller: *You Can't Do Business with Hitler* (Boston, 1941).
[16] "Bilateralism and the Future of International Trade," *Essays in International Finance,* No. 5, Summer, 1945, Princeton University, Princeton, N. J., p. 10.
[17] Ibid.

fostered by making relations politically difficult between the "dependent" country and *other* potential suppliers of capital. The tactics of "isolate and rule" are very applicable in this context.

When states, rather than individuals, trade with one another, a point is always reached where trade and politics become inextricably entangled. A monopolist with a gun in his hand, facing a lonely client, is well-nigh irresistible. The only occasions when an aggressively bilateralist country encounters a serious obstacle arise when it trades with a very strong country or when the country it deals with succeeds in keeping its own *debtor* status on current account. A characteristic occurrence told by Douglas Miller illustrates the latter point:[18]

"It was not long before most of my commercial attaché colleagues in Berlin, whose countries were working under clearings, spent a great part of their efforts in preventing shipments from their own countries to Germany, since they were fearful of running up too big a credit and finally being forced to take a loss. The Minister from Nicaragua in Berlin proudly explained that he had succeeded in stopping Nicaraguan shipments to Germany before they exceeded German goods sent to Nicaragua, and his government even went so far as to make sure that German goods entering Nicaraguan ports should actually be unloaded from the ships and placed in warehouses on the docks under Nicaraguan control before they allowed compensating products to be loaded. In that way, the little country managed to keep on the debtor side and could avoid the high-pressure tactics of the German debtor. Other countries were less cautious. They swallowed the German bait, hook and all, enthusiastically shipping commodities with little thought of how they were eventually to be paid."

The fact that trade was depressed throughout the world helped the German tactics, of course. Experience shows that the growth of bilateralist trade is very far from being an unmixed blessing to all parties concerned. The *clearings*[19] mentioned by Mr. Miller worked in such a way that the country with an export surplus would acquire a bank balance in Germany which could be only

[18] Douglas Miller: op. cit., pp. 74–5.

[19] Clearings "provided that as a rule no transactions were to be for cash but that exporters in Germany would ship, for example, to Yugoslavia and be credited with the mark value of their shipments by the German Reichsbank. Yugoslav exporters to Germany would be credited by dinars by the central bank in Belgrade, with the two banks balancing accounts. Payment was credited to the exporters in each country in their local currency, and at the end of each year the balance would be carried forward in favor of one or the other country to apply against next year's transactions." Douglas Miller: op. cit., p. 73.

used for the purchase of goods on German terms, often goods to be selected from a limited list offered by Germany. The alternative to buying these goods on these terms was to remain indefinitely the owner of blocked marks. The more widespread the use of bilateral settlements, the greater was the premium attached to the possession of *free* currencies that could be spent in the markets of the world at their owner's discretion. The Germans developed many devious techniques for the acquisition of such free balances.

Another quotation from Douglas Miller's book will round up the picture:[20]

". . . the South African government, under pressure from domestic wool growers, sold its entire wool clip to Germany against the future delivery of German locomotives, automotive equipment, and similar commodities. Unfortunately, as time elapsed, the South Africans were unable to get deliveries of German automobiles at prices which were at all in line with the cars offered from the United States and other countries. German locomotive plants seemed unable to deliver equipment which would suit the South African railroads, and the export of different types of electrical equipment, machinery and tools was prohibited, as these products were needed for the German army . . ."

The South Africans had German marks on the books of German banks but obtained no much-needed merchandise in return for their wool. Since, however, at that time world markets were shrunken, they went on selling wool to Germany and accumulating mark balances. The only way out for them would have been to find other outlets; the only way of checking the spread of bilateralist exploitation is to promote the growth of multilateral trade.

Douglas Miller's accounts are quoted here for a purpose other than telling a good story. They illustrate the abuse that can result from state-controlled trade if the state in question is strong and ruthless. Except under wartime conditions, full-fledged government control of foreign trade can only exist in an authoritarian country or in one moving in the direction of totalitarianism; and thus the check upon arbitrary governmental actions, which is provided, in free societies, by an independent and articulate public opinion, is generally missing. The examples quoted above relate to Germany; but the reason for the state of affairs they serve to illustrate must be found in the fact that Germany was

20 Ibid., pp. 76–7.

a strong and ruthless country of which the government had full control over its economic life and, in particular, over its foreign trade and payments. Analogous developments must be anticipated whenever a powerful governmental monopoly of foreign trade decides fully to use the powers that it possesses. The world learned the lesson that it "could not do business with Germany"; but can business be done with *any* totalitarian economy, with *any* state monopoly of foreign trade? This is one of the most important questions with which we are faced when making plans for the reconstruction of a world economy.

4.

A free-enterprise country finds itself in a position of comparative weakness when confronted with a country of comparable economic strength whose foreign trade is entirely controlled (or even operated) by the state. The former appears as a geographic entity embracing a large number of individual concerns; the other enters world trade as a single monopolistic corporation armed with all the monopolist's powers often supported by all the politician's wiles. It can practice discriminations and use economic, political, even military power to reach its foreign-trade objectives. The free-enterprise country is faced, in consequence, with two major hazards:

(1) Its market in the state-controlled country is dependent upon the good will of that country's government; it can be expanded or contracted by administrative fiat, often in response to political rather than economic considerations; if it is an important market, the free-enterprise country finds that its own prosperity may depend upon the arbitrary decisions of an authoritarian foreign government.

(2) Its markets in third countries are subject to the competition of a foreign-trade monopoly that can easily practice dumping, subsidize exports, use various means of pressure to promote its own interests.

If the private companies of the free-enterprise country go to *their* government for help and support, the result is an introduction of state controls into that country also. In that manner state control of foreign trade tends to spread to free-market countries which are put on the defensive by state-controlled partners or competitors. The thirties provided telling examples of such spread of controls. But this is clearly undesirable from the point of view of those who favor the maintenance of free markets and private economic activity. It is also undesirable from the point of view of economic internationalism because the spread of government powers means a corresponding increase in the scope of nationalism. What, then, are the alternatives?

An international convention on "rules of the game" accepted by both free-market and state-monopoly countries is conceivable and should certainly be aimed at; but it would not be wise to place too much reliance on it.[21] But regardless of whether such a general agreement is attainable or not, countries which favor the maintenance of free enterprise and multilateral trade can accomplish a great deal by creating as wide an area of free payments and relatively unobstructed trade as possible. Membership in it must be opened to all countries of like convictions and policies and to these countries only; its advantages must be such as to make it attractive to countries which are wavering between state-controlled and free-market trade. It is important that free-enterprise countries should, by adopting liberal commercial policies, provide markets for the produce of countries that, in the absence of such outlets, might fall into complete dependency on some authoritarian state's trading monopoly.

Relations between free-market and state-controlled economies should be very cautious and circumspect. The following broad principles might be suggested to govern these relationships:

(1) Trade agreements should be reached by which the advantages of the "multilateral group" mentioned before could be extended to the controlled economies, provided these renounce:

(a) bilateralism in their relations with *all* countries;
(b) the use of their monopoly powers to control their imports in a discriminating way;
(c) the use of their monopoly powers to withhold exportable goods or to promote exports by means of subsidies, dumping and political pressures.

---

[21] In 1937 M. Paul van Zeeland, then Prime Minister of Belgium, was entrusted by the French and British governments with the task of working out proposals for a general reduction of obstacles to international trade. His report published in 1938 was largely inconclusive; in his attempt to find a formula acceptable to *all* the leading countries, including those that practiced full state control and bilateralism, he was unable to produce a single concrete suggestion.

(2) In the absence of such trade agreements trade with state-controlled economies (foreign trade monopolies) should be kept at as low a level as feasible. Reports should be issued periodically by the governments of the free-market countries making public the details of the trade relations with countries whose foreign trade is state controlled, and warning, whenever necessary, against excessive involvement of particular industries and of the national economy as a whole. It should be made abundantly clear that these reports are entirely nonpolitical in their intent, and that they are issued only on account of the risks resulting for a private-enterprise economy from becoming too dependent upon any single monopolistic market.

(3) Finally, an international trade organization should be established in order to supervise and co-ordinate the various agreements and to promote the spread of multilateral, nondiscriminating trade. Concrete proposals for the establishment of such an organization have been formulated by the United States Government and the matter has reached the preliminary stages of international action; we shall revert to it in Chapter XI.

BOOK THREE

Towards a World Economy

CHAPTER VII

International Trade, National Prosperity, and Employment

WE SHALL BE mainly concerned in the present chapter with a novel and troublesome "chicken-and-egg" argument over the relationship between domestic "full employment" and thriving international trade. Statements on that subject could fill a sizable pamphlet; one or two representative opinions follow as a starting point for our discussion. Thus we find the following observations in the statement on *International Trade, Foreign Investment and Domestic Employment* issued in 1945 by the Research Committee of the Committee for Economic Development (hereafter designated as C. E. D.):[1]

"We recognize that the level of employment in the United States is not primarily dependent on international trade. It would be possible to have practically everyone within our own borders employed even if we discontinued imports and exports absolutely, but it would cause a great readjustment, much inefficient production, and a lower standard of living. Those defending exports on the ground that they are indispensable to high employment misstate the case. . . ."

Three members of the committee took exception to that statement and appended to it dissenting footnotes. Mr. John F. Fennelly wrote:[2]

"I cannot accept the assumption that the volume of foreign trade has little or no direct bearing on the level of domestic employment. . . . Full employment is clearly possible without foreign trade in a totalitarian economy. It seems equally clear, however, that high levels of employment can only be maintained in a system of private competitive enterprise under conditions of rising standards of living. From this, it follows that foreign trade for a free society is intimately connected with the domestic employment problems. . . ."

Messrs. Harry Scherman and Paul G. Hoffman commented at length, emphasizing that "everybody always, in thinking and talking about this matter, assumes—and quite properly—that

[1] *International Trade, Foreign Investment and Domestic Employment* (Research Committee of the Committee for Economic Development, 1945), p. 100.
[2] Ibid., p. 11, footnote.

our present standard of living shall be maintained and even raised." And, they go on to say:[3]

". . . when this is assumed, importing on a large scale—as well as exporting—are indispensable to high employment *in the kind of economy with its high standard of living* that Americans now enjoy. . . . the *existing pattern of American production,* and with it an established occupational pattern . . . is to a very large extent determined by our exchanges of goods with other countries, and particularly by the incoming side of that trade. Obviously, then, if that pattern of employment and production—with the resulting high standard of living—is to be kept at a high level, trade with other countries in large volume is indispensable. . . ."

A widely circulated report, *World Trade and Employment,* issued in June 1944 by the Committee on International Economic Policy in co-operation with the Carnegie Endowment for International Peace, takes a position similar to that of the preceding two quotations, namely:[4]

"International trade is not an aim in itself. It is a means to an end. Steady employment at remunerative work yielding high living standards is the primary goal at which economic policy must aim.

". . . Employment is more than a national problem. It is an international question, the solution of which can only be found in an expansion of world trade and economic cooperation. As peacetime production in the United States gains momentum, its demands upon the rest of the world for imports will accelerate the economic recovery of other countries. They in turn will offer expanding markets for American exports. The traffic must be two-way. . . ."

On the other hand, we find, in the British publication *Planning,*[5] a strong affirmation of the contrary direction of causal relationship:[6]

"Readers of previous issues of *Planning* will be aware of the overriding importance which P.E.P. attaches to full employment, primarily, of course, as essential to contentment and prosperity, but also as a *pre-condition* of healthy world trade, i.e., as distinct from the popular near-fallacy that healthy world trade is a pre-condition of full employment. . . ."

[3] Ibid., p. 11. Italics in the text.
[4] *World Trade and Employment* (Committee of International Economic Policy, 1944), pp. 3–4.
[5] Published by P.E.P.—"Political and Economic Planning,"—a well-known group which leans strongly toward state planning of the national economy.
[6] *Planning,* No. 243, January 7, 1946, p. 9. Italics in the text.

Here the "chicken-and-egg" argument appears in its purest and clearest form! Writing in a similar vein, Sir William Beveridge asserts, in his *Full Employment in a Free Society,* that:[7]

". . . the greatest service that Britain can render to other countries, as to herself *and to the development of international trade,* is forthwith to adopt a policy of full employment at home. . . ."

Finally, let us quote a few observations by Professor Alvin H. Hansen:[8]

"The experience of the interwar periods shows that the volume of international trade is highly dependent upon the level of employment in the great industrial nations. When employment and prosperity are high, trade has flourished even though hampered by tariffs and other restraints on trade. Domestic high employment and prosperity can override fairly serious obstacles to trade and have, in fact, despite these obstacles produced a high level of international trade. Moreover, the condition of full employment is favorable for the removal of excessive barriers to world trade. Without high levels of employment and purchasing power, the real motive force behind international trade is lacking."

We are thus faced with a variety of points of view on the relations between international trade and domestic full employment. Some of the assertions made by the above-quoted spokesmen are self-evident; others must be considered erroneous; and the remainder indicates a difference of emphasis which may have serious repercussions upon the future of world economy.

2.

It is self-evident that there is more opportunity for trade between prosperous economies than between depressed ones. Since depressions are accompanied by unemployment, it is entirely logical and correct to say that unemployment grows as international trade declines, or that international trade declines as unemployment grows. No clear causal relationship is involved, indeed there is most likely a two-way causality (or interdependence) between these two phenomena. Since in times of pros-

[7] Op. cit., p. 33. Italics added.
[8] Alvin H. Hansen: *America's Role in the World Economy* (New York, 1945), pp. 179–80.

perity opportunities for employment grow but the relative size of the labor force tends to decline, as compared with a depression,[9] it is not quite certain that foreign trade and employment always grow together. Also, with a reduction of the barriers to trade, the international division of labor may make more headway, bringing about a change in the structure and efficiency of production and in the occupational composition of the population; consequently trade may expand without a corresponding increase in employment. This qualifies the first part of Professor Hansen's statement; if we should reformulate it to read: "international trade is highly dependent upon the level of economic activity in the great industrial nations," we would obtain a statement that is correct but entirely self-evident.

The second part of Professor Hansen's observations is much more questionable. It is true that trade can expand, in spite of tariffs—*if tariffs are stable;* growing tariffs, however, interfere with the growth of international trade and may even bring about its decline. It is true that in the interwar years the volume of trade expanded in spite of growing obstacles to it; but there were compensating factors to account for this:

In the twenties trade expanded *because* of the international credit expansion, mostly originating in the United States, and *in spite* of the rising tide of trade restrictions; the pay-off came when the credit expansion gave way to contraction and the volume of international trade drastically declined, while many credits failed to be repaid. The breakdown of international trade played an important role in spreading and deepening the depression of the thirties.

In the thirties there was an expansion of German and Japanese trade, due to the practices that were described in the preceding chapter. This happened to the detriment of other trading nations and at a severe cost for the countries that were partners in bilateralism of the Axis countries.

On the whole, the interwar experiences would indicate that growing trade barriers are a menace to economic stability even though general prosperity should reign while they are being erected. Professor Hansen is right when he says that "the condition of full employment is favorable for the removal of excessive

---

[9] In prosperity young people start to work later than in depression, go to school longer; old men retire earlier; fewer women go to work.

barriers to trade," but that opinion must be qualified in two ways: *one,* full employment should not be sought through nationalistic planning behind a wall of trade restrictions; and *two,* there must be a desire to make changes in the structure of foreign trade in spite of the fact that everybody is employed. Now, the first of these qualifications would seem evident but it is often disregarded; this is a very vital point to which we shall revert in a later part of this chapter. The second qualification is much less evident yet very important. The lowering of tariffs, the removal of import quotas, the liberalization of exchange restrictions, all affect the volume and the structure of imports and, consequently, the competitive situation in the domestic market. Adjustments become necessary—and they may involve certain losses to investors and a certain amount of transitional unemployment.[10] The costs of these adjustments are worth bearing because of the advantages accruing to the whole population through an expansion of the division of labor and of multilateral trade. But in order to become aware of that we must introduce into our discussion a second criterion besides the level of employment, to wit: standards of living. At times, should the two clash, it may even be necessary to subordinate the former to the latter.

This brings us back to the passage of the C.E.D. statement quoted at the beginning of the present chapter. The footnotes contributed by Messrs. Fennelly, Scherman, and Hoffman deserve most careful attention. *Some* countries could exist without foreign trade—the United States is one of them—and, since they could exist in complete economic isolation from the rest of the world, they could also maintain full employment within their boundaries—provided they knew how. *Most* countries—including Great Britain—could *not* exist without foreign trade, certainly not after having acquired a population too large to be fed by even the largest domestically obtainable output of foodstuffs. But evidently, even in the United States, we are not interested in bare survival but in the maintenance of high and growing standards of living. The real question we should ask is that which is raised in the dissenting footnotes: is the level of employment in the United States, obtained under the industrial and occupational conditions required for the maintenance of the prevailing standard of living, dependent upon foreign trade

[10] See Chapter XIV.

or independent from it? And the correct answer to that question is that under the described conditions, *foreign trade is necessary for the maintenance of employment.*

There is nothing surprising in that answer: without imported raw materials, various industries would have to go out of business, thus creating unemployment; without export markets, other and important industries would have to curtail their output and reduce their labor force. Both of these considerations are equally important, though the first is so often disregarded that it cannot be stressed too emphatically. With their eyes glued to the surface of observed phenomena, modern mercantilists consider imports as occasioning a loss of employment; they forget that without imported materials domestic production (both for domestic consumption and for exports) would be jeopardized; they forget that there might not be any homemade substitute for the imported article and that the fact of importing foreign goods does not necessarily "take away employment" from domestic labor to "give it" to foreign workers; they forget that all expansion of imports creates employment in shipping and merchandising the imported goods and that import trade provides *directly* both employment and income; finally, they forget that the total volume of work to be done in the world is not static but dynamic [11] and that an expansion of both imports and exports creates primary and secondary employment all over the world—at home as well as abroad.

In this connection it might be well to emphasize the great scope which both imports and exports offer to small and medium-sized business. In addition to the major items of international trade, such as raw materials, staple agricultural products, mass-produced manufactures—there are thousands of articles—consumer goods, luxuries, very specialized instruments, etc., that can enter foreign trade or stay out of it according to the skill, resourcefulness, and enterprise of individual importers and exporters. This implies that there are many interesting opportunities for self-employment and for employment of others in the development of new lines of import and export trade in inessential but useful goods—a fact that has received, in the United States at least, far less recognition than it deserves.

[11] The older mercantilists held similar static notions.

3.

The experience of the thirties shows that an economic depression can exercise a devastating influence upon international trade, especially when it occurs in a highly nationalistic world. This problem can be analyzed on the assumption that a depression originating in one great industrial area spreads to other countries, or by envisaging a general depression which develops in a number of countries more or less at the same time.

Starting from the first of these assumptions, the case is well analyzed by Dr. Ragnar Nurkse:[12]

"Suppose a depression occurs abroad. The country's exports will fall as a result in the fall in foreign demand. There will be a loss of income and employment in the export industries. If nothing is done, the depression in the export industries is likely to lead . . . to a general and cumulative depression in the home-market industries as well. After a point, the depression at home will bring about a reduction in imports large enough to balance the fall in exports. Equilibrium will have been restored in the balance of payments, but only by rendering the depression general."

What can be done about it? Dr. Nurkse suggests two remedies: Domestically, "the country we are considering must endeavor to offset the fall in foreign expenditures on its exports by an increase in domestic expenditure." [13] Internationally speaking, the country will have a balance-of-payments deficit due to a fall in its exports. "The country pursuing an 'offsetting' policy must be prepared to give up temporarily some of its international currency reserve in order to meet this deficit." [14] Dr. Nurkse goes on to show that the "offsetting" procedure will result in larger balance-of-payments deficits than would be experienced in its absence because it will tend to maintain imports while exports are below their "normal" level. Hence there will be a need for increased international monetary reserves. We shall not trace the argument any further; what has been quoted so far is sufficient in the present context.

It must be noted that since the "offsetting" procedure increases

---

[12] Ragnar Nurkse: "Conditions of International Monetary Equilibrium," *Essays in International Finance*, No. 4 (Princeton University, 1945), p. 11
[13] Ibid.
[14] Ibid.

the balance-of-payments difficulties cumulatively, even the largest international reserves would, in time, prove inadequate to fill the gap—unless, of course, the foreign depression would come to an end first. In the event reserves would come close to being exhausted, the country in question would adopt various devices to restrict its imports. Since on the assumption of stable economic activity in the country, imports would not shrink spontaneously, tariffs might be increased, quotas imposed, or even exchange restrictions introduced in order to bring them down to the level of reduced exports. Thus an impetus would be given to increased economic nationalism.

The "offsetting" procedure, by means of which domestic (governmental?) expenditures would be increased when exports decline, has been advocated by many writers primarily concerned with full employment who adopt the overly simplified view that the maintenance of employment in a country depends on the maintenance of *total* expenditures within that country's economy. This line of approach ignores the very important *structural* features of economic activity. Domestic expenditures cannot "take the place" of foreigners' expenditures because the former would be directed towards other goods and services than the latter. The expansion of domestic expenditures will not keep export industries going. One cannot have the advantages of an international division of labor and the advantages of economic isolation at one and the same time. Division of labor increases living standards but involves a dependence of the national economy upon world-market conditions; isolation makes it possible [15] to seek stable full employment by national measures alone but at the price of lower living standards. Between the two it is necessary to choose.

Dr. Nurkse further observes that: [16] "In the gold standard days, the correct behavior for each country was to keep on a level with the others—to rise with the tide and sink with the ebb of the general business cycle." This, he considers, is "out of the question today" for "most, if not all, advanced industrial nations." In his opinion: "Rather than float helplessly up and down as the level of world economic activity rises and declines, countries will

---

[15] For such countries only as *can* live in isolation—and there are very few such countries.

[16] This and the following quotations are from p. 22 of the quoted essay.

seek stability by regulating their domestic money income and expenditure . . ." But this is precisely the position taken by the "new" economic nationalism. Its result must inevitably be the breakup of the world economy into "insulated" compartments, with all the frictions and conflicts this entails. The alternative is for the various countries to get together and seek economic stability in collaboration, not in isolation. The "world economic activity" is the aggregate of national economic activities of the several countries. By working in full international solidarity, nations *may* achieve an all-round economic stability; but if each nation seeks stability independently from the rest of the world, the only *certain* result will be international anarchy and confusion.

The assumption that a depression starts in some one country and spreads from there to the rest of the world is very much favored by economists of the "national-planning-for-prosperity" school of thought. They often make it appear that depressions are essentially imported evils, while prosperity is due to the virtues of undisturbed national planning by the country's own economic authorities. Actually, of course, business cycles occur everywhere; not only has no country a monopoly on wisdom in the planning for economic stability, but, in actual fact, no country has as yet achieved such stability. It is quite true that localized depressions occasionally happen and some of them tend to spread to other regions; but the *great* depressions are, in their very nature, phenomena of the world economy. The depression of 1929 and the following years is a case in point.

Now an international depression may be tackled by means of nationalistic policies of the separate countries, or by means of internationally planned action. Nationalistic anti-depression policies lead to the following state interferences with foreign trade: Varied import restrictions for the purpose of "protecting" the home market and of "creating" work for the unemployed, as well as for the purpose of improving the country's short-term balance-of-payments position; promotion of exports by means of subsidies, currency depreciation, and other devices, in order to expand domestic employment; further import restrictions to keep out the artificially promoted exports of other depressed countries. It will be readily seen that these measures defeat their purpose if they are adopted by several countries at once. In the end everybody's difficulties are aggravated and the volume of world trade shrinks, thus curtailing markets and employment.

We are thus brought back to the previously reached conclusion, that international action is required to achieve world economic stability (which involves, of course, the stability of each particular country), under conditions of economic "good-neighborliness." The alternative is chaos and economic strife from which, in the end, no country benefits.

4.

We can now revert to our "chicken-and-egg" argument. In a world subject to more or less violent fluctuations of economic activity, international trade alone cannot assure continued employment and prosperity. It is necessary to achieve a considerable degree of co-ordination among the national business-cycle policies and to supplement them by appropriate international measures. And, as a part of the program, all national policies that interfere with the international division of labor must be ruled out outright, or be subjected to the supervision of an international body.

So much about the "employment-through-world-trade" side of the argument. The other side, the "world-trade-through-full-employment" argument is a dangerous vehicle, helpful in the propagation of economic nationalism. Sir William Beveridge, one of the most eloquent advocates of national planning for full employment, makes this illuminating comment on the future of international trade:[17]

". . . strong central planning of Britain's internal affairs will make her more, not less, useful as a partner in world affairs. International trade, both for imports and for exports, will on the whole have to come under public management, in place of being left to market forces either competitive or monopolistic.[18] The organs which serve for planning at home will serve also for planning in a wider sphere."

Sir William is entirely consistent in his arguments throughout his *Full Employment in a Free Society;* his only inconsistency is the use of the word "free" in the title of his book. He out-

[17] Op. cit., pp. 240–1.
[18] Very curiously, Sir William Beveridge doesn't seem to regard as monopolistic the centralization of foreign trade under government control!

lines a blueprint for a society centrally planned for the purpose of maintaining full employment. Inevitably this takes him into the camp of economic nationalists and advocates of government monopoly of foreign trade. We have examined at length, in the preceding chapter, the consequences of that point of view; and we have found that, as concerns world unity, these are catastrophic. Planning for full employment, if carried out by national governments in a way which subordinates international order to national objectives, is likely to result in a decline of world trade and in a partial breakup of the international division of labor, and to bring about economic conflicts between nations. The contrary opinion expressed by the P.E.P. in its report quoted earlier in this chapter [19] would appear, in the light of available evidence, far too optimistic.

The conclusions of the foregoing discussion can be stated very briefly: in the interest of prosperity for every nation and for all of them we need an expansion of internationalism, not its restriction. We need active anti-depression policies [20]—internationally planned and carried out with the help of an appropriate international agency. In addition to the indispensable *passive* internationalism, which consists in the absence of arbitrary interferences with trade and capital movements, we need the *active* internationalism of a concerted attack upon the problem of economic instability. National prosperity—involving high and steady employment *and* rising standards of living—is an international problem.

[19] P. 124.
[20] Or, more generally, business-cycle policies.

CHAPTER VIII

World Economy and Peace

IN THE PRECEDING CHAPTER our main concern has been with prosperity and welfare. We have reached conclusions favorable to unfettered international trade, critical of restrictive controls, and emphasizing the need for international—and even supernational—action in dealing with the problem of business cycles. But welfare is not the only preoccupation of nations; another and overriding concern is over the maintenance of peace and freedom. Peace without subjection is the craving of most nations; peace with power is the ambition of some of them. In either case, other than welfare considerations enter the picture. We have seen that even Adam Smith considered national security as more important than national prosperity, and that Richard Cobden viewed free trade as a means of achieving durable peace. Conversely, Fichte, who was almost a contemporary of Adam Smith, and List, who was a contemporary of Cobden, were primarily concerned with national independence and national power. The writings of Adam Smith and Cobden, as well as the latter's actual political campaigns, paved the way for the establishment of a world-wide free market—a goal never as yet accomplished. Fichte and List laid the intellectual groundwork under the policies of self-sufficiency and under the conception which makes of economic relations between nations a corollary of their political aspirations. In the present chapter we are going to direct our attention upon the relations between international trade and peace. And first of all, of course, we must be concerned with the age-long controversy over origins of war; are wars due to economic or non-economic causes—or maybe to a combination of both?

The idea that wars result primarily from economic factors is very ancient, though it is the Marxists who gave it its most sophisticated form and who promoted it widely and effectively. Today it is accepted without a shade of hesitation by orthodox Marxists, and by so-called "liberals," by conservative bankers, and by many presumably non-Marxist members of the public. If widespread repetition alone (without proof) of some statement would make it true, the attribution of war to economic causes would be the truth. Actually, causes of war are considerably more complex. Some wars have undoubtedly been caused by economic factors; probably no major war was solely so caused, and in the causation of many, maybe most, wars economic factors played an entirely subordinate role. Let us look a little more fully into the matter. Three main economic reasons for war have been advanced, at one time or another, by philosophers, historians or social scientists:

The "naïve" economic theory of war (probably the most correct of the three as far as it goes) attributes war to the urge to increase one's national wealth by additions of territory, resources and population. This explanation of war, which goes back to Plato, accounts for an important factor which appeared often in ancient times, and, as we shall presently see, is not fully absent from the modern world. There is one rather evident—and exceedingly important—comment to be made on this explanation: why resort to territorial expansion and to war instead of depending upon trade? And, indeed, the growth of trade greatly reduced the incidence of that particular cause of war. For each of two reasons, however, a nation may regard an outright acquisition of land, people and resources as *economically* beneficial (quite apart from any possible military and political considerations): *one* of them is the net addition to the personal wealth of the "ruling classes" of the conquering nation and possibly of all its citizens, through looting and expropriating the properties of those vanquished; furthermore, the acquisition of cheap slave- or serf-labor which adds further to the nation's wealth; trade calls for a *quid pro quo*—not so the booty of war. The *other* reason, of much more recent origin, is the extension of the area over which the national government can plan the country's economy; territorial expansion makes sense in terms of the state-socialistic belief in the connection between planning and prosperity.

In the case of Nazi Germany, both these factors played a considerable role, and the fact that in this case the plans were made for war and not for welfare doesn't make the argument any less valid. Reference has been made before to the writings of Fichte, famous German philosopher and first *Rektor* of the University of Berlin. In his *Closed Commercial State* (1800) [1] he attributes wars to trade relations between nations and advocates absolute

---

[1] Johann Gottlieb Fichte: *Der Geschlossene Handelsstaat,* 1800.

self-sufficiency as a means of preserving peace. There is, however, an important fly in that particular ointment. In order to be capable of self-sufficiency a country must first reach its "natural boundaries," in the determination of which it is sole judge. Since this may require territorial expansion at the expense of its neighbors, the country, says Fichte, is entitled to wage war for the purpose of reaching its "natural boundaries," so that afterwards it might enjoy a lasting peace! We thus get a dash of "geopolitics" thrown into the Platonic explanation of war. Of the two philosophers, Plato is by far the more realistic because, unlike Fichte, he allows for the conflict of competing expansionisms. Incidentally and importantly, Fichte urges the country which seeks its natural boundaries not to give up trade too soon but, on the contrary, to obtain as much power as possible by means of it—so that when the show-down with its neighbors comes, these might be intimidated into acquiescence rather than to be fought. One hundred and thirty-odd years later, Fichte certainly became a prophet in his own country when Germany preached autarky,[2] practiced state-planned foreign trade, intimidated her neighbors. and expanded her territory.

2.

This brings us to the second, more elaborate, economic explanation of war. Economic resources are elements of political power. This is quite evident with respect to raw materials, to communications, to population. The first of these is generally singled out for special consideration—was so in the international discussions of the late thirties, in the text of the Atlantic Charter,[3] in other international documents; the importance of the second is underscored, e.g., by Great Britain's concern over the "life-line" of Empire communications; the third, however, population, is generally underestimated. Yet France has long felt inferior to Germany as a political and military power, on account of its smaller and more stationary population, while dur-

[2] Or "self-sufficiency." The spelling used here, *autarky,* is to be preferred to the more current *autarchy;* these two spellings have different Greek derivations: the former properly means self-sufficiency, the latter self-government. (See *Shorter Oxford Dictionary*.)

[3] Point 4 of the Charter reads, in part: "They will endeavor . . . to further the enjoyment by all States . . . of access, on equal terms, to the trade and to the raw materials of the world which are needed for their economic prosperity." But if prosperity alone were intended, why single out raw materials?

ing the past war Australia went through a period of near-panic on account of the relatively small size of its population. In addition,[4] the availability of foreign assets that can be readily sold for cash in times of war emergency increases a country's strength. This consideration, in a slightly different form, was very familiar to the mercantilists and accounted for their concern over accumulating precious metals, the best "war chest" in those days— and not a bad one in ours. The partial liquidation of British foreign assets in the course of World Wars I and II was an important factor in Great Britain's economic mobilization for war. Thus the acquisition of resources under its own sovereignty makes a country more powerful in war and stronger, therefore, in Lionel Robbins's words, "in diplomacy involving appeal to war." But to say this is *not* the same thing as to say that wars are *due* to economic causes!

In the case under consideration, long-range objectives of war-conscious diplomacy stress the importance of "owning" resources instead of securing them through trade. We have seen above two *economic* reasons for preferring territorial expansion to trade; here we are faced with a strong *political* and *military* motive. This may, at times, as in Fichte's scheme, involve war; such a war is generally localized (or intended to be so) and its object is to make the aggressor (who expects, of course, to win) stronger in case of a possible future and less limited war for power. At first glance this may look a little complicated, yet history is full of examples of wars waged for the purpose of acquiring a strong position for a future, more crucial conflict. Such were Germany's aggressions against Austria and Czechoslovakia in 1938, and against the remainder of Czechoslovakia and Poland in 1939. And the guarantee given in 1939 by Great Britain to several prospective victims of Germany's expansion—one of them was Poland—was largely inspired by the realization that Germany was gradually getting ready for the "great" conflict with the West. Thus the "limited" expansion led straight into another world conflagration—and Germany was defeated. But what might the outcome have been had she been allowed quietly to "occupy" all of Central and Southeastern Europe and to obtain an economic stranglehold over a part of South America?

[4] Cf. Lionel Robbins: *Economic Causes of War*, London, 1939. See especially Chapter IV.

If the elaboration of the "naïve" economic explanation takes us into the very center of international power conflicts, the third explanation of war remains largely in the realm of more or less "sophisticated" economic arguments. It is the Marxian explanation of imperialism and war which, in turn, can be broken up into two major theories. One is what Jacob Viner calls the "scandal theory," according to which, "every recorded case in modern times of imperialism, of aggressive war by strong against weak countries, was the result of the influence over statesmen exercised by particular and identifiable capitalists who saw an opportunity for profits for themselves in such aggression." [5] The other theory is "expounded by more theoretical-minded socialists and by many 'liberals,' and often distinguished as the Neo-Marxian theory, or the theory of the 'three surpluses,'" according to which:[6]

". . . as capitalism evolves toward maturity, industrial productivity, population, and capital accumulation develop beyond the capacity of the internal economy to employ them. There results on the part of the strong powers a three-fold struggle: for export markets to take off the surplus goods, for colonies for settlement of the surplus population, and for external fields for safe investment of surplus capital. From this struggle, war naturally arises."

Of these three economic interpretations of war, the "scandal theory" is the least plausible a priori as well as the least easy to substantiate by an appeal to history. The inquiries by Viner, Robbins, Staley,[7] and others point to the opposite conclusion. To quote Professor Viner:[8]

"In almost all of these cases [in which capitalists are alleged to have provoked war], the capitalist, instead of pushing his government into an imperialistic enterprise in pursuit of his own financial gain, was pushed, or dragged, or cajoled, or lured into it by his government, in order that, in its relations with the outside world and with its own people, this government might be able to point to an apparently real

[5] Jacob Viner: "Peace as an Economic Problem," Chapter V of *New Perspectives on Peace*, George B. de Huszar, editor (Chicago, 1944), pp. 88–9. See also Viner's article; "International Relations Between State-Controlled National Economies," op. cit., especially pp. 320–9.

[6] Jacob Viner: "Peace as an Economic Problem," op. cit., p. 91.

[7] Eugene Staley: *War and the Private Investor* (New York, 1935).

[8] Jacob Viner: "International Relations Between State-Controlled National Economies," op. cit., p. 323.

and legitimate economic stake in the territory involved which required military protection against unfair treatment or general misgovernment by the local authorities or against encroachment by other powers." [9]

As for the theory of the "three surpluses," it has a much greater superficial plausibility, although it is based on a theory of a chronic capitalistic under-consumption and over-saving which many economists, including the present writer, find it impossible to accept. What is true, however, is this: in a world the economy of which is built on the basis of an international division of labor, foreign markets are indispensable to maintain the existing structure of production. We have discussed various aspects of this question in the preceding chapter, and we have seen that in times of depression "beggar-my-neighbor" policies lead to ill-feeling and to conflict. But do they lead to war? What examples have we to confirm such an allegation? And does "normal" international competition for markets lead to war? It did frequently in the age of mercantilism; it did very rarely in the nineteenth century. This was not purely accidental: the struggle was for special privileges, for monopolistic powers, or, indeed, to break open doors that were held closed by another power. It is not surprising that struggles for markets became less violent and the incidence of war less frequent in the age of free trade when the greatest colonial power, Great Britain, practiced in her possessions an "open door" policy.

Population pressures are by no means peculiar to capitalism—just as the struggle for markets is not its distinctive feature; they are the result of restrictions on the freedom of migrations. If movements of populations were free across the surface of the earth, no conflicts would originate on that score.

As for international investment outlets, these may only lead to conflicts if financial penetration is used as an instrument of political pressure. Nor does the protection of investors' interests bring about wars—though it has been known to bring about "naval demonstrations."

The Marxian "case" is very weak—and it is surprising that it enjoys such a widespread acceptance. Political passions, the quest

[9] Viner makes one major exception from that statement, namely, the case of the Congo where "private profit was clearly the major, if not the sole objective. But the profiteer and the imperialist statesman were here the identical person, King Leopold of Belgium. . . ." Ibid., p. 323.

for power, the emotional appeal of "superiority" gained over weaker nations by armed might, all this, which *really* is at the bottom of great wars of conquest, involves much that is "irrational" and, therefore, difficult to comprehend. Economic explanations are "rational" and seem simple. This may be a reason —an important reason—for their wide acceptance. The fact that they contain an element of truth makes these explanations all the more difficult to refute.

3.

They contain, we said, an element of truth. There are, among many others, also economic causes of war, because economic factors play an important role in the phenomenon of political power. There are clashes of economic interest because there are clashes of broader national interest. As Lionel Robbins puts it, in conclusion of his *Economic Causes of War:* "The ultimate condition giving rise to those clashes of national economic interest which lead to international war is the existence of independent national sovereignties. Not capitalism, but anarchic political organization of the world is the root disease of our civilization." [10]

The existence of trade restrictions makes the case for territorial expansion and for colonial imperialism more plausible than would be the case under free trade. According to Professor Robbins, "It is not in the power to manipulate or to restrict trade that the advantage of wide territorial jurisdiction consists, but rather in immunity from the manipulations and restrictions which might be practiced by other states if the area of jurisdiction were narrowed. The British Empire is not an asset in the sense that the policy of exclusion permits large positive gains at the expense of the rest of the world. . . . But insofar as, for the inhabitants of the Empire, it keeps open at least some channels of economic freedom, it means that the division of labor is more extensive, the productivity of factors of production is greater than might otherwise have been the case. As a safeguard against loss it is very important indeed." [11] This Robbins calls "the nega-

[10] Op. cit., p. 99.
[11] Lionel Robbins: *The Economic Basis of Class Conflict and Other Essays in Political Economy* (London, 1939), essay entitled "The Economics of Territorial Sovereignty," p. 99.

tive gains of Empire"; in our times they are likely to greatly outweigh the "positive" gains.[12]

The "have-and-have-not" controversy also derives whatever real meaning it has from the existence of restrictions on the economic intercourse between nations. In a free-trade world everybody would be a "have" because everybody would have equal access to all the resources of the globe. In a tariff-ridden world (not to mention all the other, more effective restrictions), everybody is a have-not—even the United States, as shortages of strategic materials and other goods during the recent war have amply demonstrated. But countries with lesser territory, countries without colonies can present to the world a seemingly plausible case of grievances. How much we have heard, in the thirties especially, about unsatisfied nations! How greatly we were taken in by these complaints! The fact that the poorer countries, like Greece, or Yugoslavia, or some smaller Latin-American republics never complained, and that Germany could hardly be mistaken for an "underprivileged" country didn't seem to make her claims appear as absurd as they really were. Actually, in order to be a successful "have-not," a country must be very powerful. Then it can threaten the world and exact fulfillment of at least some of its demands. The lessons of the interwar years are very eloquent in that respect. Right here it may be useful to attack another widely accepted fallacy: that poverty breeds war and prosperity favors peace. It is true that in a country torn asunder by depression and discontent adventurers can more easily come to the fore than in a prosperous country. Alvin Hansen makes much of that argument in *America's Role in the World Economy:*" [13]

". . . the great depression fanned the flames of a new world conflagration. It required four years of mass unemployment to bring Hitler to power in Germany. . . .

"There was a very good chance—though no absolute certainty— that in the absence of the great depression a solution might have been found for the central problem of Europe, namely the place of Germany in international relations."

This diagnosis is open to serious objections. It was because the German nation was in favor of expansion and not averse to war,

[12] On the question of imperialism see also Moritz J. Bonn: "Imperialism—A Sketch," *Approaches to National Unity,* Fifth Symposium of the Conference on Science, Philosophy and Religion, New York, 1945, pp. 92–131.
[13] Op. cit., pp. 16, 23.

that there developed an aggressive militaristic regime. The depression may have contributed the collectivistic tinge of the new regime by bringing the National Socialists into power, but Germany was on the warpath even in the twenties. Nor did the depression produce any dictators or war-tendencies in Great Britain or the United States. And the *really* poor countries of Europe were never any danger to anyone, save passively, by being such an easy prey to aggression. In order to be able, in our times, to wage war a nation must be industrially very efficient, economically very strong. This is the verdict of common sense and, indeed, the lesson of history.

4.

The following conclusions emerge from our discussion. So long as politically autonomous "sovereign" states practice policies of economic nationalism, the economic factor will be a contributory, if not a basic, cause of international friction, conflict, and war. The growth of socialistic planning makes the situation more serious by the added emphasis it places upon a country's territory and boundaries and upon a national rather than international approach to its problems. Freedom of private enterprise and freedom of trade would tend to minimize the destructive influence of economic factors upon the peace of the world. In fact, the less governmental and the more private economic relations there are between nations, the better it is for international friendship and peace.

But private enterprise is on the decline over large areas of the world and is eliminated completely in the Soviet Union, while socialistic national planning is on the upgrade. Under those circumstances, international agreements and institutions are more than ever important and necessary.[14] The following are the indispensable components of an international economic program:

(1) The establishment of rules of commercial policy to be followed by all nations for the promotion of nondiscriminatory, multilateral trade. An international trade organization would be put in charge of administering these agreements.

[14] Even in a free-trade world there would be scope for such agreements as long as separate "sovereign" states continue to exist. Cf. Albert O. Hirschman: *National Power and the Structure of Foreign Trade* (University of California Press, Berkeley, 1945), Chapter IV.

(2) The acceptance of the principle that the promotion of autarky by a national government is an unfriendly act, aimed at making the country better able to envisage an act of aggression and, thereby, become involved in war. This requires, of course, the establishment of a reliable system of political security.

(3) The development of economic policies aiming at the promotion and enforcement of collective security. These should involve not only *post-factum* sanctions against an aggressor nation, but also *preventive* sanctions against a country that is known to be preparing for aggression (see point 2).

(4) The promotion of international investments and of stable monetary relations between nations, associated with free international payments. The institutions devised at Bretton Woods will presumably take care of these requirements.

(5) Because purely national planning of economic stability strengthens economic nationalism, thus making for friction and conflicts, an international agency for dealing with business cycles on a world-wide scale is urgently needed.

(6) In order to deal internationally with the problem of population pressures, and in view of immigration restrictions adopted by most (or all) countries, there should be established an International Migration Board.

(7) One of the means of action of an authoritarian country preparing for war consists of stepping up production and keeping living standards low. The International Labor Office can perform a most useful function in standing guard against such policies.

Such policies, and institutions entrusted with their execution, can make a distinct and vital contribution to the organization and maintenance of peace. Their ultimate success will depend, of course, upon the success of the political organization of the world.

CHAPTER IX

How *Not* to Build a World Economy:
Some Lessons from the Interwar Years

THE PROBLEMS with which the peace-builders—and that, in one way or another, means all of us—are confronted at the end of World War II present some parallels with those which had to be met at the end of World War I. Political and social circumstances are more complex at the present time; the destruction of wealth and of social order is greater in Europe and Asia than it had then been; the disintegration of world economic relations is, if possible, more severe. But some of the basic problems remain the same: the construction of a political world organization from a multiplicity of separate states, the construction of a workable world economy amidst prevailing economic nationalism, the rebuilding of confidence (now more than ever shattered by two world wars and one protracted world-wide depression) without which neither the political nor the economic tasks can be fulfilled. The attempt made after 1918 at the construction of a world economy failed, very completely, as we know. That failure casts a long shadow over our present endeavors. But even failure can be instructive; if in solving the problems of our day we can avoid repeating the mistakes of thirty years ago, we shall stand a better chance of seeing our efforts crowned with success. "What not to do" is often as good an advice as "What to do"; sometimes it may even be better, inasmuch as it is well to be forewarned about the pitfalls which one is likely to meet on one's way.

The last peace was lost on the economic front in the *early* twenties. The fundamental reason for it was, probably, the fact that the "war to end all wars" ended in a peace which failed to inspire confidence. The settlement was, in part, not radical enough; in part it was incomplete. The menace of Germany was not eradicated, as the French, for one, perfectly well realized. Other European nations, especially in Eastern Europe, soon had reasons for sharing these apprehensions. The Treaty of Locarno (1925) made a differentiation between Germany's eastern and western borders, of which only the latter obtained additional guarantees, thus weakening the Covenant of the League of Nations, which in its Article 10 assured all the members alike of their territorial integrity. The well-known campaign against the *alleged* iniquities of the Treaty of Versailles also had a disturbing effect upon the state of confidence and paved the way for the comeback of a militaristic and aggressive Germany.[1] Indeed, in the late twenties one heard a lot about Germany's secret rearmament.

Thus the general political climate deteriorated very fast. What made it still worse was the progressive weakening of the League of Nations. In the first place, the failure of the United States to join that organization deprived it of the firm guiding hand of its spiritual and political parent; a loss from which it never recovered. In the second place, certain constructive elements of the Covenant were soon whittled down, instead of being built up and implemented.[2] This gradual process of destruction through interpretation of the main security provisions of the Covenant extended to economic as well as to the political matters. The provisions of Article 16 concerning economic sanctions to be imposed against an aggressor power were badly in need of clarification and elaboration. Article 16 stipulates, in particular, that a member of the League committing an act of aggression is to be considered at war with all other members of the League, who will be under obligation to prevent "all financial, commercial or personal intercourse between the nationals of the covenant-breaking State and the nationals of any other State, *whether a Member of the League or not.*"[3] Even granting that the word "national" was used where "resident" was intended (a point clarified later on), the text calls for a good deal of elucidation, especially in view of the italicized words. What must have been intended was the subjection of the aggressor state to complete blockade; otherwise this provision would have to remain a dead letter.

That fact was recognized by the Assembly and the Council of the League of Nations in resolutions adopted in December 1920 and February 1921 respectively which decided the appointment of an International Blockade Commission to study the practical application of Article 16. This Commission presented its report

[1] Cf. Étienne Mantoux: *The Carthaginian Peace—or the Economic Consequences of Mr. Keynes* (London, 1946); and R. B. McCallum: *Public Opinion and the Last Peace* (London, 1944).

[2] Cf. William E. Rappard: *The Quest for Peace since the World War* (Cambridge, Mass., 1940).

[3] Italics added. What measures should be taken about a *non-member aggressor* was not made clear in the Covenant.

in the fall of 1921; it is noteworthy that the term "blockade" which was the key to the whole problem appeared only in the Commission's name and was conspicuously absent from its report. After 1921 the matter was left in abeyance, and when sanctions (which should have been invoked in 1931–2 against Japan) were finally applied in 1935 against Italy, there was no ready procedure for dealing with that problem: a blockade failed to be applied, and finally sanctions fizzled out and were officially given up as a failure. That, at least, was a perfectly avoidable failure, had Article 16 been fully implemented in the course of the intervening fifteen years, and had there been a will to make it work in 1935.

Another aspect of Article 16 which was given very little attention after the League came into being, is the provision of its third paragraph to the effect that: "The Members of the League agree . . . that they will mutually support one another in the financial and economic measures which are taken under this Article, in order to minimize the loss and inconvenience resulting from the above measures . . ." It wasn't until the introduction of the lend-lease system,[4] that an instrument was devised capable of dealing with that matter. There can be no reasonable doubt that had the League of Nations used blockade and lend-lease in 1935, and had the United States collaborated, the economic sanctions against Italy might have been a great success.

The great and shattering disappointment over the actual operation of "collective security" came in 1935, but already the first few years of the League's activities resulted in a growing distrust of its security system. As far back as summer 1925, Professor Rappard addressed the Williamstown Institute of Politics in the following terms:[5]

"Sanctions were the means by which the League was to enforce peace according to the provisions and intentions of its founders. As far as applicable between the states members of the League, they were provided for solely in Articles 10 and 16. . . . By the various interpretations adopted, these articles have been so appreciably weakened, that today no responsible European statesman would venture to stake his reputation and the security of his country on the potential protection of the League in case of international disturbances."

[4] Called "mutual aid" by the British.
[5] William E. Rappard: *International Relations as Viewed from Geneva* (New Haven, 1925), pp. 143–4.

And this, mind you, in 1925! That uncertainty explains the maintenance of high-cost agriculture in Western Europe, the development of high-cost industries in Eastern Europe, the protection of "key industries" everywhere. With Germany growing stronger and "collective security" growing weaker, a basis was lacking for any effective action against economic nationalism.

2.

The League's Covenant devoted little space to the problem of building up a world economy. Whereas President Wilson's *Fourteen Points* provided, in Point 3, for:

"The removal, so far as possible, of all economic barriers and the establishment of an equality of trade conditions among all the nations consenting to the peace and associating themselves for its maintenance,"

the corresponding statement in the Covenant, buried in paragraph (e) of the all-embracing Article 23, dealing with *Social and Other Activities,* simply stated that

"Subject to and in accordance with the provisions of international conventions existing or hereafter to be agreed upon, the Members of the League . . . will make provision to secure and maintain freedom of communications and of transit and *equitable treatment for the commerce of all Members of the League. . . .*" [6]

That was a considerable weakening of the Wilsonian text; even though there was room for a good deal of elaboration had there been any disposition to do so. By interpreting the term "equitable treatment," one might have injected a great deal of meaning into it, while the enforcement of that laconic provision might have given rise, in the twenties, to the establishment of that International Trade Organization, which now, after so much further suffering and distress, is at long last under official consideration.

Instead, in the twenties, we got a series of increasingly disappointing international conferences.[7] Since in the future we are

[6] Italics added.

[7] Cf. League of Nations Publications, II. Economic and Financial, 1942, II. A. 6, *Commercial Policy in the Interwar Period: International Proposals and National Policies;* Wallace McClure: *World Prosperity as Sought Through the Economic Work of the League of Nations* (New York, 1933); William E. Rappard: *Postwar Efforts for*

undoubtedly going to be treated to a great many more conferences, the experiences of the interwar years may, if assimilated, be quite helpful in making future performances more successful. The Bretton Woods Conference of July 1944 seems to indicate that a good deal has been learned from the mistakes of the past.

The first conferences, which met in Brussels in 1920 and in Genoa in 1922, were overshadowed by monetary and financial preoccupation (as was Bretton Woods, but here the analogy ends). So were other international endeavors, some of them very effectively carried out under League of Nations auspices. Inflations were spectacular, international monetary disturbances very disquieting; it was felt that no effective agreements on tariffs, etc., could be reached under conditions of widespread monetary chaos. It is true that a series of recommendations on commercial policy was drafted at Genoa, but they were very much on the "timid" side.

The fact that monetary stabilization is an *international* issue was not fully acknowledged in those days. Inflations, quite properly, were linked with budgetary deficits (though other forces were at work as well); and exchange instability was, far too exclusively, attributed to domestic inflations. That many countries required foreign help in order to stabilize their currencies was recognized and such help was forthcoming. That a country's balance-of-payments difficulties might be beyond that country's own control and result from complex international situations received less recognition, if any at all. International help for national solutions to the stabilization-of-currency problem—that was the generally accepted formula. The result was that the gold standard was re-established without any international agreement concerning its functioning, and that many *ad hoc* changes were introduced into its functioning without any preliminary study of their international implications.[8] The result was a hybrid construction, far less consistent than the "old" gold standard, and entirely unable, as events were shortly to prove, to withstand the shock of an international financial crisis.

Freer Trade, op. cit.; and *Le Nationalisme Economique et la Société des Nations,* Recueil des Cours de L'Academie du Droit International de la Haye, 1937, III.

[8] Such as the limitations of convertibility under the "gold bullion standard," or the use of U. S. dollars and other currencies based on gold as "backing" for other currencies to take the place of gold. On this whole subject, see: *International Currency Experience —Lessons of the Inter-war Years* (League of Nations, 1944).

It is noteworthy that the Genoa recommendation (of 1922) to call an international conference of central banks was never acted upon and that the founding of the Bank for International Settlements was decided upon as late as January 1930 at the Hague Conference dealing with the problem of reparations, as a by-product of the "Young Plan" for the reparation settlement. The Bank came into being too late and was given too small resources and too meager prerogatives to be of real help in the financial crisis of 1931 and the following years. Still, it became at least a regular meeting place of central bankers and an international center for the study of monetary phenomena. Had the Genoa recommendation been heeded, the world might have had this kind of an institution by 1923 or 1924 and the monetary reconstruction of the twenties might have been far more successful.

The intellectual "divorce" between money, finance, and trade, deeply rooted in the departmentalization of academic curricula, and very mischievous in its practical repercussions, is responsible for the fact that problems of commercial policy and of capital movements were largely disregarded in the monetary arrangements of the twenties. While the "new" gold standard was being erected by trial and error (mostly the latter), tariffs went on growing while capital movements followed a considerably more erratic course than was the case before New York became the greatest lending center of the world. Lacking the experience of the London investment houses, their American counterparts paid insufficient attention to the economic soundness of loans and were too exclusively concerned over earning high rates of interest. The reckoning came when the flow of capital became irregular in the late twenties and then reversed itself, and when an unprecedented volume of short-term funds started its panicky dance across the world, while tariff-restricted trade lacked the necessary flexibility to preserve the upset equilibrium of international payments.

As we have seen, no major frontal attack on economic nationalism was envisaged in the Covenant of the League of Nations. President Wilson's fight for freer trade was over and, after his electoral defeat, the United States returned, in 1921, to a high-tariff policy (after the short-lived movement in the opposite direction promoted by the first Wilson Administration and expressed in the Tariff Act of 1913). In Europe and elsewhere, economic nationalism was spurred by the feeling of insecurity, to which reference was made before, and by a widespread resistance to change. War has brought in its wake many economic upheavals: traditional trade routes have been disturbed, new productions had to be started in many countries, even at high cost, to take the place of needed but unobtainable foreign goods; agricultural output was increased to meet war needs and, later, to compensate for the decline of production in war-torn areas; and great financial obligations—war debts and reparations—had to be met. In addition, the war speeded up the rate of technological advance which brought about lasting changes in the international structure of "competitive advantages" and called for corresponding changes in the international division of labor and in the structure of foreign trade. All these changes failed to be met squarely in the postwar years.

3.

The Genoa Conference produced, as has been mentioned before, a series of rather timid recommendations. In line with these, "substantial progress was made up to 1930 in liberating the trade in raw materials, in removing prohibitions [on exports and imports], and in extending the operation of the most-favoured-nation clause; commercial treaties were gradually re-established, though on a short-term basis. After 1930 progress in all these directions ceased and there was a general reversal of policy." [9]

But the greatest amount of work was devoted, in the early postwar years, not to an onslaught on trade barriers but to a fairly "safe" international problem: the simplification of customs formalities. A diplomatic conference was convened to deal with that problem. It met in Geneva in October 1923, arrived at a convention that obtained a very wide international acceptance and was, according to Professor Rappard, "the most successful economic treaty ever drafted in Geneva." [10] It is symptomatic for the "Spirit of the Age" that the convention dealt with purely technical matters and that its terms, again in Rappard's words, were "anything but drastic."

It wasn't until 1927 that the world was ready to deal with the fundamental issues of international economic relations and with

[9] League of Nations: *Commercial Policy in the Interwar Period,* op. cit., p. 23.
[10] William E. Rappard: *Post-war Efforts for Freer Trade,* op. cit., p. 21.

the increasingly precarious condition of the world economy. The World Economic Conference which met in Geneva in May 1927 has produced the most comprehensive report of its kind, a well-reasoned document, carefully prepared and culminating in a large number of recommendations.[11] These favor, of course, the freeing of international trade through lowering tariffs and eliminating their instability, through a revival of long-term treaties of commerce with the M. F. N. clause, and through the elimination of export subsidies, dumping, discriminations, and import and export prohibitions.

Volumes have been written about that conference which was, indeed, the greatest event of its kind during the whole interwar period. It is a matter of utmost regret that the conference had no powers to draw up a convention which might involve actual commitments on the part of the various national governments. It was not a "diplomatic conference." Its recommendations were read and studied by experts, by professors, by students of international affairs; they were read (one hopes) and pigeonholed by cabinet members and parliamentarians.

After this high point of international endeavor had been reached, other, increasingly futile, conferences followed about which little need be said in the present context. When the crisis of 1929 developed, the world was utterly unprepared to deal with it by collective action. Meeting an international crisis by national means resulted in a general *sauve qui peut*, every nation looking out for itself, in a growth of neo-mercantilism and state planning, and in a dramatic disintegration of world trade, world finance, and world monetary stability.

The international conferences of the twenties teach us two most important lessons: *one,* that in order to counteract a strong trend it is necessary to hit at it and to hit hard; and *two,* that resolutions and recommendations adopted by international gatherings are of no practical value unless they actually influence the national policies of the various countries. It is useless to arrange conferences, reach resolutions, and then carry on as if nothing had happened. The public is merely lulled thereby into a false sense of security, mistaking words for deeds. It should become the habit of tomorrow to have conferences reach commitments that, once

[11] Cf. League of Nations: *The World Economic Conference. Geneva, May 1927. Final Report.*

ratified by the governments, would influence the future course
of national policies. *Commitments instead of resolutions* might
be a useful slogan for future international conferences.

The last great economic conference to meet before the outbreak
of World War II teaches us an additional lesson. The Monetary
and Economic Conference, which met in London in June 1933 [12]
and was an unqualified failure, was a gathering which should not
have taken place at all at that particular moment. Not only did
two preparatory meetings held in Geneva reveal very serious
differences of emphasis between the viewpoints of the major protagonists, but the coming of Hitler into power in Germany between the time the Conference was called and the time it met,
made the political atmosphere entirely unfavorable to an economic "demobilization" of the world. The fact that the American
"New Deal" began a few months before the Conference was to
meet and that, in its early stages it was inspired by doctrines of
nationalistic "insulation," made the fate of the Conference even
more precarious. It is a gross exaggeration to say that President
Roosevelt torpedoed the Conference—because the Conference
was moribund anyhow and would have ended in any event without reaching any significant agreements; but it is true that his
celebrated message to the London conferees acted as a *coup de
grâce*.

Apart from these most unfavorable circumstances under which
the Conference deliberated, the principal reason for its failure was
the lack of preliminary agreement concerning monetary stabilization and the lowering of trade barriers. The French and American
delegates to the preparatory meeting held in Geneva in January
1933 urged monetary stabilization upon reluctant British delegates. This would have involved Britain's return to the gold
standard which, after the 1931 devaluation and the formation of
a spontaneous "Sterling Area" in 1931 and 1932 was viewed in
London with extreme disfavor. Nor was England at that time
greatly interested in the tariff problem, having its own brand-new
protective tariff and enjoying the competitive advantages due to
the devaluation of the pound. In Geneva the British argued, therefore, that monetary stabilization should be postponed till after
an agreement had been reached on the reduction of trade barriers. The argument advanced on the other side was that ex-

[12] Cf. Leo Pasvolsky: *Current Economic Issues* (Washington, D. C., 1933).

change instability made it well-nigh impossible to lower tariffs in view of the disturbing effects of future devaluations upon international price relationships.

At the Conference this basic conflict persisted, with the United States changing its position and opposing monetary stabilization, and Britain very passively adopting a middle-of-the-road position. The Conference discussed monetary problems and problems of commercial policy separately, and was unable to reach an agreement in either field. No major effort was made to take a global view of international economic relations, and to tie monetary, financial, and commercial issues into an integrated set of agreements.

And therein lie the *negative* lessons of the London Conference. It might be useful to remember, in respect to future conferences, the following two principles:

One: it is most important that the major countries represented at a conference should reach a substantial agreement beforehand on the principal issues with which the conference is to deal. The purpose of the conference is to generalize the agreement to other countries, and to amend and improve it on the basis of suggestions received from countries which have not been parties to the preliminary agreement.[13]

Two: whenever possible, an inclusive and integrated view of economic relations between nations should be taken, especially when discussing the reconstruction of the world economy or its improvements.

The second of these "principles" applies, of course, not only to international conferences but to the whole question of international economic relations. It is particularly important that it should be stressed at the present time, when we are taking new— and it is to be hoped—bold steps towards world organization.

4.

The failure to build a new world economy immediately after the end of World War I had very grave consequences. In the first place, structural maladjustments in the various national econo-

---

[13] This procedure was successfully followed in connection with the Bretton Woods Conference of July 1944.

mies not only remained uncorrected, but received tariff protection. New maladjustments grew behind new protective walls. No
positive measures were taken to meet international emergencies
in a spirit of co-operation and confidence. Trade and finance were
developing, each in its own way, without much relation to one
another. International investments grew fast, especially after the
end of the postwar wave of inflation; but they grew like Topsy.
The monetary reconstruction was a gold-incrusted pyramid
built on quicksands. The problem of business cycles remained in
the ivory towers of academic economists and was ignored in the
realm of action.

The crisis of 1929 was, in part at least, the outgrowth of these
developments. Its prelude consisted of the difficulties experienced
in the late twenties by agricultural countries. The relative overproduction, resulting from the war and from the postwar agricultural protectionism of certain industrial countries (Germany,
France, etc.), led to a downward pressure on prices and to balance-of-payments difficulties. So long as surplus stocks were financed through a credit expansion (the operations of the Canadian wheat pool were particularly illuminating), the crisis could
be averted; but when the credit expansion came to an end, stocks
of merchandise were thrown on the market, thus aggravating
the fall in prices. When the economic crisis developed in the
United States, its gravity was very much increased due to the
great credit inflation of the late twenties. Because of the international character of that credit inflation, very serious difficulties resulted for countries deprived of new credits and having to repay
formerly incurred short-term debts. Falling upon an economically very unbalanced world, the impact of the American depression was terrific. It was made worse by the fact that not only
America's demand for imported raw materials etc. declined as a
result of the depression, but that, in addition, the adoption in
1930 of the high Hawley-Smoot Tariff further restricted the capacity of foreign goods to penetrate into the American market.

"The disease was an international disease," rightly observes
Allan G. B. Fisher,[14] "but attention was focused almost exclusively upon its national symptoms. . . . With unemployment
rising everywhere to unprecedented heights, each government
continued to pay lip-service to the virtues of freer international

14 *Economic Progress and Social Security*, op. cit., p. 241.

trade; but as any independent relaxation of its own restrictions seemed likely to intensify its own short-term difficulties, in practice nothing was done." If only there had been in existence some international machinery to relax trade restrictions *everywhere at once,* and to bring about an expansion of the volume of transactions, the situation might have been drastically improved. Alas, there was no such machinery in existence. The failure of the twenties brought in its wake the helplessness of the thirties and the drift towards increasing economic nationalism and towards disruptive economic strife. Restrictions were heaped upon restrictions, "beggar-my-neighbor" policies came into widespread use, "insulation" became the fashion of the day, and the term "autarky" emerged from dictionaries into the wide and rapidly disintegrating world. Emergency measures were soon looked upon as being the dispensation of superior knowledge, and economic internationalism as well as the free-market economy were increasingly treated with scorn and contempt as relics of a dim past. One is tempted to observe, aphoristically, that nothing breeds nationalism so fast as the lack of international co-operation.

The experiences of the thirties are instructive in several important respects. In the first place they have demonstrated that, contrary to beliefs held in that period by certain economists and politicians, fluctuating exchange rates between national currencies are highly undesirable and that competitive currency depreciation benefits no one. The spontaneous creation of the Sterling Area, a group of countries using sterling, not gold, as the basis of their monetary systems and keeping their exchange rates stable in terms of sterling; and the Tripartite Agreement, concluded in 1936 between the United States, Great Britain, and France, then extended to Belgium, the Netherlands, and Switzerland—these are eloquent expressions of a widespread desire for exchange stability.

In the second place, these experiences have demonstrated that quantitative trade restrictions and exchange control tend to grow in complexity and amplitude the longer they operate and that they lead to a decline of world trade. In the end no country derived any lasting gain from this process; no one won anything, everybody suffered losses. Ten years after the outbreak of the Great Depression—and despite the national rearmament programs—prosperity had not been restored in the world. We have here a kind of "negative proof" of the virtues of international trade.

In a special and sinister sense, there were, of course, some beneficiaries of this protracted crisis. These were the totalitarian nations plotting their dark schemes of aggression. We have described, in Chapter VI, the principal aspects of Germany's foreign-trade methods under the Nazi regime and under Dr. Schacht's guidance. The decline of world markets and the plight of smaller countries played into the hands not only of Germany, but of Italy and Japan as well. The eagerness to sell was so great that no one had the courage to inquire why these countries were buying. Nor did anyone have the wisdom and the temerity to refuse to sell. Had world trade been kept up, had the League of Nations worked out an effective system of "preventive sanctions," the Axis powers would have found their task of economic mobilization very hard indeed. But in the troubled economic waters of the mid-thirties, fishing was extremely good for them.

There are great *political* virtues in economic interdependence of nations; interdependence reduces the ability of any one nation to wage aggressive war. Policies of autarky were, as we know, a prelude to conquest. Economic disintegration made these policies possible. It would seem that these recent events vindicate Adam Smith on political as well as on economic grounds: the international division of labor and the interdependence of nations to which it leads are not only a source of welfare but a factor greatly contributing to the peace of the world.

While, in the latter part of the thirties, the totalitarian menace was increasing daily, the international bodies took no official cognizance of its economic aspects. "Totalitarian trade" has been the object of no *official* pre-war study. This was surely a serious neglect on the part of the League and of other international organizations. There is only one explanation for it: the fear of conflict. Instead, the claims of Germany that she had no adequate access to raw materials were given a sympathetic reception, and a special committee of the League of Nations was appointed to investigate the matter. Its report rejected these claims as ill-founded, declaring that "the only general and permanent solution of the problem of commercial access to raw materials is to be found in a restoration of international exchanges on the widest basis," [15] but it was left to the expert of the U.S.S.R. to put his finger on the *real* reason for the emergence of the "raw materials problem." In a supplementary declaration he urged the committee to "draw the attention of the Assembly to the fact that, in these times of political disturbance, raw materials were being used by certain States for aggressive and warlike purposes." [16]

The widespread reluctance to face the menace of totalitarian aggression and to interfere with the trade expansion of the Axis jeopardized the final opportunity of the democratic countries to jointly adopt a bold economic policy. After the conclusion of the Tripartite Agreement (which *ipso facto* included the Sterling Area as well), one final attempt was made to bring about a reduction of trade barriers. We have mentioned in an earlier chapter the mission with which the governments of Great Britain and France entrusted, in 1937, M. Paul van Zeeland of Belgium. His endeavors might have been crowned with success had the projected agreement been limited to countries of the Tripartite Agreement *plus* the Sterling Area. But once again there appeared the fear of excluding Germany and Italy—and, since these countries were committed to their totalitarian trade programs, the mission could produce no results. Shall we learn from that experience that a limited agreement is better than no agreement at all? And that countries that are governed by similar conceptions of economic organization and policy should get together whenever possible and move jointly in the direction of a "world economy"? The fact that an agreement is not universal in scope, because certain countries prefer to stay out of it, is no reason why it should be given up by those who have the desire to collaborate.

[15] League of Nations Publications, II. Economic and Financial, 1937. II. B. 7, *Report of the Committee for the Study of the Problem of Raw Materials* (Geneva, 1937), p. 30.
[16] Ibid., p. 30.

CHAPTER X

Some Problems of Transition

AT THE END of World War I, the problem of the economic disorganization of the world was much more difficult to deal with than that of material destruction. The latter was solved with a surprising speed; the former failed to be solved at all. We have seen in the preceding chapter the highlights of that failure and its dreary consequences. The depression of the thirties made the disorganization worse than ever, and, at the end of the second and far more devastating World War, we have on our hands once again these twin by-products of international conflict: destruction and confusion. We are going to leave aside in the present study the immediate rehabilitation problems, referring the reader to the reports on the activity of UNRRA—the United Nations Relief and Rehabilitation Administration [1]—which are issued periodically and contain a great deal of valuable information, and to special studies which are likely to be published as we obtain more perspective concerning the results of our handling the immediate distress resulting from the war. There are, of course, no hard and fast divisions of the subject matter of contemporary history; yet it might be useful to view the process of rehabilitation as the last phase of the war—its liquidation as it were; whereas the problems with which we are going to deal in the present chapter are the prelude to and first steps of a movement towards organized peace. The fact that both groups of problems have to be dealt with concurrently in practice, and that the dividing line between relief and rehabilitation on the one side and reconstruction and development on the other,[2] is tenuous, does not make the distinction useless.

The problems with which we are concerned in the present chapter are problems of transition. This is a frequently used term which denotes the conviction, born from interwar experi-

---

[1] See e.g., *Fifth Report to Congress on the Operations of UNRRA as of September 30, 1945* (U. S. Government Printing Office, Washington, D. C., 1946). See also the explanatory booklet *UNRRA—Organization, Aims, Progress* issued by UNRRA in Washington, D. C.

[2] To use the terms included in the titles, respectively, of UNRRA and of the International Bank for Reconstruction and Development.

ences, that time and effort will be needed to organize the world for peace and that not until much special effort will have been successfully devoted to healing the wounds of war, will the world be able to move on "in peace gear," under its own power. Until then, special measures will have to be devised to deal with particular situations, props of various kinds will have to be used, different *ad hoc* policies will be needed to forestall crises which might threaten the whole task of reconstruction.

"Reconstruction" is a misleading term, even though it is currently used. "Construction" would serve the purpose of our times better. Reconstruction means building up again something that existed and was damaged or destroyed, whereas the task that confronts our generation is one of building something new. We can derive no inspiration from looking back into the past.

Without either the possibility or the desirability of "going back," of seeking one's future goals in the contemplation of things past, the notion of a "period of transition," often used in public documents and in private discussions, calls for much elaboration. This notion brings to mind the immortal conversation between a very bewildered little girl and a very wise evanescent cat:

"The cat only grinned when it saw Alice. . . .
'Cheshire-Puss,' she began, rather timidly. . . . 'Would you tell me, please, which way I ought to go from here?'
'That depends a good deal on where you want to get to,' said the Cat."

A very sensible answer: one about which "planners," domestic and international, might do well to ponder. In the twenties, with their minds upon the past, the builders of a peaceful world had no clear notion of the goals toward which they wanted to move. In the thirties they were no less baffled than Alice—anything seemed better than the condition the world was actually in. The above dialogue, however, has a sequel, as the reader will readily recall. Answering the Cheshire Cat's observation:

" 'I don't much care where . . .' said Alice.
'Then it doesn't matter which way you go,' said the Cat.
'. . . so long as I get *somewhere*,' Alice added as an explanation.
'Oh, you're sure to do that,' said the Cat, 'if you only walk long enough.' "

Alice, as we know, got into a great many involved situations and, finally, when things got very hectic and confused, she woke up. The world of the twenties and thirties moved from war to depression and from depression to war, getting *somewhere,* to be sure, but not anywhere near where most people really wanted to get—nor was there any awakening from the nightmare.

When we speak of "transition" therefore, we must have as clear an idea as possible of the aims we seek, in order not to drift helplessly into undesired and dangerous situations. Hence our first question must be: "Whither?"

2.

To that short question no equally short answer can be given. For phrases like "enduring peace" or "one world" are evidently inadequate. We might have had both by submitting to force and by accepting the tyranny and persecutions of the Axis. We preferred war to *such* a peace and *such* a "oneness" of the world. Cultural autonomy, individual freedom, security under law, prosperity without regimentation—these values had enough appeal among people to bring about the downfall of the infamous aggressors whose thirst for power culminated in World War II. Now we want a world built in the image of our ideals. And the question arises: do we all have the same ideals throughout the world, the same goals, or are we divided as to the desired shape of the future world? There seems to be little doubt that division exists and that "one world" may not be attainable at the present time, in the sense of being a world of uniform economic and political values and standards. We cannot, evidently, deal in this study with all the phases of this perplexing situation; but its economic features are of the greatest importance for the future.

The division indicated above is not so much a sharp economic cleavage of the world into two or more parts (though this might happen and would then cast a dark shadow upon the future of the peace) as it is a gamut of conceptions of economic policy and social organization, running all the way from the free-enterprise economy of the United States to the state-owned and operated economy of the Soviet Union. In between there are various degrees and shadings of state ownership and state control, from the "mild" socialization measures in Great Britain to the near-collectivism of Eastern Europe. The situation is far from set; it is full of dynamism and is, undoubtedly, going to show many changes in the months and years to come. Actually, only the United States and the Soviet Union have at the present time crystallized economic philosophies, and there can be no doubt of the contest that is taking place in the world between the two. It may be a peaceful contest or it may degenerate into strife, according to what the ultimate, world-wide objectives of these two great continental powers will prove to be. The American objectives are clear; there is a fair amount of divergent guessing about those of the Soviet Union.

The United States aims at the maintenance of free-enterprise capitalism at home and, as far as possible, of free-enterprise world trade. The market mechanism is favored as against quantitative government controls; business deals among private partners as against intergovernmental trade. This means a strong emphasis on multilateral trade and on the principle of nondiscrimination. It is important, from the American point of view, that as large an area of the world as possible should adopt these principles for then only will the international division of labor give its full fruits and the market system its best results.

There are countries which have departed from nondiscriminatory multilateral trade under the impact of the chaos of the thirties, first, and of the war exigencies, afterwards; these countries, of which Great Britain and France are outstanding examples, may adopt these principles of policy once more if their current difficulties are resolved. There is much scope here for constructive policies on the part of the United States.

Other countries are, or may become, committed to the principle of complete state control over foreign trade. As we have seen, bilateralism is a significant feature of state-controlled trade. Whether state monopolies of foreign trade can practice nondiscriminatory, multilateral trade is a matter of conjecture. Many hopeful views have been expressed on that subject by economists and politicians, but historic evidence points to the contrary conclusions. Of course, history *may* possibly fail to repeat itself, but this only time will tell. At the present moment the conclusions reached in Chapter VI should help to guide the future trade relations between free-market and state-controlled economies. And this, specifically, also means the trade relations between the United States and the Soviet Union.[3] Eventually an agreement will have to be reached between these two countries, or better still, as a part of a general international convention, to establish "rules of conduct" to govern these inter-system trade relations. The difficulties involved in such an agreement—and in its enforcement—are greater, however, than would appear from the following opinion expressed in a recent study by Dr. Gerschenkron:[4]

". . . it may be suggested that perhaps the simplest way of solving the question would be to make a general agreement with Russia in which the latter shall undertake to be guided in the conduct of her foreign trade by commercial and not political considerations."

This comes very close to wishful thinking—not because Russia is Russia, but because it is in the nature of state-controlled trade that it cannot be divorced from political considerations. Such trade is an integral part of an over-all national program in which economic and political considerations are merged into one whole. As we have seen, therein lie serious dangers for both world trade and world peace. A totalitarian regime may be favorable to both and may be most co-operative in its foreign relations—and it may cease to be favorable to either and choose a course of autarky and territorial expansion. Only free-enterprise trade with a *minimum* of tariffs and other state interventions can take trade out of politics. In every other case the two are more or less linked—until in the case of state-socialistic countries the merger is complete.

The U. S. Government's *Proposals for Expansion of World Trade and Employment,* of November 1945[5] contain the following provisions concerning "Complete State Monopolies of Foreign Trade:"[6]

---

[3] See: "The Prospects of Soviet American Trade Relations," Institute of International Finance of New York University, *Bulletin No. 139,* August 27, 1945; Alexander Gerschenkron: *Economic Relations with the USSR,* published by the Committee on International Economic Policy in co-operation with the Carnegie Endowment for International Peace (New York, 1945).

[4] Op. cit., p. 25.

[5] See p. 197 ff., below.

[6] *Proposals,* Chapter III: General Commercial Policy; Section E: State Trading, paragraph 3.

"As the counterpart of tariff reductions and other actions to encourage an expansion of multilateral trade by other members, members having a complete state monopoly of foreign trade should undertake to purchase annually from members, on the non-discriminatory basis referred to in paragraph 1 above, [. . . members should undertake that the foreign purchases and sales of their state-trading enterprises shall be influenced solely by commercial considerations, such as price, quality, marketability, transportation and terms of purchase or sale], products valued at not less than an aggregate amount to be agreed upon. The global purchase arrangement should be subject to periodic adjustment in consultation with the Organization." [7]

These provisions can hardly be considered as adequate. The bracketed passage (from paragraph 1) ignores the great difference that exists between *limited* state trading and *large-scale* state trading or indeed complete monopolies of foreign trade. In the former case discriminations may possibly be avoided; in the latter, as has been argued before, they are almost unavoidable. The value of the agreement proposed in the quoted passage presents many theoretical as well as practical difficulties. It is difficult to visualize on what basis such agreements could be reached or revised. Multilateral trade must be flexible, whereas the formula suggested by the U. S. Government is full of rigidity. The problem is admittedly most difficult and no satisfactory formula can ever be evolved unless all the complexities and pitfalls of the matter are taken into serious consideration.

The problem of economic relations between free-market economies and those whose foreign trade is fully controlled by the state is the most important single matter affecting the future of the world economy as well as the future of free-enterprise capitalism. As viewed from America, the goal of the future is to help the establishment of as wide an area as possible of multilateral free-enterprise trade; and—without giving up our own economic principles—to reach a *modus vivendi* with countries whose economic organization involves a comprehensive state control over economic life.

To that end several intricate problems of transition will have to be dealt with, quickly and efficiently. The following will be briefly discussed in the balance of this chapter: the recovery by

[7] The proposed International Trade Organization.

Great Britain of a durable balance-of-payments equilibrium; the German settlement, a condition of the reorganization of Europe; and the place and role of the Soviet Union in the European reconstruction.

3.

Britain's problem is easy to state, though it is difficult to solve. It is the result of the decline of British exports during the war, of the losses in shipping and overseas investment and of the income derived by the British economy from these sources, and of the growth of Britain's foreign indebtedness. It will be convenient to discuss the British difficulties in two parts: first, the problem of paying for imports; next, that of paying her debts. The second point involves the question of blocked sterling balances. Both points call for a consideration of the Sterling Area and of British exchange controls.

Before the war in the years 1936–8 approximately 55 per cent of Britain's imports were paid with the proceeds of exports; 12 per cent with income from shipping; 23 per cent with income from foreign investments; 5 per cent with income from commissions, insurances, etc.; and there was a deficit of about 5 per cent.[8]

As result of the war, income from British exports fell from 471 million pounds in 1938 to 258 million pounds in 1944. Net shipping losses amounted by June 30th, 1945, to 28 per cent of the September 3rd, 1939, volume, Britain's merchant marine having declined from 22.1 to 15.9 million deadweight tons. This leads, of course, to a substantial loss of income from shipping. Income from foreign investments declined from about 200 million pounds in 1938 to a little less than 100 million pounds in 1945. This is due to the sales of overseas investments for an amount of about 4,500 million dollars (between September 1939 and June 1945), of which 2,270 million dollars represent sales of British investments in the Sterling Area and 1,725 million dollars, sales in the United States and Canada.[9]

---

[8] These figures are based on data released in the mimeographed bulletin for December 10, 1945, of the British Information Services in New York.

[9] Cf. *Statistical Material Presented during the Washington Negotiations*, a White Paper (Cmd. 6707) presented by the Chancellor of the Exchequer to Parliament, December 1945. Also: Institute of International Finance of New York University: *Bulletin No. 136*, of February 19, 1945: "The Postwar International Financial Position of Great Britain."

It follows that Britain is going to face most serious difficulties in paying for her imports in the years to come. "It is widely believed," writes a careful student of the British balance-of-payments problem, "that, in volume terms, exports would have to rise by at least 50 per cent above the 1938 level, or five times above the 1944 level, if even the 1938 volume of imports is to be paid for." [10] But actually, owing to reconstruction requirements, the import needs of Great Britain, unless consumers' demand is to be curtailed through drastic governmental restrictions, are likely to be much in excess of the 1938 level.

In addition there is the problem of British foreign indebtedness which has increased from 1,920 million dollars on August 31, 1939, to 13,525 million dollars on June 30, 1945. Of the latter figure, 10,975 million dollars represent indebtedness within the Sterling Area.[11] The reason for that large proportion of Sterling-Area debt will easily be found in the fact of American Lend-Lease and of Canadian gifts to cover British war expenditures in these countries, whereas expenses incurred in India, Burma, Egypt, etc., resulted in a British sterling debt. Ninety per cent of British foreign liabilities are short-term or "quick" liabilities, and the sterling debt consists of sterling balances owned by the respective countries in London. These balances are mostly blocked, i.e., the owners cannot use them freely to purchase goods in Great Britain, nor can they obtain for them dollars or other foreign exchange. In order to pay off this debt, Great Britain would have to increase her exports still further. In that respect, being already in great need of expanding her exports in order to pay for her current imports, Great Britain is in the position of Alice in Wonderland:

"Now, *here,* you see [said the Queen to Alice], it takes all the running *you* can do, to keep in the same place. If you want to get somewhere else, you must run at least twice as fast as that!"

How this feat is to be accomplished, is the perplexing problem faced by Great Britain at the end of World War II.

[10] Arthur I. Bloomfield: "The British Balance-of-Payments Problem," *Essays in International Finance,* Princeton University, Autumn 1945, p. 13.
[11] This can be further broken up as follows: Dominions—1,550 million dollars; India, Burma, and Middle East—6,980 million dollars; other Sterling Area countries—2,495 million dollars.

As regards the foreign sterling debt, it will eventually have to be scaled down and repaid over a long period of time, thus reducing to manageable proportions the necessary addition to annual exports. We shall not deal with that matter here, except to point out that it is situations like this one that illustrate dramatically the intimate connection between international trade and international capital movements, the more theoretical aspects of which were discussed in Book I.

In "normal" times, once an appropriate framework of economic policies, domestic and international, is set up, the equilibrium of balance of payments more or less "takes care of itself." Normally, therefore, our main concern needs to be over the establishment of a workable framework, not over the position of the balance of payments. But this is not the case when major disturbances cause great and sudden changes in one or more groups of a country's foreign transactions and make further major changes necessary in order to restore the balance. In the case of Great Britain it is necessary either to drastically reduce the volume of imports or very considerably expand exports. The former would impair the tasks of domestic reconstruction and lower dangerously the living standards of the population; the latter would require the accomplishment of an economic *tour de force* of unprecedented scope.

A drastic curtailment of imports, combined with the development at home of substitute industries would involve the perpetuation of exchange controls and of other restrictive devices, and a substantial degree of central economic planning of the entire national economy (in order to determine the relative importance of various kinds of imports, and to establish scales of "priorities," allocating "scarce" foreign exchanges for one or another among many competing demands). Since Britain's standard of living depends to a considerable extent upon her imports, this could never provide an effective "solution" of her problem; it could not be successful even as an emergency measure. The slogan "Export or Die," often heard in the past few years, is appallingly true.

The difficulty is aggravated by the psychological consequences of Britain's interwar experiences. As result of a faulty choice of parity in the 1925 stabilization of the pound sterling, British prices expressed in terms of foreign currencies became too high to be competitive, and there appeared a need for deflationary measures.[12] As these encountered much opposition, Britain's export trade suffered, and throughout most of the twenties her economy was afflicted with chronic unemployment. This, incidentally, accounts for the discredit into which the gold standard has fallen in England. The system itself is being blamed for what was, in essence, an error of judgment in 1925 in deciding to return to the pre-1914 gold parity of the pound, which, in point of fact, was depreciated at that time by about ten per cent. Actually, the foregoing explanation is far from complete. The British industry had lost much of its earlier "drive" and spirit of enterprise; plants failed to be modernized; sales methods lagged behind those of Britain's competitors in world markets; too much reliance was placed on cartels; competition was regarded with suspicion and apprehension.[13] The devaluation of 1931—which, under the circumstances, should have been carried out in the late twenties—helped a great deal to improve Britain's competitive position vis-à-vis the United States, etc., while, at the same time, a group of countries tied their currencies to the sterling rather than to gold, which preserved London's position as a financial center. Britain's experiment with reverting to protection, in 1931, was far less conclusive.[14] On this latter occasion a group of outstanding British economists, mostly connected with the London School of Economics, formed a committee to examine anew the tariff issue. Their conclusions, dated August 1931, are worthy of quotation:[15]

"We have surveyed once more, in the light of to-day, the well-trodden fields of this ancient controversy. After that survey we should all think it a disaster, if the policy of Free Trade which has served Britain so well materially, as through her it has served as an inspiration to all who in any land have worked for good understanding among nations, were to-day to be sacrificed to ignorance or panic or jealousy or specious calculations of a moment's gain."

12 Cf. J. M. (Lord) Keynes: *The Economic Consequences of Mr. Churchill* (London, 1925).
13 Cf. André Siegfried: *England's Crisis* (New York, 1931). See also the recent detailed study by Alfred Edward Kahn: *Great Britain in the World Economy* (New York, 1946).
14 Cf. Frederick C. Benham: *Great Britain under Protection* (New York, 1941).
15 *Tariffs: The Case Examined*, by a Committee of Economists under the Chairmanship of Sir William Beveridge (London, 1931). The passage quoted is the concluding part of the preface. Signatories: F. C. Benham, W. H. Beveridge, A. L. Bowley, T. E. Gregory, J. R. Hicks, W. T. Layton, A. Plant, L. C. Robbins, G. L. Schwarz.

It is rather sad to reflect upon circumstances that have caused Sir William Beveridge, chairman of that committee, finally to succumb to panic and to advocate—fourteen years later—a course of policy for Great Britain which involves a complete denial of the above-quoted principles.

The fear of competition and the distrust of any international monetary system that would be even vaguely reminiscent of the gold standard—these are the two principal reasons (apart from doctrinal leanings towards a state control of economic life) for the current wave of economic nationalism in Great Britain, to which we have referred in preceding chapters. That economic nationalism is based not on the British Isles alone—for insulation within such narrow confines is clearly impossible—but on the Sterling Area. Its advocates would wish to insulate that whole area, within which Britain's economic predominance is indisputable, from the rest of the world. In relations outside the area, various controls and discriminations would be used—their scope varying with particular predilections of the individual spokesmen. In relations within the area, Britain would either practice a limited kind of multilateral trade, or use its power to play the bilateralist game—again according to the philosophy of particular spokesmen. The more extreme of these have learned a great deal from Dr. Schacht!

The great issue before Great Britain is the choice between coming into the same system of multilateral trade with the United States, Canada, etc., or remaining within the orbit of the Sterling Area. It is the choice between trusting efficiency and engaging in free and fair competition in world markets, thus helping to restore a world economy based on multilateral trade, on the one side, and relying upon the *power* of a centrally run Sterling Area to obtain from the outside world advantages which are believed to be unattainable through competitive channels on the other.

There can be no doubt about the long-run advantages for Great Britain of the multilateral solution. Yet, if the balance-of-payments deficits that are certain to exist in the next few years, until exports have recovered and substantially exceeded their prewar level, are not paid out of an adequate volume of "cash reserves,"[16] England is likely to step into the bilateralist solu-

[16] Gold or dollars.

tion. The Sterling Area enthusiasts and the "Anglo-Schachtians" will have come into their own. The question can, of course, legitimately be raised as to whether the members of that area would remain content with such arrangements. One can hardly doubt that some, at least, would prefer free dollars to blocked sterling if only they saw a chance of expanding their trade with the United States. On the other hand, the use of the powers Great Britain, backed by the Sterling Area, could exercise in economic bargaining would very likely precipitate an economic conflict with the United States. This country is almost certain to be victorious in such a struggle—but in the course of fighting it our free-enterprise economy might well suffer a deathblow.

In order to help Britain surmount her difficulties within the framework of multilateral trade, negotiations for an American loan were conducted in Washington in the fall of 1945, resulting in the agreement of December 6, 1945. That agreement and the "Understanding Reached on Commercial Policy," as well as the Joint Statement on the "Settlement for Lend-Lease and Reciprocal Aid, Surplus War Property and Claims," all signed on the same occasion, constitute the cornerstone of the future Anglo-American economic relations. The "understanding" on commercial policy, which is a most important part of the agreements, will be discussed in the next chapter; as for the financial arrangements, they involve (1) the cancellation of 25 billion dollars of Lend-Lease indebtedness; (2) a loan of 650 million dollars to pay for the settlement of surplus war property and net Lend-Lease deliveries made by the United States after V-J Day; (3) a loan of 3,750 million dollars in the form of a line of credit, which may be drawn upon before December 31, 1951. The repayment is to begin on that date and be spread over fifty years. We shall leave aside the technical details of the loan agreement.[17] What must be noted, however, because it is an important innovation in the field of international finance is that interest payments on the loan may be waived in any year in which Great Britain experiences serious balance-of-payments difficulties. As Lord Keynes—the principal British negotiator of the loan—put

[17] See, however, the full text of all three agreements in Publication 2439 of the Department of State: *Anglo-American Financial and Commercial Agreements* (Washington, D. C., December 1945).

it in his speech of December 18, 1945, in the House of Lords: "We pay no interest in any year in which our exports have not been restored to a level which may be estimated at about 60 per cent in excess of what they were pre-war [in volume]."

For the United States, the purpose of the loan is to assist Britain's reconstruction and her return to multilateral trade. Unless England and the British Commonwealth drop the stringent exchange controls and other restrictive measures that keep this country out of most of the Sterling-Area markets, the revival of American exports will be handicapped while the achievement of a multilateral, non-discriminatory international trading system will be made well-nigh impossible. Instead we might be faced with a widespread conflict among hostile economic blocs. Lord Keynes's pertinent comments in the conclusion of his House of Lords speech of December 18, 1945, are worth quoting in this connection: [18]

". . . much of these policies [agreed upon by England and the United States] seem to me to be in the prime interest of our country, little though we may like some parts of them. They are calculated to help us regain a full measure of prosperity and prestige in the world's commerce. They aim, above all, at the restoration of multilateral trade which is a system upon which British commerce essentially depends. You can draw your supplies from any source that suits you and sell your goods in any market where they can be sold to advantage. The bias of the policies before you is against bilateral barter and every kind of discriminatory practice. The separate economic *blocs* and all the friction and loss of friendship they must bring with them are expedients to which one may be driven in a hostile world, where trade has ceased over wide areas to be co-operative and peaceful and where are forgotten the healthy rules of mutual advantage and equal treatment. But it is surely crazy to prefer that. Above all, this determination to make trade truly international and to avoid the establishment of economic *blocs* which limit and restrict commercial intercourse outside them, is plainly an essential condition of the world's best hope, an Anglo-American understanding, which brings us and others together in international institutions which may be in the long run the first step towards something more comprehensive. Some of us, in the tasks of war and more lately in those of peace, have learnt by experience that our two countries can work together. Yet it would

[18] *Parliamentary Debates* (Hansard), House of Lords, Vol. 138, No. 41, 18 December 1945, Col. 793–4.

be only too easy for us to walk apart. I beg those who look askance at these plans to ponder deeply and responsibly where it is they think they want to go."

Needless to say, the American loan by itself, and the removal of the most obtrusive trade barriers and the revival of multilateral trade, will not suffice to solve Britain's postwar problem. In order to achieve and maintain the high volume of exports which is needed to preserve a new equilibrium in Britain's foreign payments, British industry must lose its fear of competition and acquire a zest for improvement and a love of efficiency. The latter must also govern the behavior of British labor. Nationalization, as the *Economist* once very wisely observed, is no substitute for rationalization. A new wave of economic pioneering and risk-taking is necessary. Faith in the power of initiative and of inventiveness of individual men and women, and the creation of conditions favorable to the exercise of these twin motors of dynamic economies, can do more for England in the end than faith in the miracles of state-ownership and state control. In that field there may be much scope for constructive collaboration between American and British industries: exchange of technological "know how," market research, etc., collaboration, in short, for the purpose not of restricting competition but of increasing the vitality of private enterprise in industry and trade. It is along the second line that the reintegration of Great Britain and the other members of the Sterling Area into a system of multilateral trade may *both* solve the British financial predicament and create an environment favorable to the reintroduction throughout a large part of the world of the spirit of economic internationalism.

4.

The British problem is a financial problem reaching into the realm of trade policies and of industrial efficiency. Its solution—or a failure to solve it—will have important repercussions on the future shape of the world economy and of world politics as well. The problem of European reconstruction is, by contrast, primarily a political problem, though the political solution will have to be guided by certain economic considerations and, in turn, will affect the future of international economic relations.

In the heart of Europe, geographically as well as economically, lies Germany, defeated and weak in 1918 and 1945, strong and aggressive in 1914 and 1939, and, who knows, maybe strong and aggressive again in the future.

Economically, politically, and socially, Europe is completely broken up and disorganized at the end of World War II. In the East the Soviet Union extends its political and economic influence; in the center lies the unsolved problem of Germany; the West is in a turmoil, but there is a distinct possibility that it will retain some, at least, of the basic tenets of a free-market economy, even though the nationalization program of France may go further than that of Great Britain. It is not our purpose in this book to provide a topical survey of current events, which would be obsolete almost as soon as written and certainly as soon as published. Nor is it our intent to engage in the booming but precarious pursuit of prophecy. As, in addition, the length of this discussion must be very limited, we shall merely highlight the most important issues. The first among these is the future of Germany.

As has been emphasized in Chapter IX, the insecurity that jeopardized the fate of international economic organization after World War I may be traced, in part at least, to the failure of the victorious powers to destroy effectively the menace of German militarism. We must not repeat that mistake again. Yet there is real danger that it *will* be repeated and that its repetition will be justified on economic grounds. It is argued in many places, on both sides of the Atlantic, that the German industry is indispensable for the prosperity of Europe and for the recovery of world trade; that minor controls are sufficient to prevent it from becoming again a tool of war;[19] that a new and de-Nazified Germany will be a trustworthy and peaceful member of the international community.[20]

Let us leave the last point aside even though it is often made;

[19] Thus e.g., Harold G. Moulton and Louis Marlio in *The Control of Germany and Japan* (Washington, D. C., 1944), propose to control the use of power in Germany and so to limit its output so as to make Germany dependent on importation of electric power from its neighbors.

[20] E.g., Antonin Basch in *A Price for Peace* (New York, 1945) writes: "Our objective should be not to keep Germany isolated and controlled for an indefinite period but to bring a reshaped German economy back into genuine cooperation with the rest of the world, *assuming* that a new Germany will prove worthy of trust and of admission into the family of nations" (p. 144, italics added). It is impossible to take such an "assumption" seriously as a guide to policy! In reality it is just wishful thinking.

wishful thinking, however desirable its content, is never a prac-tice to be indulged in, lest it stultifies practical action. It is risky to believe in the efficiency of "minor" devices and of seem-ingly efficient short cuts to a real solution. Most of all, we must guard against underestimating our enemy. An otherwise remark-able report, prepared by one of the Congressional committees, deprecates the "fear of the bogey of a Germany, reduced in its boundaries and stripped of its warmaking capacity as modern Germany is," and warns that "if the whole future recovery of Europe is to be geared" to this fear, "the recovery of Europe be-comes a hopeless proposition."[21] Now it should be observed that the territorial changes agreed upon at Potsdam leave Ger-many's major war potential *within* her reduced borders, since it is located in the western part of the country; and that the re-moval of the equipment from Germany's war plants is a measure which cripples her militarily for a limited time only, because, eventually, new plants can be built and new and more modern equipment installed. The real problem is not to make Germany weak for the next few years—but to make her indefinitely un-able to wage war. After two world wars due to German aggres-sion, it is surely a peculiar usage of terms to speak of "bogey" when referring to the dangers of a German comeback.

Actually, four main courses of action are open with respect to Germany:

(1) To allow her to keep her industries going, subject to "minor" direct controls and to a general supervision by the United Nations; this solution appears as very precarious and unreliable because such controls would grow easier and easier to evade and more and more difficult to enforce as time went on Some day Germany would be readmitted to the world com-munity of nations and then controls would be dropped alto-gether. At that point the danger of a new German aggression would become very real indeed.

(2) To prevent her heavy industries from operating and to close, partly at least, her coal mines. This solution would destroy the German menace for as long as the United Nations would be disposed to enforce the prohibition, if necessary with military

[21] *Economic Reconstruction of Europe,* Eighth Report of the House Special Com-mittee on Postwar Economic Policy and Planning, William M. Colmer, Chairman, November 12, 1945, Government Printing Office, Washington, D. C., p. 40.

measures. The solution would be costly, in purely economic terms, on account of the "lost" output of industries and mines prevented from operating.

(3) To segregate from Germany the western industrial areas of the Ruhr, the Rhineland, and the Saar and to place them under international control. This would prevent the German state from controlling the output of these regions and would correspondingly reduce the German war potential. The weakness of the proposal lies in the pitfalls of international controls. In the world that has emerged from World War II it is almost impossible to expect a harmonious international administration of so crucial an area as western Germany. Major frictions would almost certainly develop among the great powers; they would, very likely, be stimulated, later on, by the effects of German diplomacy. Eventually Germany might be allowed a representation on the control boards—and eventually the object of destroying her war potential would most likely be placed in jeopardy.

(4) To separate completely the Ruhr, the Rhineland, and the Saar from Germany and to integrate them with France, Belgium, and the Netherlands. This course of action calls for some further comments.

In reading the literature about the reconstruction of Europe and the settlement with Germany,[22] one is struck by the fact that the geographical boundaries of Germany are generally regarded as something given and immutable. The Potsdam agreements that made major territorial changes in the east of Germany should have shattered that peculiar belief, but it seems to live on with respect to western Germany. We read about how Europe needs German industry, how the economic weakening of Germany would affect adversely the living standards of other countries,[23] and so forth, but actually the question might be asked: What *is* Germany, geographically speaking? Boundaries are man-made and can be changed by men. The German "geopoli-

---

[22] See e.g., Henry Morgenthau, Jr.: *Germany Is Our Problem* (New York, 1945); Antonin Basch: *A Price for Peace,* op. cit.; the Report on *Economic Reconstruction of Europe* (two parts), op. cit.; Moulton and Marlio: *The Control of Germany and Japan,* op. cit.; etc., etc.

[23] E.g., the Royal Institute of International Affairs, London, published in 1943 a Report on *The Problem of Germany* in which it is stated that: "Deliberately to ruin German productive capacity, both industrial and scientific, would involve the further depression of the standards of living of other European countries" (p. 42; quoted in Basch, op. cit., p. 131).

tics" has given geographical advice for that country's expansion, guided by the desire to increase the power of the German state. What we need now is *geopolitics in reverse gear;* we must so change the boundaries of Germany as to reduce the power of the German state. The separation of the western industrial and mining regions from Germany would serve that purpose better than anything else we could do.

Some further advantages of the fourth course of action are the following: it is a definitive solution, allowing for no such further wrangles, frictions and intrigues as would very likely develop under the operation of an international control agency; Germany deprived of these districts would be too weak ever to contemplate a comeback; [24] the resources of the Ruhr, Rhineland, and Saar would be integrated into the economies of three countries that are peaceful and trustworthy—France, Belgium, and the Netherlands—and thus would add to the prosperity of Europe and of the world.

This course of action with respect to Germany would, if adopted, allow a radical reshaping of the European economy. It might usefully involve the conclusion of a customs union by France, Belgium, the Netherlands, and Luxemburg. Furthermore, both Great Britain and the United States should take an interest in the organization and integration of such a large and promising free-trade area in western Europe that would result from the adoption of the discussed program. There would be much scope for capital investments, especially through private channels and through direct industrial ventures of American and British companies; and there would be a large outlet for American and British technicians. This western European economic union would become a large market for the agricultural surpluses of central, eastern, and southeastern Europe—provided that appropriate trade relations can be established—a problem which will presently be examined. Incidentally, the removal of the Ruhr, Rhineland, and Saar from Germany will make the new and reduced German state much more self-supporting in food than would otherwise be the case.

[24] It may be argued that Germany's bitterness would breed war. But bitterness is incapable of resulting in war, if those who are bitter are also weak. The aftermath of the Civil War in America is a conclusive proof of that assertion—for no *second* Civil War (war of revenge) has ever followed.

If Europe is to become a peaceful continent, its reconstruction must be approached in an imaginative and constructive spirit. Here more than anywhere else perhaps "construction" rather than "reconstruction" is the proper term with which to describe the task ahead. Nor can we afford to be guided by economic criteria alone. The problem of Europe is primarily political; it must be solved in a way which is politically sound, even if it should be one that is economically costly. Along some such path as outlined above we stand a good chance, however, of achieving at the same time the purpose of destroying the war potential of the German state and that of using to the best economic effect the resources of the European continent.

5.

As envisaged in these pages, the economic reshaping of Europe involves extensive trade relations between eastern and western Europe. But, on the other hand, the division of the world into different trading and economic systems, to which we have devoted the earlier part of this chapter, becomes especially acute on the European scene. The House Special Committee on Postwar Economic Policy and Planning (known, by the name of its chairman, as the Colmer Committee) has dealt with that question at some length in a report issued in November 1945.[25] Certain passages from the Committee's report are so important as to justify the following lengthy quotation:[26]

"Russia, for several reasons, will play a critical part in the establishment of a stable world economic order. . . . Russian influence in the countries of eastern Europe at the present time determines the possibility of economic operations in those zones by other powers and the character of the economic as well as the political systems of a very large part of Europe. In spite of the heavy losses of the war, the Russian population within the new Soviet boundaries is something approaching 200,000,000 and constantly increasing because of a high birth rate. Direct control is presently exercised in Europe over another 100,000,000 people. Russian power extends over the resources of the Polish mining and industrial areas, Czechoslovak mining and industrial areas, and

[25] After the return of a delegation of its members from an eight-weeks trip through Europe and the Middle East.
[26] *Economic Reconstruction in Europe,* op. cit.; the passages quoted appear on pp. 29–30; 32 and 33.

the food and industrial areas of Hungary, Austria, Yugoslavia, Rumania, and Bulgaria, together with the Rumanian oil fields and the mineral resources of this entire territory. . . .

"A major economic problem of Russian relationships is the form of Russia's own organization and its relation to the possibilities of increasing world trade. It is proposed to leave to a later section a detailed discussion of the possibilities of dealing with state trading monopolies; at the same time it is possible here to indicate several problems which Russia's political and economic organization present in considering the possibilities of world recovery and particularly of American foreign trade:

"(a) Russia is at present working out trade agreements with the states which she effectively controls in eastern Europe. These might be described as barter arrangements. The terms of these treaties have not been made available to any of our diplomatic missions, even those most intimately concerned, or to the Department of State. The terms of the arrangement which Russia has made with Hungary have just been announced, in accordance with which at least 50 per cent of Hungarian production seems to be tied up by Russia, if press reports are to be believed. Some sources give 90 per cent of Hungary's present industrial production as going to Russia. What is needed are more reliable facts. . . .

"(b) In the second place, no real basis for evaluating the Russian economy exists so long as secrecy as to official statistics of production and as to future production plans is maintained. The committee was told that with the war over details of the 5-year plan would soon be published and the annual statistics thereafter. Official statistics are not sufficient; there should be opportunity, freely accorded by other countries to Russian observers, for journalists and others to look at the facts upon which these production statistics are based. Not only during the course of the war but up to the present time the entire American productive mechanism was thrown wide open to Russian inspection, and the opportunity was fully utilized. Carefully guarded industrial secrets which would not be revealed to domestic competitors were made available to Russia under the general conception of our lend-lease aid. No such parallel freedom has been accorded to American observers; indeed, it has not been possible to find out, in many cases, what products were being manufactured.

"The committee feels that it is necessary that American and other technicians be permitted to look at Russian industrial installations and to estimate the basis of Russian statistics in the matter. Perhaps the United Nations Organization may later be utilized to internationalize and generalize this type of information and technical inspection. It cannot see how, at present, without uncensored and independent estimates by our own representatives, including those of the properly accredited press, there is any sound basis for judging the adequacy of Russian statistics or her ability to repay loans. . . .

"The whole question of opening up the waterways, the communications and transportation systems of Europe rests very largely in the hands of Russia today. . . ."

These are weighty observations and they reveal to some extent the scope of difficulties that will be encountered in dealing with the overall problems of European reconstruction. In one of the passages quoted above reference is made to the Committee's "discussion of the possibilities of dealing with state trading monopolies." Since this is *the* crucial issue to be dealt with in connection with the building of an enduring world economy, the relevant observations by the Colmer Committee are also quoted in full: [27]

"It is clear that the pattern of future world trade is greatly conditioned by the existence of state trading monopolies. The Russian system constitutes the most powerful example of this. The system has been reproduced in all the eastern European countries under Russian control and tied into Russia by secret trade treaties, as well as by political control.

"It is by no means limited to these governments, however. The British Government has announced a policy of continuing state purchases for all the basic essentials of its import program in raw materials. The probability of the extension of this system into other purchases as an adjunct of exchange control seems strong. France is in effect achieving the same pattern. Although ordinary importers may be used as private channels in the manner noted above, the effect of pooling the disposal of the goods imported and selling them through state-controlled prices achieves the results of a state monopoly. This pattern appears to be one that may be widely followed in other nations. It is generally defended as a part of the need for controlling the volume of imports during a period of severe pressure on the exchanges.

"The committee recommends that two policies should be followed in dealing with state import monopolies:

"(a) In the instance of Russia it is necessary to deal with the state monopoly (Amtorg) as an inherent feature of the Russian system. At the same time every effort should be made to have private American business accorded more flexible channels of approach to Russian in-

[27] Ibid., p. 45.

dustrial concerns than through the single channel of Amtorg in New York.

"(b) It does not seem to be necessary to recognize the same completely controlled system in other countries. The foreign-trade policy of the United States should do everything possible to discourage trading with state monopolies and should facilitate direct trade with individuals in the countries concerned. Such a policy will be considerably strengthened if it is integrated with our postwar foreign lending program. In general, loans should be made in such a way as to secure the greatest possible amount of trade between individuals. In particular, care must be taken that any loans to these state monopolies do not result in disruption of existing channels of private trade and commerce."

Note on the Sterling Area

SEVERAL REFERENCES have been made, in section three of the pre-ceding chapter especially, to the Sterling Area. It may be useful to append a brief analysis of its nature and functions by quoting from an article by Mr. Paul Bareau.[1]

"The sterling area was originally a grouping of countries thrown, almost involuntarily, into some form of monetary cohesion by in-stinctive defence against the currency turmoils of the early 1930's and the disintegration of the international gold standard system. Con-venience, the pull of the British market and the long tradition of maintaining exchange reserves in London were the main architects of this currency 'bloc,' which gave its members in the 1930's the double benefit of almost complete exchange stability within the area and of insulation from the forces of deflation which continued to afflict the countries that clung to their gold parities.

"With the coming of war, the sterling area changed both its mem-bership and its character. It immediately lost its neutral adherents. Like everything else forming part of the texture of the British Com-monwealth of Nations it became an instrument of total war. The gradual evolution of sterling exchange control was built within the frame of the sterling area. That area acquired something it had never had before: statutory definition. It became one of the essential means of defence for sterling, used consciously and openly for canalizing trade where strategic demands required it to be canalized, providing the means for every kind of discrimination both in commercial policy and in directing the flow of capital to and from the various members of the area. As with so many of the metamorphoses brought about and justified by the needs and arguments of total war, this one has found a strong and vocal body of permanent supporters. The debates on Bretton Woods have revealed how strong is the body of opinion which wishes to preserve the sterling area not as what it was, but as what it is: an instrument of economic warfare; a battering ram with which to open the door to unwilling markets; a spiked fence of dis-criminatory devices with which to keep unwanted goods from un-wanted sellers out of the Empire market.

"... Although the sterling area emerged in definite recognizable

---

[1] Paul Bareau: "The Sterling Area—Its Use and Abuse," *The Banker*, London, March 1945, pp. 131–3. See also two articles by David Sachs: "Exchange Control in Transition," *The Banker*, London, August 1945, and "Exchange Control after Wash-ington," *The Banker*, London, January 1946. Very much valuable material can be found in the excellent *Annual Reports* of the Bank for International Settlements, Basle.

form from the turmoil that attended the breakdown of the gold standard in 1931, the system which then appeared to crystallize was not new. Within the framework of the gold standard—and particularly of the gold exchange standard—many countries that were nominally 'on gold' were, in effect, 'on sterling.' They kept the bulk, not merely of the exchange reserves needed for their current trade, but of the more static reserves required as backing for their currency, in the form of sterling balances and other short term assets. Most of these countries decided, in September, 1931, when the pound left gold, to keep their exchanges stable in terms of sterling and not of gold. This group included all the members of the Commonwealth, with the important exception of Canada, whose dollar went some of the way with sterling in its depreciation in terms of gold, but later linked itself to the U. S. dollar and not to sterling. South Africa hesitated for a few months before joining—no doubt fearful of the effect on her basic gold mining industry of the disintegration of the gold standard. Certain non-British countries, including Portugal, joined the sterling group immediately. Others joined it later: the Scandinavian countries in 1933, when the U. S. dollar lost some of its lustre, Iran and Latvia in 1936. Apart from the recognized adherents of the group there were several countries, including Argentina and Japan, which for many years kept their exchanges stable in terms of sterling, but without keeping appreciable reserves in London.

"This grouping of countries within a common currency area was extremely loose and wholly informal. There was no attempt by the countries concerned to pursue a common monetary policy, though the fact that most of them kept their monetary reserves in sterling provided some kind of mechanism of contraction and expansion which caused them to keep more or less in step with the central reserve country. The stability maintained within the area was not rigid. There were several changes of parities, among them by New Zealand and Denmark. They were made wholly on the initiative of the country concerned, as the result of unilateral decisions and without reference to Britain. The only intrusion of formality into the structure of the sterling area was the monetary resolution of the Ottawa conference of 1932 which, in effect, defined the general aims of monetary policy within the sterling area as being the stability of sterling prices. The system of Imperial preferences initiated at Ottawa was, moreover, a factor tending to bind the economic ties of the Empire countries more closely and, therefore, to strengthen the informal currency alliance which found expression in the sterling area. The 'success' of the sterling area in the 1930's is evident in the fact that it ensured exchange stability within a large area and that it did so without providing a physical basic standard such as gold.

". . . Came September 1939 and, with it, a considerable transformation of the sterling area. In the first place, its neutral adherents were frightened away from it by the sharp depreciation of sterling which occurred on the outbreak of the war. In any case, their continued membership would hardly have been compatible with the requirements of neutrality. In the second place, the sterling area became one of the corner stones of the system of sterling exchange control. Within this area, movement of funds, whether for current or capital purposes, remained free. The fence of exchange control was placed round the whole sterling area.

"Another change in the character of the sterling area brought about by the war was the Exchange Pool Agreement into which all members of the sterling area entered at the beginning of the war. By this agreement, the signatories undertook to do what, in fact, most of them had done voluntarily before the war: namely, to sell their foreign exchange income to Britain and thus maintain the whole of their exchange reserve in the form of sterling assets. In exchange for this undertaking, the member countries were guaranteed from the pool such hard currencies as they required to pay for absolutely essential imports from the countries in question. Since the wartime imports into these countries have been determined by the inter-Allied organizations controlling materials and shipping, this guarantee has not seriously invalidated the effective centralized control of the British Treasury over the foreign exchange income of the sterling area. The original pooling agreement has been modified in certain special cases, and notably in that of India, which in 1944 was granted special concessions allowing her to retain a part of her U. S. dollar income."

Writing after the Anglo-American agreement had been signed in Washington in December 1945, the editor of the London *Banker* made the following pertinent observations which bring the foregoing quotation up to date:[2]

"Nor need we spend much time over the complaint that the agreement means the end of the sterling area. What it means is the end of the dollar pool; *the sterling area will revert to its pre-war form*. It may be true that sterling will not be so attractive as a depository for reserves as before the war, as is argued by some critics. . . . But it is self-evident that sterling will be a much more attractive currency with the aid of nearly four billion dollars than without it. The truth is *that the sterling area would inevitably have disintegrated without the loan and has been saved by it.*"

2 "Towards an Expanding World Economy," *The Banker,* January 1946, p. 7.

Understood in that way, the Sterling Area is no more than a voluntary and informal arrangement. If general monetary stability reigns in the world, there arises no need for such arrangements, they merge in that general organization of monetary relations. When stability breaks down over the wide area of the world, the Sterling Area provides a way of saving it over its own more limited area. It is, for Great Britain, a "second line of defense" of monetary stability. Before the war the Sterling Area was solely a *monetary* arrangement; during the war it became also an insulated trading system; now it is to be liquidated in that second capacity, but not in the first.

CHAPTER XI

International Economic Organization

THE WORLD IS DIVIDED into numerous separate states, but world peace and world prosperity are indivisible. This simple statement contains the principal reason for building a political and an economic framework of agreements and institutions with the help of which it would be possible to initiate, co-ordinate, and integrate national policies which favor international harmony, and to attenuate or eliminate national policies which are destructive of such harmony. In a preceding chapter we have examined the principal reasons for the failure of the endeavors to build an integrated world economy after World War I. We shall now see what steps have been taken, are contemplated, or should be taken in order to establish in our days an international economic organization of our planet.

The general objectives were stated, a quarter of a century ago, in President Wilson's "Fourteen Points" and in the Covenant of the League of Nations.[1] At the present juncture, there are three major declarations of policy to be considered: the Atlantic Charter of August 14, 1941 incorporated in the United Nations Declaration of January 1, 1942, the Lend-Lease "Master Agreement," and the United Nations Charter.

The Atlantic Charter, in its point 4, pledges its signatories[2] to

". . . endeavor, with due respect for their existing obligations, to further the enjoyment by all States, great or small, victor or vanquished, of access, on equal terms, to the trade and to the raw materials of the world which are needed for their economic prosperity."

The Lend-Lease *Master Agreement*[3] provides in Article VII that in the final settlement of Lend-Lease claims,

". . . the terms and conditions thereof shall be such as not to burden commerce between the two countries, but to promote mutually advantageous economic relations between them and the betterment of

---

[1] See above, p. 147.

[2] Originally the United States and Great Britain, later all the signatories of the United Nations Declaration.

[3] The first of these was the Master Agreement between the United States and Great Britain, signed on March 11, 1941.

world-wide economic relations. To that end, they shall include provision for agreed action by the United States of America and the United Kingdom, open to participation by all other countries of like mind, directed to the expansion by appropriate international and domestic measures, of production, employment, and the exchange and consumption of goods, which are the material foundation of the liberty and welfare of all people; to the elimination of all forms of discriminatory treatment in international commerce, and to the reduction of tariffs and other trade barriers . . ."

The United Nations Charter devotes its Chapters IX and X to economic and social matters and provides for the creation within the framework of the United Nations of an Economic and Social Council. The general economic objectives of the United Nations expressed are in the following statements:

"*Article 55.* With a view to the creation of conditions of stability and well-being which are necessary for peaceful and friendly relations among nations based on respect for the principle of equal rights and self-determination of peoples, the United Nations shall promote:

"(a) higher standards of living, full employment, and conditions of economic and social progress and development;

"(b) solutions of international economic, social, health and related problems; . . .

"*Article 56.* All members pledge themselves to take joint and separate action in cooperation with the Organization for the achievement of the purposes set forth in Article 55."

It is the "Master Agreement" which provides the most explicit and far-reaching directions. The Washington agreements of December 6, 1945 include an acknowledgment of Article VII. Since the settlement arrived at involves a cancellation of wartime Lend-Lease, there will be no international financial payments connected with Lend-Lease; this article of the "Master Agreement" becomes therefore inoperative, at least in the relations between the United States and Great Britain. Nevertheless it has been agreed that "both governments will continue to discuss arrangements for agreed action for the attainment of the economic objectives referred to in Article VII of the mutual-aid [lend-lease] agreement. The governments expect, in these discussions, to reach specific conclusions at an early date with respect to urgent problems such as those in the field of communication and civil aviation." [4] Furthermore, as we have seen in the preceding chapter, an "Understanding on Commercial Policy" was reached at the same time. The previously mentioned United States Government's *Proposals for the Expansion of World Trade and Employment,* which were made public on the same day as the Anglo-American agreement, provide the basis for that "understanding." To quote from the Anglo-American "Joint Statement" on this subject: [5]

". . . the Government of the United Kingdom is in full agreement on all important points in these proposals and accepts them as a basis for international discussion; and it will, in common with the United States Government, use its best endeavors to bring such discussion to a successful conclusion, in the light of the views expressed by other countries. The two Governments have also agreed upon the procedures for the international negotiation and implementation of these proposals. To this end they have undertaken to begin preliminary negotiations at an early date between themselves and with other countries for the purpose of developing concrete arrangements to carry out these proposals, including definitive measures for the relaxation of trade controls. These negotiations will relate to tariffs and preferences, quantitative restrictions, subsidies, state trading, cartels, and other types of trade barriers treated in the document published by the United States and referred to above. . . ."

It is interesting to see that the principles included in the Lend-Lease Agreement have been made the starting point of a concrete action for the liberalization of world trade. The fact that Great Britain has become America's partner in that venture is an event of incalculable importance for the future of international economic relations.

By contrast to Article VII of the Lend-Lease Agreement, the provisions in Articles 55 and 56 of the United Nations Charter are very vague and noncommittal. They fall far short even of the emasculated Article 23 (e) of the Covenant of the League of Nations. In the absence of any precise undertakings or concrete commitments, the establishment of the Social and Economic Council as a part of the new world organization is a gesture comparable to that which a young married couple make when they decorate one room in their new home with a picture of

[4] *Anglo-American Financial and Commercial Agreements,* op. cit., p. 4.
[5] Ibid., p. 3.

Dumbo on one wall and of Minnie Mouse on the other and call it "The Nursery." They don't pledge themselves thereby to have a family; similarly the United Nations are in no wise pledged to the building of an integrated world economy. There is nothing in Article 55 that an economic nationalist could not subscribe to—nor is there anything that could prevent a country, by virtue of Article 56, from engaging in policies of "insulation" as part, e.g., of a nationalistic full-employment program. The future alone will show to what use the Social and Economic Council will be put.[6] If it is to be effective, it will have to look for inspiration and directives elsewhere than in Chapter IX of the United Nations Charter. This enhances the importance of the Washington agreements of December 1945.

In reading Chapters IX and X of the United Nations Charter, one cannot fail to be impressed by the relative importance their authors seemed to attach to institutional arrangements. There are many references to agencies, old and new, but nothing is said about policies. Now a policy that requires an institutional implementation will rarely fail to obtain it, and at this juncture in world affairs policies are more needed than anything else. One must hope that the organ will create its function, or rather, that the organ and the function, leading at present an independent existence, will eventually find each other.

The above comments are not so much a criticism of the Charter as they are a criticism of the frequently encountered tendency to overestimate the value of institutional arrangements. One doesn't solve a broadly phrased problem merely by setting up an institution to deal with it. The institution must have concrete objectives as well as the powers necessary for their attainment. In the case of the Bretton Woods Agreements, the International Monetary Fund as well as the International Bank have been provided with both. The Social and Economic Council has been given neither. Probably the more general the scope of an institution is, the more difficult it becomes to obtain an international agreement on its functions and powers. It must be remembered that we live in a highly nationalistic world. Even such "surrenders of sovereignty" as are involved in the membership of

[6] Cf. National Planning Association, *International Economic Collaboration* (*Role of the Economic and Social Council of the United Nations Organization*) (Washington, D. C., 1946).

international institutions and organizations can be nullified by the act of withdrawing from the institution or organization. We have as yet no international organization from which withdrawal is impossible. When the day comes that such organizations will be established, a new era will dawn upon the world and both peace and prosperity will become more secure than they have ever been. But that day is not here yet.

2.

The other international economic organizations are "functional" in scope, that is to say they are established to deal with one particular set of problems. The *International Monetary Fund,* which was discussed in Chapter III, is entrusted with the task of promoting international monetary stability and of bringing about in an orderly manner such changes in parities as may become necessary in the course of the changing circumstances of national and international economic life. Taking the "internationalist" view of the world economy, we find that the Bretton Woods Agreements leave one major task undone, namely the establishment of a complete freedom of international payments. In an unsettled and nationalistic world more could not be accomplished; but it is well to keep in mind the fact that a compromise was made on a very vital issue. It will be essential that the United States, the country most interested in the freedom of international payments, should urge, in due time, the abolition of controls over movements of capital. Clearly, these controls are not likely to be given up as long as there is enough insecurity in an unsettled world to make "capital flights" a likely occurrence. But as the world settles down to an enduring peace, the case for the removal of *all* controls on international payments will grow stronger and ought to be pressed. Otherwise, it may happen that even the limited freedom of payments provided in the agreement on the Fund will become precarious. The Fund as it now stands affords a very auspicious starting point; it is up to the United States and other countries interested in free international payments (and in multilateral trade) to see to it that from now on evolution should move in the desired direction.

The revival of international flows of investment funds is being fostered by the establishment of the *International Bank for*

Reconstruction and Development. That institution is designed to provide capital for reconstruction and development purposes to borrowers who "in the prevailing market conditions . . . would be unable otherwise to obtain the loan under conditions which in the opinion of the Bank are reasonable for the borrower." [7] It is stipulated, furthermore, that the loans made or guaranteed by the Bank will be arranged "in relation to international loans through other channels so that the more useful and urgent projects, large and small alike, will be dealt with first." [8] Thus the Bank appears as an institution intended for the purpose of supplementing the flow of capital resulting from private and from inter-governmental transactions. We have dealt in Chapter II with the organization and the scope of the Bank; here we shall situate it within the framework of other international institutions. In that context the Bank represents a recognition not only of the great need for reconstruction of the war-devastated areas of the world, but also—and this is important—of the great urge felt in economically "backward" regions of the globe to develop the existing natural resources and to increase standards of living of the people. The growth of world trade, of the international division of labor, and of living standards everywhere will obtain a great impetus from a large-scale movement towards the industrialization of undeveloped and under-developed areas such as India, China, Russia, eastern Europe, parts of Africa, and Latin America. The view that industrialization leads to a decline of international trade because it enables people to make for themselves goods that they would otherwise buy rests upon a misapprehension. In modern times trade between industrially developed countries has become one of the major elements in world trade. Industrialization leads, of course, to changes in the structure of foreign trade and it is essential, if large foreign investments are to be undertaken, that these changes should be allowed to take place. Hence, policies promoting the structural flexibility of national economies, as well as the adaptability of international trade to changing circumstances, are a necessary adjunct of developmental programs. [9]

[7] "Articles of Agreement," op. cit., Article III, Section 3 (ii).
[8] Ibid., Article I (iv).
[9] Cf. *Industrialization and Foreign Trade,* a study issued by the Economic, Financial and Transit Department of the League of Nations (written mainly by F. Hilgerdt), League of Nations Publications, II. Economic and Financial, 1945. II. A.10. See also:

International private investment is likely to be assisted by the establishment of the International Bank in three ways: (1) a large part of the loans guaranteed by the Bank will be issued in the private capital market; (2) the development of "backward" areas will broaden the investment opportunities for investors; (3) the Bank will establish certain standards, by means of which private investors may be guided in their judgments. Thus we may avoid the repetition of the unhappy experiences of the twenties and the misdirection of funds into unproductive channels. In addition to the services that will be rendered by the Bank, other international arrangements and agreements will be necessary. Reference has already been made in Chapter II to the need of a *code of fair play* in the field of international finance. The investor wants to be protected against discrimination and expropriation, while the borrowing country wants its long-range interests protected against "colonial" exploitation. A conference should be called at an early moment to deal with this matter. The conference might appoint a special committee to prepare a project of a code, which, once accepted by the various governments, would become a part of the international economic organization of the world. The enforcement of such a code might be entrusted either to a special tribunal or to the projected International Trade Organization.

The Bretton Woods Conference was entirely aware that monetary and financial arrangements are only two parts of a more comprehensive set of arrangements and that they cannot stand up by themselves if the other matters fail to be dealt with. Hence, in its *Resolution VII,* the conference recommended to the participating governments:

" . . . to reach agreement as soon as possible on ways and means whereby they may best

"(1) reduce obstacles to international trade and in other ways promote mutually advantageous international commercial relations;

"(2) bring about the orderly marketing of staple commodities at prices fair to the producer and consumer alike;

"(3) deal with the special problems of international concern which will arise from the cessation of production for war purposes; and

---

A. J. Brown: *Industrialization and Trade,* The Royal Institute of International Affairs (London, 1943); and Eugene Staley: *World Economic Development,* op. cit.

"(4) facilitate by cooperative effort the harmonization of national policies of Member States designed to promote and maintain high levels of employment and progressively rising standards of living."

Of these recommendations, the first converges with the course of action originating with the Lend-Lease Agreement and leading, as we have seen, to the International Trade Conference contemplated in the Washington Agreements of December 1945. The second will be presently discussed, while the fourth relates to the subject matter of Chapter XII. The third recommendation deals with problems of "liquidation of the war" and need not concern us here.

3.

The question of "orderly marketing of staple commodities" has received much attention ever since the developments of the late twenties and early thirties to which reference was made in Chapter IX. Raw materials and agricultural staples are subject to considerable fluctuations in price in response to changes in the economic conditions of industrial countries. Agriculture, in addition, suffers from climatic uncertainties. In both groups it is difficult to bring about a quick readjustment of supply to demand in the case of major shifts in demand. World War I brought in its wake a large overproduction of many of these products; World War II will most likely have a similar result. The decline of production in war-torn areas led to an expansion of output in other areas, while the need to keep considerable stock piles for military purposes added to total demand and thus encouraged a further expansion of output. When the postwar rehabilitation is completed, production in the devastated areas will be resumed and another overproduction is likely to make itself felt. Now the downward adjustment of output is particularly difficult in agriculture for institutional reasons; after World War I it was never fully carried out until the depression came. Instead, various "stabilization schemes" were tried for wheat, rubber, tin, coffee, etc., through the operation of international cartels and other arrangements. In view of the anticipated difficulties of the next few years, and in order to avoid the repetition of the difficulties of the interwar years with respect to these "primary" commodities, various projects have been formulated during the war and several new "commodity agreements" have been reached.[10]

Actually the problem has two phases: there is the price instability to contend with, which is the result of wartime developments; and there is the particularly heavy impact of business-
cycle fluctuations upon prices of mineral raw materials and staple
agricultural products. The latter cause of instability must be
eventually attacked at its source, i.e., through a world-wide approach to the problem of economic instability; while the former
evidently calls for special measures. These fall into three main
categories: (1) international controls of production; (2) the
holding by governments of "buffer stocks" accumulated in times
of surplus production and sold in times of surplus demand; (3)
planned expansion of consumption.[11]

Of these three courses of action, the first and the second have
very much in common with cartel arrangements and are subject
to the same criticisms. Clearly some international policy is necessary as the pressure for both private and public arrangements of
this kind is likely to be considerable in the years following the
end of "rehabilitation." [12] In designing such policies on an international scale, it will be necessary for the participating governments to keep in mind the following principles: the programs
adopted should be temporary, i.e., should be adopted to deal
with the particular crisis resulting from the war; interests of consumers should be safeguarded; and the adoption of the necessary
measures should not be allowed to be used as an opening wedge
by the many industries aspiring to cartel arrangements.[13] As a

---

[10] Cf. International Labor Office, *Intergovernmental Commodity Control Agreements*
(Montreal, 1943); Erwin Hexner: *International Cartels,* op. cit.

[11] Cf. J. B. Condliffe and A. Stevenson: *The Common Interest in International Economic Organisation* (Montreal, International Labour Office, 1944); and Alvin H.
Hansen: *America's Role in the World Economy,* op. cit. Both books are concerned with
the subject matter of this entire chapter.

[12] As Professor Condliffe and Mr. A. Stevenson point out: "The distinction between
private and government control is perhaps not quite as crucial as might appear since
the government bodies regulating the various commodity markets have in fact been
dominated by producers' organisations or have acted largely in the interests of the
producers." Op. cit., p. 60.

[13] Cf. Corwin D. Edwards: "The Possibilities of an International Policy Towards
Cartels," essay appearing in the symposium *A Cartel Policy for the United Nations*
(New York, 1945), pp. 114–15. See also *Wheat Under International Agreement* by
Joseph S. Davis, Director of the Food Research Institute of Stanford University (Amer-
ican Enterprise Association, New York, 1945), for a brief and incisive criticism of
the performance of the Wheat Agreement. A point of view *favorable* to international
cartels will be found in *International Cartels in the Postwar World* by Professor J.
Anton de Haas (American Enterprise Association, New York, 1944).

long-run policy commodity agreements and "buffer stocks" are undoubtedly just as undesirable as private cartels. They interfere with the operations of the market economy and are likely to increase structural maladjustment instead of curing them.

The third group of measures, referred to above, is the most promising and coincides with the objectives of yet another international agency, the *Food and Agriculture Organization* (F. A. O.). This organization is the outgrowth of the Hot Springs Conference of May 1944. Its constitution was ratified by the requisite twenty governments in April 1945, and the United States joined it on July 31, 1945. The objectives of the F. A. O., as set forth in the Preamble to its Constitution, are: (1) to raise levels of nutrition and standards of living; (2) to secure improvements in the efficiency of the production and distribution of all food and agricultural products; (3) to better the condition of rural population; and (4) to contribute by these means toward an expanding world economy. The functions of the F. A. O. are described in the following terms in Article I of the Constitution:

"(1) The Organization shall collect, analyze, interpret, and disseminate information relating to nutrition, food and agriculture.

"(2) The Organization shall promote and, where appropriate, shall recommend national and international action with respect to

"(a) scientific, technological, social, and economic research relating to nutrition, food and agriculture;

"(b) the improvement of education and administration relating to nutrition, food and agriculture, and the spread of public knowledge of nutritional and agricultural science and practice;

"(c) the conservation of natural resources and the adoption of improved methods of agricultural production;

"(d) the improvement of the processing, marketing, and distribution of food and agricultural products;

"(e) the adoption of policies for the provision of adequate agricultural credit, national and international;

"(f) the adoption of international policies with respect to agricultural commodity arrangements.

"(3) It shall also be the function of the Organization

"(a) to furnish such technical assistance as governments may request;

"(b) to organize, in cooperation with the governments concerned, such missions as may be needed to assist them to fulfill the obligations arising from their acceptance of the recommendations of the United Nations Conference on Food and Agriculture; and

"(c) generally to take all necessary and appropriate action to implement the purposes of the Organization as set forth in the Preamble."

The F. A. O. is an advisory organization, not an administrative agency. It can, nevertheless, do much good through its researches, reports, and recommendations. In its operations it may frequently find itself associated with the work of the *International Labor Organization* (I. L. O.). The latter came through the war with a fine record of studies and will occupy an important position in the new international setup, watching over social conditions throughout the world and promoting agreements and policies intended to raise living and labor standards. From the viewpoint of world trade, the I. L. O. may render great services in checking on the extent to which industrial progress (in terms of increasing productivity) is translated in various countries into rising living standards of the populaton; in that way it may help to forestall the undesirable competition of cheap labor working with efficient means of production.[14] Eventually the International Labor Organization, which has been founded as a part of the League of Nations, will presumably become a part of the United Nations, although certain political difficulties must first be overcome.

4.

The interwar experiences with unbridled economic nationalism resulted in widespread demands for some international agreement concerning national commercial policies and for an agency put in charge of the administration of such an agreement. Professor Viner, for example, in his study of *Trade Relations between Free-market and Controlled Economies* (1943) declares himself in favor of an international trade conference for the purpose of obtaining a multilateral agreement to eliminate direct trade controls "on a mutually-agreed time schedule" and to establish rules of conduct and procedure in the realm of international trade. Viner makes provisions for relations with countries that would stay out of such an agreement and suggests that the "participating countries" should "formulate the procedures to be followed *in common* in trade relations with non-participating countries adhering to direct controls." [15] Finally, he suggests the establishment of a permanent international agency to supervise

14 See above, p. 80.
15 Op. cit., p. 88 (italics added).

the administration and application of the agreement and to handle questions of revision, admission of new members, etc. Penalties, through withdrawal of the benefits of the most-favored nation treatment, would be applied against countries which would be found by the international agency to have violated the agreement. Viner also suggests that non-signatory countries should not receive the most-favored-nation treatment from signatory countries. Thus membership in the proposed organization would carry distinct advantages.

We shall revert later to the question whether the contemplated international agreement should be so formulated as to be susceptible to general acceptance in a world in which free-enterprise trade co-exists with state monopolies, or whether, as Viner implicitly suggests, it should be an agreement among free-market countries alone. First however, let us examine in more detail the idea of setting up a special international trade agency. Proposals of that kind have been advanced by several prominent writers; the most careful studies on the subject came from the pen of Dr. Percy W. Bidwell, of the Council on Foreign Relations, who in a series of articles and monographs published over the past few years [16] urged the establishment of a United Nations Trade Commission, "an official body composed of appointees of member states." The Commission would collect information, organize periodic trade conferences, and in every way possible help "to make multilateral trade agreements workable and effective." It would come, eventually, under the Economic and Social Council of the United Nations.[17]

Unlike Professor Viner, Dr. Bidwell envisages a general organization which "should . . . include all the great trading nations," including apparently both free-enterprise and state-trading countries. These two points of view express the most serious dilemma encountered today when contemplating an international economic organization. Either countries believing in the principles of the free-market economy and of non-discriminatory multilateral trade will get together in an endeavor to cre-

[16] Percy W. Bidwell: "Controlling Trade after the War," *Foreign Affairs,* January 1943; "A Postwar Commercial Policy for the United States," *American Economic Review,* Supplement, Vol. XXXIV, No. 1, March 1944; *A Commercial Policy for the United Nations* (New York: Committee on International Economic Policy in cooperation with the Carnegie Endowment for International Peace; 1945).

[17] *A Commercial Policy for the United Nations,* op. cit., pp. 53 and 55.

ate as wide a trading area as possible governed by these principles, or they will try to reach an agreement with all countries, including those whose governments practice direct quantitative controls over foreign trade and foreign payments or have state monopolies of foreign trade.

The first course involves the creation of a trading area governed by principles of free-enterprise trade and of a market economy. Membership in that area must confer advantages that are withheld from non-members, thus attaching a positive premium to membership. By the very nature of things, it is in the interest of every free-enterprise economy to be a part of as wide a free-market area as possible; only thus can they reap the full advantages of the international division of labor and of multilateral trade. It follows that this trading system must be open to all countries that are willing to accept its operating principles and the international "discipline" involved in its rules. Some of the now "undecided" countries might eventually join the free-market group on account of the advantages conferred by membership; but other countries, definitely committed to state-controlled or state-operated foreign trade, will remain outside of that system. With these countries special agreements could be concluded by the free-market group acting as a whole.

The second course attempts to find a common ground among all countries in order to secure a universal membership for a world trade organization. In order to accomplish this, it is necessary to develop a formula that would be broad enough to be acceptable to both the free-market and the state-controlled economies (as well as to state monopolies of foreign trade). This entails the danger of keeping direct controls in existence indefinitely, and even of allowing them to spread to formerly free economies. The principles on which universal agreement might be obtained today, in the field of commercial policy, are not such as to make the prospects of achieving an integrated world economy seem at all bright. Instead, the perpetuation of quantitative controls is likely to lead to a progressive disintegration of the economic life of the planet.

The first course of action presents great advantages, even though it seems to underscore the division of the world into separate trading systems. Widely divergent conceptions of economic and social life and of economic policy are one of the disturbing but very real features of our times. It is better to recognize these existing divergencies and build a world organization on that basis, rather than to cover them up with broad formulae and, in the process, risk destroying the free-market systems altogether. Agreements could undoubtedly be reached between the free-market group *as a whole,* and those countries which wish to stay out; indeed, it is only if they take a clear stand as a group, that free economies can hope to maintain themselves in the contemporary world.

Events are moving, however, in the opposite direction, towards *one* trade agency of the United Nations and *one* agreement that all countries, regardless of their economic system, might sign. That tendency will certainly serve the principle of "unity"; but it will be unity at a cost—and the cost may be a gradual and progressive deterioration of free-market systems. And since the political and social implications of such a drift would be very serious indeed, in terms of human values and human opportunities, the matter is worthy of deep thought and of very careful attention. Hence the foregoing comments. It has been suggested in the preceding chapter that the future relationship between free-market and state-controlled economies is the greatest international economic issue of our time; a thorough study of the U. S. Government's *Proposals* [18] fails to reveal an adequate acknowledgment of its complexity and difficulty.

5.

Proposals for the Expansion of World Trade and Employment is the basic official American document on commercial policy, which has now received the approval of the British Government and Parliament as well and will be the basis of the forthcoming World Trade Conference. These *Proposals* are the outgrowth of the several statements of policy formulated during the war and quoted earlier in this chapter, and have benefitted from the many studies and discussions by independent students of international economic relations, to which reference has equally been made. Their spirit can be summed up in one sentence of the official "Analysis" which forms the introductory part of the U. S.

[18] *Proposals for the Expansion of World Trade and Employment,* Department of State, Publication 2411, Washington, D. C., November 1945.

Government's document:[19] ". . . the Proposals try to state fair principles acceptable to all and of benefit to all." There is no doubt that we should have had before us a different document had the U. S. Government tried to formulate "principles acceptable to free-market economies." It would also have probably been a different document had it not been drafted so as to secure the above-mentioned adherence by the British government. In its present form, the *Proposals* are essentially a compromise statement.

The *Proposals* link together problems of international trade and those of employment; in doing so, they follow a prevalent pattern which has been the object of some critical comments in earlier chapters of this study. If instead of "employment" the notion used had been that of "volume of economic activity" (including employment but also including production and productive efficiency and standards of living), the picture obtained by such a juxtaposition would have been more instructive. Actually, the *Proposals* deal principally with trade and only in a subsidiary way with employment, while the great problem of how to attack internationally the phenomenon of economic instability is left almost unanswered. It will be argued in the next chapter that another conference and another agency are necessary to do justice to it.

Once this is said, one must warmly applaud the following declaration that appears in section B of the document, entitled *Proposals Concerning Employment:* "Domestic programs to expand employment should be consistent with realization of the purposes of liberal international agreements and compatible with the economic well-being of other nations." This seems to rule out the "beggar-my-neighbor" policies which have done so much harm in the 'thirties. Furthermore, acccording to this statement:

"There should be an undertaking that:

"(1) Each of the signatory nations will take action designed to achieve and maintain full employment within its own jurisdiction, through measures appropriate to its political and economic institutions.

"(2) No nation will seek to maintain employment through measures which are likely to create unemployment in other countries or which are incompatible with international undertakings designed to

19 Ibid., p. 3.

promote an expanding volume of international trade and investment in accordance with comparative efficiencies of production. . . ."

Of these two principles the second is very sound; the second part of the sentence might have been clearer if it were couched in slightly different language, to wit: "international undertakings designed to stimulate the growth of international trade and investment and to promote the international division of labor." The danger of unclear phraseology in texts like this lies in the escape avenues which divergent interpretations provide to those who wish to break the spirit of the agreement while keeping its (ambiguous) letter. And speaking of ambiguity, it is rather unfortunate that this most unclear term, "full employment" should be used here without a trace of a definition.

More important is the fact that point 1 of the quoted statement considerably weakens point 2. Measures furthering full employment and appropriate to the political and economic institutions of a state-socialistic country are likely, by their very nature, to restrict international trade and are almost certain to interfere with the international division of labor based on comparative advantage. An agreement reached among free-market countries alone might have emphasized much more forcefully the destructive effects of centralized planning for full employment upon international economic relations, and might have stressed, in consequence, the need of internationally planned measures for the elimination of wide fluctuations in economic activity. Point 1, as it stands, and especially its second part, is a monument to the desire to please and conciliate everybody;[20] it is, to be sure, qualified by point 2, but at the same time reduces the latter's effectiveness. In a nationalistic world there is no need to tell nations that they may do as they please; what is needed is a limitation of their freedom of action—as is very properly provided in point 2.

We now reach the main part of the *Proposals,* dealing with the proposed International Trade Organization. The need for that organization is explained in the following terms:[21]

"(1) Measures designed to effect an expansion of trade are essential because of their direct contribution to maximum levels of employ-

---

[20] When will statesmen learn the wisdom of the French proverb: *"L'on ne peut pas satisfaire tout le monde—et sa belle-mère"?*
[21] *Ibid.,* p. 10.

ment, production and consumption. Since such expansion can only be attained by collective measures, in continuous operation and adaptable to economic changes, it is necessary to establish permanent machinery for international collaboration in matters affecting international commerce, with a view to continuous consultation, the provision of expert advice, the formulation of agreed policies, procedures and plans, and to the development of agreed rules of conduct in regard to matters affecting international trade.

"(2) It is accordingly proposed that there be created an International Trade Organization of the United Nations, the members of which would undertake to conduct their international commercial policies and relations in accordance with agreed principles to be set forth in the articles of the Organization. These principles, in order to make possible an effective expansion of world production, employment, exchange, and consumption, should:

"(a) Provide an equitable basis for dealing with the problems of governmental measures affecting international trade;

"(b) Provide for the curbing of restrictive trade practices resulting from private international business arrangements; and

"(c) Govern the institution and operations of intergovernmental commodity arrangements."

It will be the purpose of the Organization [22] to promote international commercial co-operation through the establishment of appropriate machinery for consultation and collaboration, to further the growth of opportunities for trade and economic development, to "facilitate access by all members, on equal terms, to the trade and raw materials of the world which are needed for their economic prosperity," and, finally, to promote "national and international action for the expansion of the production and consumption of goods, for the reduction of trade barriers, and for the elimination of all forms of discriminatory treatment in international commerce."

The provision concerning "access . . . to the trade and to the raw materials of the world" is evidently borrowed from the Atlantic Charter. Its scope is limited (and very properly so) to members of the Organization, but nothing is said about trade with non-members, a confusing omission. The formulation adopted perpetuates the memories of the "raw materials problem" of the thirties, which we have discussed in another context. Actually there is no need whatever to segregate trade in raw materials

[22] Ibid., Chapter I.

from all the other trade of the world and to single it out for special attention. Raw materials are as necessary to advanced industrial countries as manufactured goods are to underdeveloped countries; in practice, the latter suffered more from an inadequate "access to manufactured goods" than the former did from an inadequate "access to raw materials." Isn't it time we laid, once and for all, the ghost of the "raw materials problem"?

With respect to the last-named purpose of the Organization, it should be noted that "the elimination of all forms of discriminatory treatment in international commerce" would require the adoption of a very strong course of action with respect to quantitative trade controls which are, by their very essence, discriminatory. But to do this might mean antagonizing some prospective members of the Organization.

Chapter III of the *Proposals* deals with "General Commercial Policy" in a manner that calls for little special comment. Tariffs are to be substantially lowered, equality of treatment is to be furthered, the "invisible tariffs" [23] are to be, as far as possible, eliminated. Quantitative controls (quotas, embargoes, etc.) are to be eliminated, but this general rule is subject to several most important exceptions. (See Section C.1.) Among these there is one which calls for special attention; it reads as follows:

"Section C.2. *Restrictions to safeguard the balance of payments.* Members confronted with an adverse balance of payments should be entitled to impose quantitative import restrictions as an aid to the restoration of equilibrium in the balance of payments. This provision should be operative under conditions and procedures to be agreed upon."

Now this is a very dangerous principle, especially since the application of the *Proposals* is not limited to the immediate postwar transitional period. The "protection of the balance of payments" is the favorite argument supporting quantitative controls that is used by governments that are not ideologically committed to state control over foreign trade. Balances of payments are never in perfect equilibrium; what is needed is a "mechanism" with which to restore disrupted equilibrium. Once govern-

[23] The term has presumably been introduced by Dr. Percy W. Bidwell who wrote a book under that title. "Invisible tariffs" are ways of using administrative devices, customs laws and formalities, etc., in such a way as to obstruct the entrance of foreign goods into the country.

ments start to adjust imports to exports *directly,* and not through the market mechanism, the system of free-enterprise foreign trade is gravely compromised. There is no other passage in the *Proposals* whose presence in that document is as surprising and distressing as that of the passage just quoted. It strikes one as standing in complete contradiction to the often proclaimed principles of American foreign economic policy. Under an apparently innocuous technical appearance it represents, in a system of free-enterprise, non-discriminatory multilateral trade, a real "Trojan horse" of bilateralism and state-controlled trade. The fact that there is provision for "international consultations regarding balance-of-payments restrictions," attenuates the danger but does not eliminate it.

We shall pass over the question of subsidies, Section D of Chapter III. Section E, on State Trading, has already been discussed in the preceding chapter.[24] As regards exchange control, the present *Proposals* reaffirm the principles agreed upon at Bretton Woods.

The *Proposals* take a strong stand against private cartels[25] in Chapter IV on "Restrictive Business Practices." By contrast, commodity agreements which, as we have seen before, are a form of governmental cartels, meet, in Chapter V, with a far more kindly reception. The general attitudes adopted with respect to private cartels and with respect to governmental commodity agreements are difficult to reconcile—and this in spite of the repeated emphasis on the principle of economic expansion in discussing the latter kind of agreements. The language of Chapter V is far from lucid and the general effect of that part of the *Proposals* may be the sanctioning of a far-flung network of intergovernmental arrangements restricting the effectiveness of the market system. Temporary arrangements, for the "liquidation-of-the-war" period, are certainly necessary. But agreements that "should not remain initially in effect for more than five years," though they can apparently be extended beyond that time limit through renewal (Chapter V, point 6), can hardly be regarded as short-term emergency measures. If we assume that the economic policy of the United States favors the maintenance of the market sys-

---

[24] See above, pp. 162–3.
[25] Curiously, the word "cartel" is not used in the text of this chapter, although it appears in the "Analysis" which precedes the "formal" text of the *Proposals.*

tem as the basis of our economic organization, then the chapter under discussion represents a considerable lack of consistency.

The International Trade Organization towards the establishment of which the foregoing proposals are directed, will have the following functions: (1) to collect, analyze, and publish information regarding the operation of the provisions included in the *Proposals;* (2) to provide technical assistance to members; (3) to make recommendations to members regarding the provisions of the *Proposals;* (4) to interpret these provisions, to consult with members regarding disputes growing out of these provisions, and to provide a mechanism for the settlement of such disputes; (5) in accordance with rules to be established, to waive, in exceptional circumstances, particular obligations of members; (6) to make recommendations for international agreements "designed to improve the basis of trade and to assure just and equitable treatment for the enterprises, skills and capital brought from one country to another . . ."

These are very important functions, and it is to be hoped that the projected organization will be established at the earliest possible moment.

Looking at the U. S. Government's *Proposals* of November 1945 as a whole, one might suggest that they suffer from the determination of their authors to produce a statement that could be "acceptable to all." The alternative approach would have involved an outspoken and fearless statement of America's *own* principles—principles of free markets and free enterprise, of complete nondiscrimination, of multilateral trade, and free international payments. Very likely these principles would have had to be qualified to reach an agreement with other countries, even with Great Britain. But had the U. S. Government first issued a statement of America's own principles of commercial policy, notice would have been served upon the world as to the influence which this country proposes to exercise in that matter in the years to come.

The critique that precedes is addressed to the *Proposals* as a statement of United States policy; our attitude to them, viewed as an Anglo-American compromise, should be substantially more mellow. After all, the most important practical problem of the day is to find an initial common ground of action.

We have now committed ourselves to the quest for a *universal* organization. It must be hoped that the agreements reached by the World Conference on Trade and Employment will produce an environment in which free-market economies can safely live. Once the new International Trade Organization is established, we shall be able to explore the ways and means by which the various international agencies, each of which has today an autonomous existence and a separate membership, can be coordinated into one over-all system.

CHAPTER XII

International Quest for Economic Stability

THE SUBJECT MATTER of this brief chapter is, in reality, a part of that of Chapter XI. It has been segregated on account of the exceptionally great importance of the problem as well as on account of the insufficient attention that it generally receives, especially in official circles. Even the literature of the subject is strangely meager if one compares it to that of other problems of economic policy. The problem of seeking economic stability by international means is, in short, the Cinderella of economic policy —virtually a Princess among problems, awaiting the arrival of a Prince among statesmen who might translate its possibilities into reality.

There are two main reasons for the relative neglect of an international approach to the problem of attenuating business cycles. One is the problem's great complexity which almost evades careful analytical investigation. The other—and the more important—reason is the prevalence of economic nationalism. We have seen in Chapter V how economic nationalism results in conditions that make it plausible to regard business cycles as a national phenomenon; and how a nationalistic approach to business-cycle policy leads, by way of "insulation" tactics, to an aggravation of economic nationalism. So long as this attitude prevails, "full employment" policies, or "anti-depression" policies are conducted on a national basis. Occasionally—of late quite frequently—the demand is voiced that all countries should adopt "full employment" policies. Statements to that effect are included, as we have seen, in the United Nations Charter and in the U. S. Government's recent *Proposals*.

The Australian delegations at several of the wartime international conferences urged the adoption of an international agreement obligating the several governments to maintain national full employment in their respective countries. And Professor Hansen, in his recent book, declares that: "An international commitment by all countries to maintain high levels of domestic employment would contribute greatly to the success and workability of all other international economic arrangements."[1] Elsewhere, he denounces "beggar-my-neighbor" policies,[2] thus acknowledging the fact that national policies aiming at higher levels of production and employment *may* be prejudicial to other countries. It is well recognized today that the pushing of exports by means of subsidies, etc., during a general depression merely shifts difficulties from one country to another, but fails to reach the roots of the trouble. Much less widely recognized is the fact that policies of economic "insulation"[3] are also likely to have detrimental international repercussions by interfering with the flow of goods and with the division of labor, thus facilitating the growth of maladjustments in the structure of world production and trade.

We have seen, on the other hand, that the future of economic internationalism depends upon how successfully the question of fluctuations in economic activity will be dealt with. Monetary stability, i.e., the maintenance of stable parities between national currencies depends upon the "synchronization" of business-cycle developments in the respective countries. The maintenance of economic stability in the large and highly developed countries is, furthermore, of the greatest importance for the preservation of a high volume of international trade and of a regular flow of investment funds. When there is a depression in the United States or in Great Britain, this means a loss of markets for countries producing raw materials and for numberless producers of all kinds of goods in almost every country of the world. Yet it is not enough for the large economic units to seek their economic stability and "full employment" by national means alone. Their endeavors have to be co-ordinated and synchronized if international order is to be preserved. A recent very illuminating report on *Economic Stability in the Post-war World*, prepared by the League of Nations' "Delegation on Economic Depressions,"[4] strongly emphasizes the international character of the problem. The "Delegation on Economic Depressions" was appointed by the Economic and Financial Organization of the League in the fall of 1937 to prepare a report on measures that might be employed "preventing or mitigating economic depres-

[1] Alvin H. Hansen: *America's Role in the World Economy*, op. cit., p. 182.
[2] Ibid, pp. 137 ff.
[3] See Chapter V, above.
[4] League of Nations Publications, II. Economic and Financial, 1945. II. A.2.

sions." The first part of the Delegation's report (the work on which was delayed by the outbreak of the war) was published in 1943 under the title "The Transition from War to Peace Economy";[5] the second part of the Report (quoted above) followed two years later and includes a series of most important opinions and recommendations.

Among the Delegation's comments on the general scope of the problem, we find the following wise observations:[6]

"What is required is not only a high level of employment, but efficient employment. Policy must be concerned not only with the size of the national income, but also with its distribution, must aim not only at reducing the risk of unemployment, but also at an equitable sharing of its burden. It must be designed to promote the welfare not of some nations only, but of all, and to assure the smooth working of the economic system without impairing essential human liberties."

The Delegation, of its own admission, has devoted the major part of its report to national measures, "because we have thought it desirable to be as explicit as possible regarding the nature of the policies open to individual governments. . . ."[7] This is very appropriate, of course, since, under existing institutional arrangements, national policies are always adopted to meet a national problem, even if the problem is merely a national manifestation of an international phenomenon. The report recommends international action along the following lines:[8]

"(a) the adoption of more liberal and dynamic commercial and economic policies;

"(b) the creation of an international monetary mechanism;

"(c) the creation of an international institution which will stimulate and encourage the international movement of capital for productive purposes and which will, so far as possible, impart a contra-cyclical character to this movement;

"(d) the creation of a buffer stock agency;

"(e) the international coordination of national policies for the maintenance of a high and stable level of employment."

These are excellent recommendations, except, perhaps, point (d) concerning the creation of a buffer stock agency about which

[5] League of Nations Publications, II. Economic and Financial, 1943. II. A.3.
[6] *Economic Stability in the Post-war World*, op. cit., p. 22.
[7] Ibid., p. 315 ("Summary and Conclusions," para. 100).
[8] Ibid., pp. 315-16 ("Summary and Conclusions," paragraphs 100-3).

some doubts may be expressed.[9] Points (a), (b), (c) and (e) are all well taken. The first of them will presumably be taken care of by the World Trade Conference and the actions based upon its decisions; the second and third find their answer in the institutions established by virtue of the Bretton Woods Agreements. It is the fifth and last point which takes us into the very heart of the "Cinderella problem" stated at the beginning of the present chapter.

International co-ordination of national policies for the maintenance of a high and stable level of employment: how is it to be accomplished? Can it be accomplished? Is it sufficient?

The third of these questions is answered in the negative—and rightly so—by the mere fact that this particular recommendation is only one of five points. More specifically, recommendation (c) supplements it very importantly.[10] In addition, the question can arise whether and how national economic policies *can* be co-ordinated. This is a baffling problem to which there is no ready answer at the present time. As Professor Viner rightly pointed out at the 1946 session of the Harris Foundation at the University of Chicago,[11] an effective co-ordination of national economic policies aimed at the achievement of economic stability and of high employment is made very difficult, perhaps even impossible, by the requirements of national autonomy and the difficulty of co-ordinating and synchronizing the legislative processes of the various countries. He proposed therefore the establishment of a great international investment fund, in charge of an international agency. Such a set-up "could do a great deal to synchronize . . . the rate of investment in different areas without having to approach all the legislatures of the world and to try to synchronize their legislative processes," which, in Viner's opinion would be "absolutely impracticable." The new international financial institution would supplement the Bank for Reconstructon and Development. Its primary concern would not be

---

[9] Such a program *might* lead to the perpetuation of maladjustments by subsidizing chronic surpluses of certain goods. The Delegation is aware, by the way, of the pitfalls of this particular proposal. See Chapter XIX of its 1945 Report (especially pp. 265–71).

[10] See, in that connection, Lewis L. Lorwin: *International Economic Development: Public Works and other Problems,* National Resources Planning Board, Technical Paper Number 7, U. S. Government Printing Office, Washington, D. C., 1942.

[11] Cf. *Proceedings of the Twenty-first Institute under the auspices of Norman Wait Harris Foundation: the United Nations and the Organization of Peace and Security* (Chicago, 1945) (privately circulated).

with development but with stabilization; it would use its funds to operate "counter to the business cycle, lending heavily . . . at times of incipient depression and cutting off lending at times of inflationary or unduly expansionist tendencies."

The above gives only the barest outline of the idea. May it be suggested that an expert committee should be appointed at the earliest date by the U. S. Treasury, or, jointly, by the Treasuries of the United States, Great Britain, and Canada to prepare a detailed project along these general lines? The time to do it is evidently now. The projected institution is an indispensable, basic element in the new world economic organization. And, as the League's report rightly points out, in its final paragraph: [12]

"Nothing could be more dangerous nor more untrue than to assume that the maintenance of the fullest possible measure of employment can be left to each government acting in isolated independence. All will be affected by the success or failure of all others; all must cooperate in their attempts to attain the end on which we believe all agree. Even granted such cooperation, success will not be achieved lightly or rapidly."

[12] Op. cit., p. 319.

BOOK FOUR

*The United States and the World
Economy*

CHAPTER XIII

America's Rise to Economic Pre-eminence

THE HISTORY of America's growth from a semicolonial country to the world's leading economic power is one of the great epics of all times. The story is too long to be presented in the present book, but the reader will find a large literature devoted to that important and fascinating subject.[1]

In order to obtain a broad view, at least, of the principal phases of the evolution of America's international economic position, the best method is to look at the evolution of the structure of the country's balance of payments. This evolution has been the object of a pioneering study by Bullock, Williams, and Tucker, published in 1919,[2] from which the following table is derived. It divides America's balance-of-payments history from 1789 to 1914 into six principal periods, which are characterized in the following way:[3]

1st Period: 1789–1820. Excess of imports balanced by profits of our merchant marine.

2nd Period: 1821–1837. Excess of imports increased by inflow of foreign capital.

3rd Period: 1838–1849. Excess of exports due to interest payments on foreign indebtedness.

4th Period: 1850–1873. Excess of imports restored by growth of domestic gold production.

5th Period: 1874–1895. Excess of exports definitely re-established by growth of interest charges on foreign indebtedness.

6th Period: 1896–1914. Excess of exports increased by tourists' expenditures and immigrants' remittances.

---

[1] See, for example, Chester W. Wright: *Economic History of the United States* (New York, 1941); Louis M. Hacker: *The Triumph of American Capitalism* (New York, 1940); Cleona Lewis: *America's Stake in International Investment* (Washington, D. C., 1938); John T. Madden, Marcus Nadler, Harry C. Sauvain: *America's Experience as a Creditor Nation* (New York, 1937); Frank T. Taussig: *Tariff History of the United States,* 8th Edition (New York, 1931); Hal B. Lary and associates: *The United States in the World Economy* (Department of Commerce, Washington, D. C., 1943).

[2] Charles J. Bullock, John H. Williams, Rufus S. Tucker: *The Balance of Trade of the United States,* The Review of Economic Statistics, Preliminary Volume I, July 1919, pages 213–66.

[3] Ibid., p. 213. See also Hacker, op. cit., pp. 243–7 and 399–400.

From the beginning of the twentieth century onwards, the United States has been coming of age, economically speaking, with accelerated speed. Industries have expanded, the internal capital formation has speeded up. Still a debtor country, her productive equipment has become capable of turning ever larger quantities of goods for foreign markets. Under "normal circumstances," the United States might have paid off the debt over one, two, or more decades. In actual fact, World War I resulted in such heavy liquidations of foreign holdings in this country,[4] in order to pay for badly needed goods, which America's industry was able to provide in such large volume, that, on balance, the United States ceased to be a debtor country. Before the war was over, she became a net creditor of the world.[5] The need of postwar reconstruction resulted in new American loans; her creditor position became firmly established. Thus an extraordinarily drastic change in the country's international financial position took place almost overnight. Other changes ought to have followed in due course, to adapt America's balance of payments to her situation as creditor country. It is interesting to note that in the six periods established by the Bullock, Williams, and Tucker study referred to above, the pattern of development of trade and finance corresponded very closely to what we should have expected on the basis of economic theory.[6] But after 1919 the pattern ceases to conform to anticipations; as a nation we have refused to recognize the great change—its suddenness made its assimilation very difficult.

2.

Writing in 1919, Bullock, Williams, and Tucker drew their readers' attention to the changed international position of the United States, and, towards the end of their inquiry, casting an inquiring glance into the dim and uncertain future, they ventured the following previsions:[7]

[4] ". . . the aggregate investment of foreigners was reduced from about 7.2 billion dollars in the summer of 1914, to about 4 billions at the close of 1919." (Lewis, op. cit., p. 114.)

[5] Loans made by the U. S. Government between 1917 and 1920 amounted to 9.5 billion dollars. (Ibid., p. 362.)

[6] Cf. Chapters I, II and III, above.

[7] Bullock, Williams, and Tucker, op. cit., p. 254.

"Exports are certain to diminish and the *quantity* of goods imported is sure to increase markedly. Whether the *value* of imports . . . will also increase is much less certain. But whether the change is wrought solely by a diminution of exports, or is assisted by an increase of imports, the present excess of exports will come to an end. Either our exports and imports will come to a balance, or, in case continued export of capital makes us definitely a creditor nation, we may expect to have an excess of imports as soon as the process of capital exportation has had time to work out its inevitable results."

These forecasts might have been verified by events if the nation had been willing to accept the implications of the country's changed position in the world economy. Actually, the contrary happened. All the forces making for the "old-fashioned" protectionism were still at work after the end of World War I, while demands to protect industries essential for war were much stronger than in the past. Furthermore currency depreciations in many European countries resulted in demands for increased tariffs. Consequently the tariff was raised in 1921 and again in 1922, the latter increases being incorporated in the new Tariff Act of 1922. Finally, with the enactment of the Hawley-Smoot Tariff in 1930, American protectionism reached its high tide.

The reasons for the last-named tariff are not easy to find. Professor Taussig, in his authoritative *Tariff History of the United States,* emphasizes the peculiarity of the 1930 tariff which, as he points out, cannot be explained by any of the circumstances which accounted for its predecessors. He concludes that: "The explanation of the act of 1930 . . . turns on some peculiarities in the economic conditions of the decade 1920–30 and especially on those of the agricultural situation." [8] This act was to be a *limited* tariff revision prompted by agricultural interests. The revision got "out of hand," however, and due to the mutual support of special interest groups in Congress ("log-rolling") it became a general revision. There is a lesson in that experience to be kept in mind when it comes to yet another tariff revision in the future.

The American tariff history in the twentieth century shows some very peculiar characteristics. It follows a very "normal" pattern up to World War I, then moves in a direction exactly opposed to that which one would expect it, a priori, to take. As

[8] Taussig, op. cit., pp. 489–91.

the American economy grew stronger and more efficient, high protection began to taper off. The famous Underwood Tariff of 1913 (the first Wilson Administration) provided for substantial reductions of duties and marked a new departure in American commercial policy—a departure that, as we have seen, was not to prove durable. But even the Tariff of 1909 already showed a changed atmosphere with respect to protection. As Professor Taussig wrote in his *Tariff History of the United States,*[9] ". . . a somewhat different spirit from that of 1890 or 1897 was shown in 1909. Though the act as a whole brought no considerable downward revision, it was less aggressively protectionist than the previous Republican measures. . . . there was unmistakable evidence in Congress and in the community of opposition to a further upward movement. High-water mark apparently had been reached, and there was reason to expect that the tide, no longer moving upward, might thereafter begin to recede." Having written this in 1910, Professor Taussig saw himself vindicated by the passage of the above-mentioned Underwood Tariff. But after the war a protectionist reaction set in, and the course of America's adaptation to her international economic-financial position has suffered, as we saw before, a serious and regrettable setback.

The effects of that setback were at first concealed owing to the prevalent high-pressure selling of foreign bonds to the American public. As result, an export surplus remained in existence throughout the interwar period, though it fell from the high figures of the reconstruction period (4 billion dollars in 1919, nearly 3 billion in 1920), to a figure between 300 million and 1 billion dollars. The United States provided, in 1928, over 16 per cent of the world's exports, while absorbing only 13 per cent of the world's imports. In consequence, the stability of world trade became too dependent upon the continued flow of American capital, much of which was short-term, instead of being more solidly rooted in better balanced trade. Had the United States opened its domestic market more widely to foreign goods, and had the lending operations been more largely designed with reference to the economic soundness of the investment outlets, America's leadership in the world economy might have been considerably more constructive in the postwar

[9] Ibid., p. 408.

years than it has been in reality. The instability of the American economy also reduced America's chance for leadership both to forestall the boom of the late twenties and to launch an internationally co-ordinated attack against the depression of the early thirties.

The depression of the thirties not only reduced the volume of international trade, but price deflation still further reduced its value. In addition, the Hawley-Smoot Tariff very considerably restricted the importance of the American market for foreign countries. In 1938, American exports accounted for nearly 15 per cent of the world's export, $1\frac{1}{2}$ per cent less than in 1928, but American imports were down to $9\frac{1}{2}$ per cent of world imports, or one third less than in 1928. Thus the United States failed to keep her position as a market for foreign goods. The cost of that failure was not only a considerable loss in terms of trade, but also a loss of investments. Payments of debts with the proceeds of goods sold in the American market having been discouraged by the 1930 Tariff, the ensuing wave of defaults very considerably reduced the value of America's foreign assets. By September 1944 American investments abroad represented about 10.6 billion dollars, of which 7.3 billion were direct investments and only 1.7 billion were foreign-dollar bonds.[10]

At the same time as the depression-born wave of defaults depleted the American foreign investments, the United States grew in importance as haven of refuge of "frightened" foreign capital. As the war drew closer, flight capital came to the United States, largely in the form of short-term balances and of a corresponding influx of gold. By September 1944 short-term foreign deposits in the United States were about 6 billion dollars. As a study prepared in the Department of Commerce reveals, the net financial position of the United States was that of a debtor! The table is quoted from that study.

This is an interesting situation. The United States was as of that date a *creditor* on long-term account of 4.4 billion dollars and a *debtor* on short-term account of 5.6 billion dollars, leaving a net debit balance of 1.2 billion dollars. These short-term liabilities will eventually be paid off, as foreign countries start making greater progress towards reconstruction and as confidence

<hr>

10 Cf. Robert L. Sammons: "International Investment Position of the United States," *Foreign Commerce Weekly*, January 27, 1945.

INTERNATIONAL INVESTMENT POSITION OF THE UNITED STATES,
SEPTEMBER 1944

(In billions of dollars)

Assets (United States investments abroad):
    Long-term:

Direct	7.3
Foreign dollar bonds	1.7
Miscellaneous private	1.0
United States Government	.6
Total long-term	10.6

    Short-term:

Private	0.3
Official	.2
Total short-term	0.5
Total assets	11.1

Liabilities (Foreign investments in the United States):
    Long-term:

Direct	2.2
Preferred and common stocks	2.7
Corporate and government bonds	.7
Miscellaneous	.6
Total long-term	6.2

    Short-term:

Private	2.8
Official	3.3
Total short-term	6.1
Total liabilities	12.3

Net creditor (+) or debtor (−) position of the United States:

On long-term account	+4.4
On short-term account	−5.6
Net position	−1.2

returns. A part of these short-term balances will be withdrawn
in form of gold; another part will finance purchases made in the
United States; still another may become a component of the
monetary reserves of foreign central banks. The debtor position
of the United States at the end of 1944 represents, of course, a
purely transitory situation. America's capacity to invest abroad,
supported by her tremendous capacity to produce goods that the
world needs, has resulted in a resumption of private and public
lending activity. Gradually the volume of America's foreign investments will be built up again, this time, one may hope, on a
sound and enduring basis.

3.

The severe impact of the "Great Depression" led to a reappraisal
of the problem of America's foreign trade. Owing to the tireless
efforts of Secretary of State Cordell Hull, an important amend-
ment to the Tariff Act of 1930 was passed in 1934, under the
name of the Trade Agreements Act. This Act authorized the
Administration to negotiate trade agreements with foreign
countries, providing for the Most-Favored-Nation Clause and
involving reductions of tariff rates as great as 50 per cent of the
rates established in the Act of 1930. These reductions could be
made without further Congressional action, and had to be preceded by public hearings at which interested parties were given
an opportunity to present their arguments, pro and con. Countries with which such agreements were concluded were expected
to make comparable downward adjustments in their tariffs and
to apply to the United States the Most-Favored-Nation Clause.
Some special provisions were devised to deal with countries
which practiced quantitative trade restrictions, while no agreements were concluded with countries that were held to discriminate against the United States exports.

The Trade Agreements Act was established for three years,
and was renewed several times, the latest renewal taking place in
June 1945. This most recent renewal was preceded by very extended hearings and an active fight in Congress. It not only extended the life of the trade agreements program, but increased
the powers of the Administration to reduce tariffs. Henceforth
the 50 per cent reduction, representing the maximum conces-

sion the government can make, will be counted not from the tariff level of 1930 (the Hawley-Smoot Tariff) but from that of 1939.

The trade agreements program has not been able, so far, to produce its full results on account of the disturbed condition of the world economy in the later twenties, and of World War II. Nevertheless, thirty-two agreements have been negotiated with twenty-eight countries since 1934, and more are likely to be concluded in the immediate future.

The adoption and successive renewals of the Trade Agreements Act mark important stages in the process of America's acknowledging her place and her responsibilities in the world economy. They represent preparatory stages to working out a new American foreign economic policy, suitable to the realities of the world we live in. There are other indications that as a nation we have learned a good deal from the experiences of the interwar years. This is illustrated by the adoption of lend-lease during the war and by the surrender of economic isolationism.

Lend-lease forestalled the accumulation of a large volume of new intergovernmental war debts. As of October 1, 1945, "total lend-lease debt in the form of articles and services furnished . . . which was charged to foreign governments," amounted to nearly 44 billion dollars.[11] Had the World War I method of loans been used, the creditor position of the United States would look nowadays very impressive indeed—but only to create future maladjustments ending in another wave of defaults.

After the end of World War I, the Congress of the United States voted down the Treaty of Versailles and America entered into a protracted period of political isolationism, associated with the already-mentioned reversion to a dynamic high-tariff policy. In the middle-forties, America leads the way in initiating, promoting, and ratifying international agreements and institutions. The United Nations Organization and the Bretton Woods Agreements offer striking illustrations of that new attitude of leadership. The World Trade Conference and the International Trade Authority will also be largely the outcome of American initiative and American leadership. The 1919 forecast of Messrs.

---

[11] *Twenty-first Report to Congress on Lend-Lease Operations,* for the period ended September 30, 1945, p. 14.

Bullock, Williams, and Tucker,[12] which failed to be verified in the interwar years, may well come true in the *next* twenty years.

For the decades to come, the United States has a position of economic power that no country has ever possessed—save perhaps, in relative terms, England of the mid-nineteenth century. American soil and American industries are unscathed by the war; the efficiency of American industry is unrivaled; the inventive genius of her scholars, the skill of her technicians carry high promise of future achievements. Financially, she is a young creditor power which has learned an expensive lesson, and is about to start building up a large volume of new foreign investment. The American system of private enterprise has given proofs of great vitality and of impressive adaptability. Further proofs are likely to be forthcoming in the years to come. If that system is to survive in a world, large parts of which are either hostile or indifferent to it, American help in revitalizing it abroad will be very necessary. This will involve, in addition to financial help, the export of technological "know-how" and the promotion of principles of unfettered multilateral trade and free international payments.

12 Quoted on page 215, above.

CHAPTER XIV

America's Contribution to World Prosperity

THERE ARE six principal ways in which the United States can contribute to the growth of world trade, to the progress of productive efficiency in the world, and to general prosperity:

(1) The maintenance at home of high levels of economic activity, production, trade and employment;

(2) The opening of the American markets to goods produced by other countries;

(3) The extension of long-term credit for economically justified ventures in underdeveloped countries;

(4) The setting up of agencies that might internationally attack the problem of economic instability and insecurity;

(5) The revitalization and protection of market mechanisms and of economic flexibility and adaptability;

(6) The promotion of agreements for the purpose of establishing a vast area in which payments are free and trade unobstructed and non-discriminatory.

The above list—which undoubtedly might be expanded—includes the most important lines of policy by means of which the United States might carry out its economic leadership in the world. The place of each item on this list carries no implication as to its relative importance in the over-all program; actually it can be said that all six points are equally important. Points 4 and 6 qualify, incidentally, point 1 by ruling out the purely nationalistic methods of securing "full employment."

2.

The maintenance of high levels of economic activity at home is, of course, one of the most important contributions that any large economic unit can make to the cause of world prosperity. When an important market is depressed, its imports naturally fall off and other countries suffer accordingly. This is self-evident, yet this idea has of late been given as much emphasis as if it were a highly novel and original discovery. Statistical studies have been

[222]

made showing the close parallel between the fluctuations of the national income of a country and those of that country's imports. The reader will find a comprehensive discussion of these relationships, as they occur in the American economy, in the Department of Commerce Study, *The United States in the World Economy*.[1] Some writers conclude that tariffs are relatively unimportant, since it is variations in the volume of economic activity that influence most the size of imports. Let us seek "full employment," they say, and tariffs will not really stand in the way of growing international trade. That view is fallacious. In a world economy subject to violent fluctuations of economic activity, the correlation between fluctuations of various statistical series relating to the different components of economic activity is as inevitable as it is unenlightening. The question should be put in another way: given a certain level of economic activity, do tariffs (and especially changes in tariffs) affect the size of imports? To that question the answer should most certainly be in the affirmative.

Coming back now to the matter of domestic employment, we hear frequently statements like these:

"The greatest single contribution which we can make to an expanding world trade after the war will be to run our own economy full blast."[2]

or:

"The greatest single contribution the United States can make to the postwar world in economic affairs is to maintain her domestic economy at levels of high income and employment."[3]

or:

"World security and world peace depend in a very fundamental sense upon how good a job we do in managing our own economy. Prosperity and full employment in the United States are a basic prerequisite to world political and economic security."[4]

or:

"The maintenance of a high level of employment in the United States is the most fundamental condition for keeping in operation a program of international trade expansion."[5]

[1] Op. cit., pp. 37 ff.
[2] Milo Perkins: "Can our Foreign Customers Pay?" *Atlantic Monthly*, September 1945.
[3] Buchanan, op. cit., pp. 215–16.
[4] Hansen, op. cit., p. 178.
[5] Calvin Hoover: *International Trade and Domestic Employment* (New York, 1945).

All of these statements express the same, evidently correct, idea that a prosperous America is essential to a prosperous world. This is what in logic is called "a necessary condition"; but is it a "sufficient condition"? We have seen that "full employment" can be secured by very different means and that some of these involve policies of insulation of the domestic market from outside influences. Now it is essential *not only* that the American economy should be prosperous, *but also* that the American market should be open to foreign-produced goods. When economists discuss this question in terms of imports of primary commodities, raw materials especially, they have no difficulty in proving that the growth of domestic production brings forth a growth of imports. Their argument loses much of its validity, however, if applied to imports of manufactured goods and, in general, of nonessentials. Yet—and this is an often neglected fact—the growth of international trade must be to a very considerable extent a growth of trade in nonessential goods, in goods whose enjoyment forms the pleasant aspects of higher living standards.

The argument that America's greatest contribution to the world's prosperity consists of being prosperous herself is morally too facile. In addition, it is economically inadequate because it places the spotlight on the obvious instead of directing it upon more complex and less evident aspects of the problem: the role of the United States in setting up methods of action for an *international* quest for prosperity,[6] and the ways and means of making the prosperous American market a dynamic factor in the world economy. Before we turn our attention to these questions, let us observe in passing that there is an idea abroad that greatly requires qualification, to wit, that the instability of the American economy is *the* most dangerously upsetting factor in the world economy. This idea has been promoted by American enthusiasts of "full-employment" planning as well as by advocates of "insulation" policies in other countries. The latter can quote views of the former to the effect that so long as the United States fails to plan effectively for "full employment," the world is faced with major hazards. Insulation from the American instability becomes a wise and necessary course of action for other

[6] See above, Chapter XII.

countries. There is much water here on the isolationist's mill! Actually, of course, no country has a monopoly of economic instability, and, as has been pointed out in an earlier chapter, the American crisis of 1929 had deep international causes. The British economy was more stable than the American in between the two wars, but it was chronically depressed during most of that time, while the instability of Germany at least matched that of the United States.

Unless we come to grips with the world-wide problem of cyclical movements of economic activity, we shall be unable to avoid the nationalistic implications of domestic full-employment programs. Sir William Beveridge is giving dangerously bad advice when he asserts that: "Each country must work out its own full employment problem";[7] on the contrary: all countries must get together in order to solve in common the "full-employment" problem of the world.

3.

In the discussion that follows it will be assumed that the United States will do its utmost in the future to promote and maintain high levels of economic activity by methods compatible with the operations of a free-enterprise economy and with the growth of multilateral foreign trade.

This being postulated, what can be done by this country to actively promote the prosperity of the world? We have already mentioned the different lines along which constructive policies might be devised; let us now deal in more detail with some of them.

In the first place, let us consider the importance of foreign trade for the United States. It is often argued, with a plausibility which is so frequently associated with economic fallacies, that American foreign trade is unimportant; since this country sells abroad only a small fraction of its output—the frequently mentioned figure is eight or ten per cent—exports are of little importance to the national economy. The argument then goes on to say that the whole question of foreign trade is for the United States a matter of limited interest and that the wise course of ac-

[7] Beveridge, op. cit., p. 234.

tion consists in concentrating upon the domestic market. The actual situation is very different, as is demonstrated by the following table:[8]

*Exports in percent
of National
Production (1929)*   *Commodities*

50 to 60 per cent	Cotton; sardines; gum raisin; gum turpentine; paraffin wax
40 to 50 per cent	Tobacco leaf; borax; dried fruit; linseed oil; phosphate rock
30 to 40 per cent	Rice; sulphur (crude); copper (refined); carbon black (paint); lard; office appliances
20 to 30 per cent	Agricultural implements and machinery; canned fruit; corn starch and corn flour; benzol; printing and bookbinding machinery
15 to 20 per cent	Wheat; refined mineral oils; medicinal preparations (biologicals); carbons and electrodes; safety razors and blades
10 to 15 per cent	Petroleum asphalt; coal tar colors, dyes, stains, etc.; mineral oils and chemical pigments; salmon; industrial machinery; automobiles; aircraft and parts; dental instruments and supplies.

In the light of these figures it is quite evident that the present structure of production in the United States calls for the maintenance of world trade at high levels in order to enable important branches of our economy to preserve their prosperity. For these industries total sales include considerable exports; without an adequate access to foreign markets, these lines of production cannot avoid a depression.[9]

Under the impact of these inescapable realities, the United States is becoming gradually more and more export-minded. But a proper appreciation of the role of imports remains a great stumbling block on the path of developing a comprehensive foreign-trade policy. In 1928 manufactured goods accounted for

[8] This table is based on the detailed data published in *Summary of Foreign Trade of the United States, Calendar Year 1941*, U. S. Department of Commerce (Washington, D. C., 1944).

[9] See Amos E. Taylor: *The "Ten Per Cent" Fallacy*, Committee on International Economic Policy (New York, 1934).

only 25 per cent of all the American imports. After the adoption of the Hawley-Smoot Tariff and at the end of the first recovery period of the thirties, this percentage stood at the even lower level of 20 per cent in 1927. What is needed here is, first of all, a tariff revision so that manufactured goods can enter the country more freely. But more than the suppression of high-tariff protection will be required. In order that the American market should absorb an expanding volume of foreign-made goods, it is necessary that the public should acquire a taste in these goods. High living standards involve a growing variety of nonessential goods. Imports can greatly increase the variety and price range of such goods and thus contribute to the consummation of higher standards of living.[10]

The expansion of imports calls not only for a lowering of tariffs but also, and very importantly, for the development of better merchandising techniques in the field of import trade. Foreign producers must find means to stimulate the interest of the American public in their wares, using methods comparable to those employed by American manufacturers about to launch a new product or increase the market for an old one. It is very likely that foreign producers will find it necessary to enlist the help of American merchandising and advertising firms. There is scope here for much constructive partnership between American and foreign companies.

It might be noted, in this connection, that foreign trade affords much scope to the initiative of private merchants and even of small businesses. It takes much inventiveness, versatility, and risk-taking to introduce foreign-made nonessential goods into a given market, but rewards of success are usually very high. The variety of such products is almost indefinitely great. Each of them may, taken individually, involve only very small amounts; compared to the total volume of foreign trade it may be "small fry"; taken in aggregate, and promoted with all the instrumentalities of modern advertising and merchandising methods, these small separate items may add up to impressive totals. The freer international trade and the larger its volume, the greater the prosperity of the great trading nations and the greater the absorptive capacity of their markets, and the more

[10] See Percy W. Bidwell: "Imports in the American Economy," *Foreign Affairs*, October 1945.

scope there is for the "pioneering" element in international commerce. From the point of view of America's general attachment to the system of free enterprise, this aspect of the problem is worthy of careful attention.

4.

In order that the United States should be able to liberalize world trade, the American tariff itself must be thoroughly overhauled. The Hawley-Smoot Tariff of 1930 represented, as we know, a great backward step on the road of America's adaptation to world condition; and the actual application of the Trade Agreements Act of 1934, to which reference has already been made, has amounted, in practice, to a tariff truce combined with moderate tariff reductions. A new tariff act which would take account of America's changed position in the world economy is badly needed and long overdue. It might be mentioned, incidentally, that never before in American history has a tariff act been in effect as long as the Hawley-Smoot Tariff; there is nothing unusual, therefore, in a request for a new act.

What should the new act involve? Evidently, lower tariff rates. How much lower and on what articles is a question, however, that is not easy to answer. Let us start, therefore, from the other end and inquire into the purposes of the American tariff.

In earlier days, the tariff was a major source of revenue for the Federal Government and an instrument of protection for "infant industries." It has long ceased to be either. In 1939, the tariff provided six per cent of the normal Federal revenue. As for the American industry, it has very long since become the most "grown up" industry in the world. The tariff has become gradually an instrument of protection for industries which could muster enough political influence to limit the competition of foreign-produced goods by this method. We have seen that most of the arguments used to justify the protective tariff are fallacious and misleading. The price paid for that protection is being borne unwittingly by the public in the form of higher costs of production and higher prices. Only two kinds of protection are justified in a country having as exceptional a productive efficiency as that of the United States. One is the protection of strategic industries necessary for national defense. It will be remembered that Adam Smith, himself, allowed this exception from his general principle of free trade. The other is the protection against dumping and against discriminatory practices of other countries. All this does not imply that the existing tariff could or should be scrapped overnight. Quite on the contrary: careful planning spread over a number of years will be indispensable to *liquidate* a tariff system that has grown obsolete.

Tariff protection is nothing else, in the last analysis, than a form of *subsidy* given to the protected industries. As we have seen before, it is a peculiarly uneconomic kind of subsidy, and one of which the cost to the public is concealed and difficult to ascertain. It has been suggested, therefore, to subsidize directly those industries the assistance of which is considered necessary in the national interest.[11] There are several important advantages that the method of *direct* subsidy might have over the method of *indirect* subsidies by means of the tariff. In the first place, the public would know exactly who the recipients of the subsidy are and what is the cost involved. Secondly, subsidies can be limited to "marginal producers" rather than extended to *all* the producers.[12] Thirdly, public pressure to improve productive techniques can be brought to bear upon the subsidized industries; the fact of spending the taxpayer's money has a greater appeal to the instincts of economy of the man in the street, than the fact of paying (often without knowing it) a higher price than is necessary for products of industries enjoying tariff protection. Finally, direct subsidies allow a greater degree of flexibility in giving or withdrawing assistance from particular industries in accordance with changing requirements of the situation. This is an important consideration when subsidizing productions necessary for national defense.

To be sure, subsidies would be certain to give rise to much political maneuvering, lobbying, and logrolling. In this respect the situation would resemble that which exists at present in the realm of tariff policy. Since, however, the scope of subsidies might be very limited, as compared to that of existing tariffs,

11 Cf. Beardsley Ruml: *Tomorrow's Business* (New York, 1945), pp. 150–8.

12 The various companies producing a given commodity, whether in mining, agriculture, or manufacturing, have different costs of production. Only "marginal" producers, unable to meet foreign competition, require assistance, whereas the tariff spreads the benefits to *all* producers.

the area of abuse would be correspondingly reduced. (This would also be the case, of course, if tariff protection were to be limited to strategic industries.)

The suggestions presented here involve a drastic curtailment of protection, limiting it to the objectives mentioned above. As for the remaining assistance, should it be given through tariff protection or through direct subsidies? It is not likely that a generalized system of subsidies taking the place of *all* the import duties would prove a practical possibility. Subsidies should definitely be preferred, however, to tariffs as a means of protecting "strategic" industries. The aim of national defense is to have an adequate production of certain goods, such as rubber, and an adequate supply of certain services, such as shipping. Once the necessary supplies are assured, no further expansion of the industries providing them is necessary. Subsidies can—and tariffs cannot—limit in that manner protection given to strategic industries.

5.

The proposed transition to a system of much freer trade is certain to encounter a great deal of opposition. Part of that opposition will be due to an emotional reluctance to discard old political taboos and traditional patterns of thought. In answer it can be pointed out that we are living under very novel circumstances and we must adjust ourselves to present-day conditions or suffer from the consequences of a bad adaptation to our environment. Other sources of opposition will be more objectively founded: opponents can emphasize the extent of economic dislocations that would result from such sweeping changes in our commercial policy. This is a weighty objection to our proposals; in answer, it might be emphasized that the transition from the old system to the new must be *gradual* and carefully planned, so that *the burden of adjustment should not be borne exclusively by those directly affected by the change, but be spread as equitably as possible among the entire population.*

What, exactly, is involved in the transition from the present tariff to this new system of substantially freer trade? Particular firms in certain industries will have to go out of business and people employed by them will be out of jobs. At the same time, however, there will arise new opportunities for the development of production in other fields, due partly to an expanding volume of exports and partly to new demands resulting from the cheapening of the hitherto protected, and therefore, necessarily more expensive products.[13] We shall witness, therefore, shifts of resources towards more productive industries and shifts of manpower into new and more efficient employment. All of these cannot be left purely to chance. Even in a free-enterprise society much constructive planning on a local, regional, and national basis will be needed to speed up and facilitate the required adjustments. Not only will it be necessary to achieve a close collaboration between the government, business, and labor, but, as has been mentioned before, the cost of the transformation will have to be spread equitably.

The anticipated change in the economic structure of the United States will make this country more efficient and, in the long run, more prosperous than it has been before. Thus the benefits of the change will extend to the nation as a whole; yet the immediate costs will be borne only by one sector of the population whose investments or jobs will have been placed in jeopardy. It is necessary, therefore, to work out a system by which the immediate "victims" of the change should be given an appropriate amount of compensation for their losses, as well as all possible help in finding new opportunities for employment. A positive program for a *subsidized transition* from a high-tariff economy to a nearly-free trade economy is the only effective answer that can be given to those who object to such a change by reason of the dislocations that it must inevitably produce.

These proposals necessitate a major departure from America's traditional policies. The adoption of a new and bold foreign economic policy will require a good deal of imagination on the part of our political leadership and a good deal of understanding on the part of the public. It is tempting, at the end of the war, to go back to prewar habits and to prewar patterns of individual and social behavior. However, in our day such a return to the past carries no promise of securing prosperity and peace either economically or politically. It is imperative that we adopt new

---

[13] For example, a person who will pay $2.50 for an imported pair of shoes that had cost him $4.50 when the tariff was in effect will now be able to buy $2.00 worth of other goods in addition to the shoes, thus increasing the demand for other articles.

attitudes and new policies in the matter of international relations.

Our suggestions relate only to basic principles of policy. Much painstaking work will have to be done in elaborating the detailed practical applications of these principles before they can be brought to the blueprint state. This is, evidently, a task beyond the means of any single individual. A first step leading to practical realizations should consist in the appointment of a National Commission on the Tariff comparable in scope and importance to the famous Monetary Commission whose painstaking studies and well-considered report paved the way for the establishment of the Federal Reserve System. The Commission on the Tariff should have as members men with a distinguished public record and well-known to the public, none of whom would have personal connections with any organized interests and any pressure groups. The Commission should secure the collaboration of the best technical talent available. Among its tasks would be an inquiry into the real protection afforded by the existing tariffs to various branches of the American economy and the practical consequences of removing, or substantially reducing, the various items of the tariff. On that basis the whole tariff question could be viewed with a fresh eye. Proposals could then be drafted for an *orderly* reduction and, in many cases, liquidation of the existing tariffs.

The consideration of new tariff legislation is always a risky matter. A limited revision, as in 1929, may become a general revision. A general revision intended to reduce the tariff rates might even lead to their increase on account of the organized pressures of special interests. And yet the working out of a new and *low* American tariff is a "must" on our national agenda for the future.

A bold new approach to our foreign economic policy, along the suggested lines, will have two consequences, both of them immeasurably important:

(1) *Materially,* it will result in opening the vast and growing American market to the goods of other countries, thus giving a great impetus to the growth of world production and world trade;

(2) *Morally,* it will serve notice upon the world that America "means business" when advocating a world economy based on free markets, multilateral trade, and fair competitive standards.

6.

A nation's foreign economic policy is a major issue which must be decided by the public opinion and the political institutions of the country. By joining the United Nations, this country has declared itself in favor of international collaboration for the purpose of building an effective world order. By joining international financial institutions and other agencies, we have expressed our interest in the development of a well-working world economy. There is no doubt now that we shall work together with other nations, in the pursuit of international peace and economic prosperity. Indeed, in the years to come, it is entirely likely that we shall take new initiatives in the field of economic organization, along the lines, for example, indicated in Chapter XII of the present book.

To be a good member of international institutions, however, will not be a sufficient contribution on our part to the building of a world economy, unless we also shape our domestic economic life and our national policies in a way favorable to the achievement of our international goals. Two lines of approach have been indicated above to building domestic foundations under our foreign economic policy: we must do all in our power to promote a steady growth of our national economy, avoiding booms and depressions, and seeking both economic and social stability; and we must open our domestic market to the goods produced by people living in foreign lands. Only thus can we obtain for ourselves and provide to others all the advantages of an international division of labor. By an appropriate credit policy, we can stimulate the economic growth of other countries, just as our own continent has been developed with the help of foreign capital in years gone by. But if we are to be repaid, we must accept eventually a *net* inflow of foreign goods and services.

Instead of protecting our least efficient industries by ever-higher trade barriers, let us make change easier and adaptation to technological advance smoother. If the public is to contribute to the costs of economic change, let this be done in a way that will encourage progress rather than to assist inefficiency, that will increase living standards at home and abroad, rather than to lower them the world over. And let us insist that other countries act likewise.

It is a strange reflection of the mood of our times that, on the one hand, economic internationalists are often compared unflatteringly to the dodo, while, on the other hand, world peace and world organization are generally proclaimed as our highest goals. If we really want to achieve an enduring peace, we must adopt a far more kindly attitude towards the doctrines of economic internationalism and be willing to pay the price of translating them into practice. For neither peace nor stable prosperity can be secured in a "bargain basement."

The quest for world organization, when the tide of nationalism runs high, can hope for success only if that tide is effectively stemmed in at least one area of international life. The area in which this can best be attempted at the present time is that of international trade, and the United States is placed today in a unique position to accomplish that historic feat. By opening its market to foreign goods, by promoting effectively multilateral trade and free international payments, by initiating an international attack upon the problem of economic instability, and by extending a helpful hand to less fortunate nations whenever they need assistance, the United States can lead the world towards a better day. Rising weak but alive from the ashes of war and pointing the way towards the future, economic internationalism, thus resurrected by America's efforts, might well take for its emblem not the dodo-that-was but the eternal phoenix.

BOOK FIVE

*Economic Reconstruction in an
Insecure World*

CHAPTER XV

Economic Nationalism
versus International Trade (1945–50)

I.

EXPERIENCE between wars—1919–39—led me, in Chapter IX, to formulate some advice on how *not* to build a world economy. "Shall we learn from that experience that a limited agreement is better than no agreement at all?" I asked; in spring 1951 a melancholy "no" could be supplied. We had not learned that lesson when the U.S. Government put its weight on the side of an International Trade Organization with universal membership. "We have now committed ourselves to the quest for a universal organization. It must be hoped that the agreements reached by the World Conference on Trade and Employment will produce an environment in which free-market economies can safely live." Such, the reader will recall, is the conclusion of Chapter XI, written at the end of 1946. Now that five years have passed, the regret that lay between these lines has been justified by the fate that befell American ambitions for the establishment of a universal ITO. And the wistful hope for a new economic environment was duly disappointed.

The United Nations Conference on Trade and Employment was held in Havana from November 1947 to March 1948. It was preceded by two conferences of a Preparatory Committee held, respectively, in London in October and November 1946, and in Geneva from April to September 1947. In the course of the preparatory work, a draft charter was worked out in which emphasis was gradually shifted from liberalizing world trade to safeguarding, through trade restrictions, national planning programs that would—in the views of their authors—promote either "full employment" or economic development. The U.S. Government, as I have shown in Chapter XI, was off to a bad start because it aimed at universal membership in the future International Trade Organization and because it accepted the notion that a country in balance-of-payments difficulties was justified in restricting its imports by quantitative controls. Because it desired universality, the U.S. Government found itself impelled to sacrifice, one by one, all the principal tenets of American foreign economic policy. Most of the participating governments were animated by a fierce spirit of economic nationalism, and the American negotiators were determined to humor them; hence the many qualifications, exceptions, and escape clauses that, in increasing numbers, adorned the successive drafts of the ITO Charter and progressively weakened the organization. The authors of the Charter "redoubled their efforts after they had forgotten their aims," the "forgotten aims" being, of course, the restoration of freer multilateral world trade through the elimination of import quotas, exchange controls, and discriminatory practices, and the progressive lowering of import duties.

For the sake of co-operation from Britain, American negotiators introduced in the original "Proposals"[1] the escape clause concerning "restrictions to safeguard the balance of payments." And American delegations to successive ITO Conferences were incapable of checking the drift toward what has become the Charter's most objectionable single article—Article 21.[2] Because of the pressure of American agricultural interests for special favors and because American high-tariff interests insist on an escape clause of their own, the State Department's position was further weakened in the arduous negotiations that followed. Nevertheless, the Department might have checked the Conference's drift toward economic nationalism by refusing at certain points to accept further compromise.[3]

The ITO Charter as it was finally adopted by the Havana Conference represented a victory for those forces in the world which placed complete freedom of national action above requirements of international co-operation. It was a disappointing outcome to what started out as a very worthwhile effort. It revealed disappointing things about the frame of mind of a great many governments of the world. It revealed serious weaknesses in American leadership. And it entailed the loss of several years during which, instead of following the will-o'-the-wisp of a universal organization, the United States and other countries of like mind might have set out to organize effective economic

[1] See above, pp. 197–204.
[2] See Appendix I, pp. 289–90.
[3] See my article: "How the U.S. Lost the ITO Conferences" (*Fortune,* September 1949).

co-operation among nations willing and able to work to-gether.

In the United States the ratification of the Havana Charter gave rise to great controversy. The advocates of the Charter made claims barely substantiated, if at all, by the tangled text of the document. Freely using omission and misrepresentation,[4] advocates of the Charter managed to play on the idealistic feel-ings of that sector of the public opinion which tends to respond favorably to anything that sounds like international co-opera-tion. One group of the Charter's opponents, also misreading and misinterpreting the document, made an appeal to that sector of the public opinion for which anything implying international co-operation and freer trade is *ipso facto* objectionable. There remained those who opposed the Charter because they were resolute advocates of freer trade and uncompromising oppo-nents of quantitative restrictions and discriminatory practices. This group—of which I was a member—found itself fighting a two-front battle against those who upheld the Charter in spite of its failings and those who opposed it for reasons of economic nationalism.[5] It is of course difficult to predict the way in which a document as involved as the Havana Charter will be applied in practice. Some writers are inclined to be optimistic,[6] while others feel that the weight of past experience—such as the ITO debates themselves—forces a pessimistic anticipation. No experi-mental test is likely to settle the issue. The U.S. Government has decided not to press the ratification of the Havana Charter and, since other countries were only interested in an ITO that would

4 See for example the *Guide to the Study of the Charter*, prepared by an official of the State Department, and published by the Department in September 1948, together with the text of the Havana Charter. This "guide" plays down all the escape clauses and qualifications of the Charter, omits all reference to some of its most unwholesome provisions, and succeeds in giving the lay reader a completely misleading picture of the contents of the document.

5 All through the work of the ITO Conferences the International Chamber of Commerce urged that the successive drafts be revised in the direction of a document more favorable to the rebuilding of multilateral trade. See its reports submitted, respec-tively, to the Geneva and Havana Conferences, in April and November, 1947: *Trade and Employment*, Brochure No. 106, and *A Charter for World Trade*, Brochure No. 124. To the same school of thought belongs the criticism of the Havana Charter published in 1949 by the National Association of Manufacturers, *The Havana Charter for an International Trade Organization: An Appraisal*. So does Philip Cortney's provocative and important book, *Economic Munich* (Philosophical Library, New York, 1949).

6 See, for example, the comprehensive study by William Adams Brown, Jr., *The United States and the Restoration of World Trade*, published by the Brookings Institu-tion, Washington, D.C., 1950.

include the United States (for reasons given in Appendix I), the entire project, in its present form, has become obsolete.

2.

There remains, as a legacy of the ITO Conferences, the so-called GATT: The General Agreement on Tariffs and Trade, and the Contracting Parties to it. The Contracting Parties are a group of countries informally organized for the purpose of negotiating multilaterally to reduce their respective tariff rates. The General Agreement, in addition to expressing this determination to negotiate tariff reductions, also contains—and that is its weak point —a comprehensive selection of articles from the ITO Charter. This Agreement was set up in Geneva in 1947 and then coordinated with the Havana Charter. It has never been formally ratified, has only a temporary secretariat, and leads an altogether precarious existence. Several long conferences have met under the auspices of the Contracting Parties and have made some progress toward the lowering of tariff rates, but that progress might have been far greater if international trade had not been so thoroughly hamstrung by import quotas and exchange control—two instruments of trade restriction far more effective than tariffs.

Should GATT be maintained? The "general provisions" of the Agreement make this undesirable. If the Havana Charter obstructs rather than helps the growth of multilateral world trade, so do these "general provisions," which but repeat the Charter. Possibly an organization based on a much simpler charter might be maintained for the purpose of multilateral trade negotiations.

It is surely a mistake, when attempting to liberalize international trade, to concentrate on tariffs alone when quantitative restrictions are so prevalent and so damaging. Nor is it possible to seek universal, or even general, agreements in view of the particular problems faced by individual countries. It would seem to be much more realistic to make the attempt by means of bilateral negotiations between the United States (which alone can take the lead in such a program) and other individual countries. The agreements to be negotiated should be comprehensive enough to cover all kinds of trade restrictions and to provide, on the part of the United States, a sufficiently attractive *quid pro quo*. The problems of eliminating the major trade restrictions and restoring convertibility of currencies are only different facets of the same fundamental reality. What is the good of lowering tariffs if trade continues to be restricted by quotas and exchange control? What is the good of liberalizing the application of import quotas if exchange control can be applied all the more effectively for the same restrictive purpose—or vice versa? It is useful to recall that the great movement toward free trade in the second half of the nineteenth century was made possible by bilateral treaties the results of which were generalized through the application of the most-favored-nation clause. A hundred years after the decline of mercantilism had set in there were neither import quotas nor exchange controls in existence in the Western world—and by adopting a free-trade policy of her own Great Britain placed herself in a position to exercise effective leadership through bilateral negotiations. The lesson for the United States to ponder is that of *multilateral trade reached through bilateral agreements.*

3.

Thus our commercial policies wasted several precious years, and ended in a deadlock that can only be broken by a drastic new departure in American foreign economic policy. It was the widespread—and excessively nationalistic—concern with full-employment planning and with economic development which brought about the ultimate failure of the ITO Conferences.

The connection between national planning for full employment and the "new" economic nationalism has been examined in Chapter V. We have seen that full-employment planning led its advocates to favor policies of national economic "insulation," rather than free national participation in the activities of the world economy. In order to underline the importance of dealing with the problem of economic stability within the framework of the world economy, the international quest for economic stability has been made the theme of a separate chapter (Chapter XII). I suggested in 1946 that the problem of seeking economic stability through international means was "the Cinderella of economic policy—virtually a Princess among problems, awaiting the arrival of a Prince among statesmen who might translate its possibilities into reality." [7] What I should have added, of course, is that the Prince would have to be a scholar as well as a statesman—because this challenging problem of statecraft had not yet been solved by scholars. The five years since 1946 have failed to bring us nearer to a solution.

Although in 1946 I was sufficiently conscious of the importance of this problem to devote a chapter (albeit only a token one) to it, I did not feel brave enough at the time, nor do I feel brave enough now, to propose an outline of a positive solution. Instead of acknowledging such a display of intellectual modesty, some of my reviewers took, alas, the view that I should have either played Prince to the "Cinderella problem" or desisted from all criticism of the national (and nationalistic) full-employment planners. This is hardly a reasonable attitude to take! It is perfectly legitimate to consider—and state—that a certain line of policy is wrong in terms of its results, and yet have no alternative solution to offer. The absence of a counter-proposal does not invalidate justified criticism. When a critic says that a book is bad it is not incumbent upon him to write a good book on the same subject!

At the end of 1949 there appeared the United Nations' report on *National and International Measures for Full Employment,* a joint project of a Committee of Experts brought together under U.N. auspices to play collectively Prince to our Cinderella problem. Now this is not the place to analyze the Experts' Report in detail.[8] Let us note that the document displays an unlimited faith in the ability of national governments to manipulate the economic system to secure stability of employment at high levels, and displays as well an utter disregard of many elements to which economists traditionally pay considerable attention, such as the changing structure of production, the operation of free markets, and the need to avoid cumulative inflationary pressures. Of particular interest, however, to students of the trade

[7] See p. 205.

[8] See, however, Professor Jacob Viner's brilliant analysis of the report, entitled "Full Employment at Whatever Cost" (*Quarterly Journal of Economics,* August 1950); also Philip Cortney's "United Nations Experts Propose U.S.A. Finance Nationalistically Planned Economies" (*Commercial and Financial Chronicle,* February 23, 1950); and "Maintaining a High Level of Employment in a Democratic World," a report by the Study Group on Full Employment of the United States Council of the International Chamber of Commerce (New York, February 1951).

of nations, is the attitude of the experts toward economic nationalism and multilateral trade. Their report accepts—indeed, favors—economic nationalism as a way of life; it expects that all these independent nationalisms, meeting at a conference table, will prove capable of working out a harmonious and well-balanced international trading system. But does this not assume the existence of an "invisible hand," infinitely more powerful—and infinitely less probable—than that invoked by Adam Smith and so often derided nowadays by adepts of the "new economics"?

That collectivism and collectivist planning lead to economic nationalism and the breakdown of world trade is borne out by logic and by experience. The authors of the U.N. report, while hoping for the best, evidently place national collectivism ahead of international order, just as they place the avoidance of unemployment as an objective of economic policy ahead of the avoidance of inflation. (Nor do they devote any thought to the deflationary consequences of a broken-down inflation—or to the deflationary consequences of a breakdown in international trade.) Yet, by crippling the world economy, economic nationalists not only would lower the standards of living everywhere (through the loss of benefits derived from the international division of labor), but would also pave the way for international conflicts and frictions. They seem to be blissfully neglectful of these aspects of the problem. They regard multilateralism and currency convertibility as lower-grade economic objectives, and they are prepared to accept bilateralism and exchange control as normal. This attitude is best exemplified by the following discussion, appearing in paragraph 65 of the U.N. Experts' Report:

"While the return to multilateralism and currency convertibility is the declared aim of the great majority of nations—alongside the policy of internal stability and full employment, as laid down in the Charter of the United Nations—it is important to realize clearly how far these aims are complementary and how far one is a pre-condition of the other. The system of bilateral trading and exchange control is undoubtedly a most powerful weapon for maintaining full employment and a high level of production within the countries participating in such a system, in the face of serious fluctuations emanating from non-participating countries. It is not, however, in itself a major source of economic instability and cannot therefore be regarded as an obstacle to the successful pursuit of domestic full employment policies by any country. The justification for bilateral methods of trade will undoubtedly disappear once the present structural disequilibrium in international trade has been removed and countries have succeeded in eliminating major fluctuations in their balances of payments arising from inadequate or unstable effective demand. However, in the successful attainment of the twin goals of full employment and the creation of a relatively free multilateral trading system, the former must certainly take precedence over the latter; while countries can pursue full employment policies even without a multilateral trading system, the restoration of multilateralism without the attainment of internal economic stability in the trading countries is impossible."

The above speaks for itself—and also explains, *ex post facto*—why so many of the Havana conferees, animated as they were by similar considerations, were so little interested in the restoration of multilateral trade, although this was supposed to be their principal objective.

Neither the ITO discussions nor the Experts' Report, and the discussions to which it gave rise, have indicated how one might promote simultaneously a reasonably high degree of economic stability and a free expansion of multilateral trade. At the same time, a growing practical experience with national planning gives little reason to expect that such policies, carried out behind the walls of trade restrictions, will provide their beneficiaries with well-being as well as employment. Indeed, Professor A. J. Brown of the University of Manchester notwithstanding—he claims that the "suggestion that world prosperity is primarily dependent on the volume of world trade is, surely, at variance with all the findings of economic research in the field in the last generation" [9]—countries that have reduced their links with the

---

[9] A. J. Brown's review of *The Trade of Nations*, appearing in *International Affairs*, Royal Institute of International Affairs, London, April 1949. Surely, Keynes's essay *On National Self-Sufficiency* (Yale Review, 1933), and the school of writing which followed in its footsteps and deprecated the importance of international trade, must not be mistaken for "all the findings of economic research" in the field of international economics! (The word "primarily" is, of course, question-begging.) Professor Brown, who seems to have specialized in reviewing my book, also writes in the March 1949 issue of *Economic Journal* that it dismisses "the essential truth in the dictum that national prosperity [meaning an appropriate internal investment policy] is an international duty." That is high-sounding enough, but what exactly does it mean? Surely, this is a very loose application of the word *duty*, and surely no government in the world would fail to regard the prosperity of its population as one of its top objectives. The question is *how to do it;* and there the "planners" have little to offer save self-assurance.

postwar world economy through exchange controls and import quotas have failed to keep pace with countries that followed more liberal and internationally minded policies.

So far it has not been shown by either argument or experience that the benefits of international trade and international capital movements can be forsaken or curtailed without causing serious damage to the standard of living of the man in the street. The principal objective of economic policy should be the reconstruction of multilateral trade, unhampered by quantitative restrictions and hampered as little as possible by tariffs. Within such a framework one must seek, both by domestic policies and by international agreements, to maintain economic activity and employment at high and relatively stable levels. Absolute stability is probably unavailable outside of prisons and of totalitarian countries; this is increasingly recognized in current economic literature.[10] There are many methods by which domestic policies could foster economic activity and stability. In the choice of methods, governments should be guided by two limiting considerations: (1) the need to minimize inflationary pressures, and (2) the need to avoid measures that disrupt international economic equilibrium. *Under no circumstances must balance-of-payments difficulties generated by domestic inflationary pressures be regarded as a legitimate excuse for the adoption (or maintenance) of exchange controls or import quotas.*

4.

The economic development of underdeveloped areas of the world is an old economic problem that has in recent years acquired a great deal of new political significance. Reference has already been made to it in Chapter II of this book,[11] and the role of foreign investments in speeding up the process of economic growth and development has been emphasized and explained. Also stressed were these facts: (1) nationalistic governments can discriminate against foreigners engaged in business or investing

[10] Special attention should be directed here to the series of four articles which appeared in *The Economist* during December 1950 under the general title: "Is Full Employment Secure?" These articles are one of the most brilliant, constructive, and thought-provoking contributions made in recent years to this important and intricate subject.

[11] See above, pages 23–9.

capital in their country; (2) governments of capital-importing countries can do damage to foreign investors through the practice of exchange controls; and (3) the principle of "equality of treatment" of foreign and native investors is inadequate when applied to the administration of exchange control—even if nationals of a country cannot freely transfer their funds abroad, foreign payments to a foreign investor should not be similarly restricted. I also remarked: "This . . . is an area in which much work remains to be accomplished—unless, of course, we should witness in the future the restoration of a full freedom of international payments."

Five years later, international payments are still subject to drastic restrictions and controls, and difficulties on the path of revived capital movements are very considerable indeed. Much has been said on this subject in international conferences, in United Nations committees, in intergovernmental negotiations, but little, if anything, has been done about it. Meanwhile the problem of economic development has acquired even more prominence than it had immediately following World War II. The reasons for this are several: (1) the politicians and statesmen in underdeveloped countries—some of which acquired their political independence since the end of the war—found that the promise of rapid economic development was a valuable argument (or slogan) in political campaigns at home; (2) economic development was used as an excuse for policies of economic nationalism, such as drastic trade restrictions; (3) economic assistance for "backward" areas was increasingly regarded, in the United States in particular, as a powerful weapon against Communist propaganda and infiltration. (Hence the emphasis on the so-called "Point Four" program).

Although the phrase "economic development" has thus become a widely used political slogan, its implications in terms of concrete economic policies have remained largely unexplored. Nor has much attention been paid to the place of economic development in the reconstruction of a workable world economy. At the ITO Conferences "economic development" was given great prominence—a separate chapter was devoted to it in the Havana Charter—but it must, alas, be noted that all these discussions and consultations made no positive contribution to the problem. All that the delegations of the governments concerned fought for was the right of underdeveloped countries to practice policies of trade restriction at will, and after protracted and harrowing negotiations they obtained full satisfaction. Accordingly, Chapter III of the Havana Charter [12] stipulates that economic development programs can legitimately be invoked as a reason for quantitative trade restrictions. This is another victory for economic nationalism, another setback for multilateral world trade.

Their nationalistic outlook has prevented the governments of many underdeveloped countries from assuring fair treatment to foreign investors. This was quite evident in the Havana Conference discussions over the "foreign investments articles" of the ITO Charter; even the still unsatisfactory final text of Article 12 was obtained only after long debate.[13] The same attitude was apparent in the first two reports issued in 1947 and 1948 by the United Nations Sub-Commission on Economic Development. The fair-treatment issue is of key importance because the world's exportable capital is predominantly in private hands, while the economies of the capital-importing countries are chiefly government controlled. The (often nondoctrinal) collectivism of underdeveloped countries and the arbitrary action to which it leads create special risks for the private foreign investor; among these the following call for particular attention: [14]

Nationalization programs. Should his investment fall within the scope of a nationalization program, the investor will want to be assured that he will receive a compensation corresponding to the actual value of the nationalized investment; that he not only can use the compensation within the foreign country itself, but can transfer it into his own currency at will; and that the compensation will be paid quickly and will be transferable abroad within a very short time, so that he can avoid additional risks resulting from a possible depreciation of the currency in which the compensation is made.

Restrictions on transfer of investment income. Although very frequently income from foreign investments is reinvested in the

[12] Supported by Article 21, 4(b) of Chapter IV. See Appendix I.

[13] For a critique of the article, see *International Code of Fair Treatment for Foreign Investments* (Brochure No. 129 of the International Chamber of Commerce, Paris, 1949), Appendix, pp. 18–19.

[14] The following few paragraphs are taken from the writer's essay on "Private Means of Implementing Point Four" (*The Annals* of the American Academy of Political and Social Science, Philadelphia, March 1950), pp. 60–1.

same country, the investor wants to be assured that there will be no restriction on his right to take that income out of the country.

Discriminatory treatment of foreign enterprises. The investor wants to be assured that his treatment by the foreign government in matters of taxes, administration, access to courts, and so forth will be the same as that accorded to nationals.

Interference with operation of enterprises. It is necessary that the investor be free, under the laws of the country in which he operates, to run his enterprise so as to achieve maximum efficiency, that he be under no limitations in the importation of technicians, raw materials, or machinery, and that he be subjected to no special requirements as to the nationality of directors, shareholders, or employees. Neither should the growth and development of his enterprise be subject to special limitations.[15]

Interference with repatriation of investment. The investor wants to be assured that he can gradually liquidate his investment and regain control of his capital for other uses. This assurance must be based on appropriate rules governing the transfer of depreciation and amortization and of the proceeds of the sale of all or part of his investment to residents of the country.

The practices against which foreign investors need to be protected arise from two sources: (1) the existence of governmental controls over a country's trade and payments (import quotas and licenses and exchange control); and (2) discrimination against foreign enterprise and foreign investors. The protection that the investor would require before venturing with his funds into a foreign country amounts to a pledge of nondiscrimination, plus specified exemptions from trade restrictions and import quotas which may be in existence in that country and which, if not qualified in his favor, would seriously jeopardize his legitimate interests. Almost no investor can by himself settle these matters with the foreign governments; they are the proper subjects of negotiations and agreements between governments. Hence the increasing importance of what are currently termed "investment treaties."

All these matters were considered in a "posthumous" League

---

[15] Restrictions on the importing of machinery and technical help may interfere very effectively with the organic growth of an enterprise.

of Nations report on *Conditions of Private Foreign Investment,* published in 1946, from which the following might be quoted:

"The responsibility for establishing and safeguarding the conditions conducive to private foreign investment falls largely on governments. . . . Private foreign investment will thrive if there is national and international political security, price stability, exchange convertibility and freedom of trade."

The work of the League of Nations was carried on by the International Chamber of Commerce, which from 1947 on published a series of reports concerned with the revival of private-capital movements across the world.[16]

The U.N. Sub-Commission on Economic Development has become aware of the uniquely important contribution private capital can make to the cause of economic development. It has also become aware of the prospective investors' concern over the "climate" in investee countries. The International Chamber of Commerce published, in June 1949, an *International Code of Fair Treatment for Foreign Investments.*[17] That Code received the Sub-Commission's careful attention, and at the time of that group's 1950 session at Lake Success the views of the I.C.C. were sought through direct consultation.[18] The final report of the Sub-Commission represents an important step forward on the road to mutual understanding between capital-exporting and capital-importing countries. Only when further progress is made in that direction, and when the spirit of economic nationalism gives way to a sense of international partnership, will real advances in the economic development of the "backward" areas of the world become possible.

Contrary to popular belief, economic development is a painstaking, slow, and cumulative process. Economic development

16 See the following publications: *Foreign Investments and Economic Expansion* (I.C.C. Brochure No. 107, Paris, 1947); *International Code of Fair Treatment for Foreign Investments* (I.C.C. Brochure No. 129, Paris, 1949); *Financing Economic Development* (I.C.C. Brochure No. 142, Paris, 1950); *Governmental Guarantees to Investors* (I.C.C. Brochure No. 145, Paris, 1951).

17 The International Chamber of Commerce is one of the Category A Consultative Non-Governmental Organizations to the United Nations, and all its resolutions and reports are submitted to the U.N. Economic and Social Council.

18 It was my good fortune to represent the I.C.C. on that occasion, and I found much more receptivity to I.C.C. views at that time than I did when representing the Chamber at the Havana Conference.

must not be confused, as it often is, with industrialization—the latter is merely a particular case of the former. Economic development cannot be exported: a country that seeks to speed up its economic growth must rely upon the vigor, resourcefulness, and enterprise of its own population, the wisdom of its government, and, of course, the natural wealth of its territory. The foreign contribution, in terms of capital, of technical know-how, of managerial advice, can initiate and accelerate the process of development; but this contribution, for all its importance, is essentially a marginal factor in the developmental process. Much reliance is placed today upon "technical assistance," but technical assistance can be of major significance only if it is supported by an adequate capital investment. Any attempt to provide technical assistance without an appropriate supply of capital resources is likely to end in disappointment and frustration.

The governments of underdeveloped countries should attempt to attract the largest possible foreign participation in their economic development. This they can only achieve, however, by forsaking policies of economic nationalism and by adopting measures broadly favorable to the trade of nations. Long-term stability of capital movements is essential; it can best be secured when foreign investments are based on the hard-headed notion of mutual advantage. Neither colonial exploitation nor philanthropy is a sound basis on which to build enduring relations between "advanced" and "underdeveloped" countries. Prosperous countries are under no obligation to help the growth of poorer ones—but modern history clearly demonstrates that a growing prosperity in poor nations has a favorable effect upon the condition of rich ones. Enlightened self-interest has usually proven to be a sound guide to economic policy; it is given much new scope through the emergence of economic development as a major political objective.

Recently the Colombo Plan [19] of the British Commonwealth and the American Point Four program [20] have focused much constructive thinking on this subject; we may expect a great deal of achievement in the next decades.

[19] "The Colombo Plan for Co-operative Economic Development in South and South-East Asia," Report by the Commonwealth Consultative Committee (His Majesty's Stationery Office, London, 1950), Cmd. 8080.

[20] See "Partners in Progress," A Report to the President by the International Development Advisory Board headed by Nelson Rockefeller (March 1951).

5.

The full rehabilitation of international trade on the basis of multilateralism and free-market processes demands freedom of international payments between countries; i.e., mutual convertibility of national currencies.[21] This is a field in which relatively little progress has been made since 1945, even though international monetary conferences held successful sessions even before the end of hostilities, and the Charter of an International Monetary Fund [22] was adopted as early as June 1944. Despite all its considerable resources the IMF has been unable to contribute effectively to the cause of monetary reconstruction between 1945 and 1950.[23] Indeed, on several occasions, progress made by individual countries was achieved in disregard of the IMF's regulations (as in the case of France) or with the Fund's agreeing to take a less than literal view of some provisions of its Charter (as in the cases of Italy and Canada).[24]

Let us examine, first of all, the reasons for this unhappy frustration. True, much progress has been achieved, with the aid of the Marshall Plan, in production and in the material rehabilitation of Western Europe. True, the balance-of-payments positions of the Sterling Area and of most of the Western European countries have improved in a spectacular way. True, the material conditions of life in most of the continental countries of Western Europe are back—or almost back—to prewar. And still the recovery of world trade lags behind, and a return to convertible currencies and free international payments is generally considered to be remote. An explanation is in order.

[21] See above, pages 14–18.

[22] Henceforth designated as IMF.

[23] At the Havana Conference (1947–8), offices assigned to the various international agencies represented there bore the initials of the respective agencies. On the door of the Monetary Fund's office one could read, however, not I.M.F. but F.U.N.D., which, as a witty delegate remarked, must have stood for the warning: "From Us No Dollars!"

[24] As these lines are being prepared for the press, there appear strong indications that the Fund will become far more active in the future than it has been in the past, as a champion of freer international payments. Reference is made to the Fund's *Second Annual Report on Exchange Restrictions*, issued in April 1951 and strongly recommending a relaxation of exchange controls by countries whose international financial position has shown sufficient improvement. The publication of this very important report may well prove to be the opening shot in the second phase of the post-World War II fight against trade and payment restrictions.

Since the war's end, experts who considered that a return to currency convertibility was impossible "at the present time" have given many rather sophisticated reasons for their views. The disruption of production was an early explanation; on the whole, it was a valid one. So was the exceptionally heavy post-war demand for imported goods, coupled with the disorganized condition of export markets. These conditions required remedial action; so did the loss of foreign assets and of "invisible exports," experienced by such countries as the United Kingdom [25] and the Netherlands. There remained also a widespread fear of capital flights; the idea that capital movements had to be controlled for an indefinite time to come, even if current transactions were freed from restrictions, became a dogma of the new economic orthodoxy.

Probably the most popular and plausible arguments in favor of exchange control were provided by the "dollar shortage." At the end of the war certain countries found themselves with reduced dollar earnings (due to the loss of foreign assets and the disorganization of export markets) while their needs for American-produced goods were exceptionally heavy. These countries experienced, not unnaturally, the symptoms of a "shortage" of dollars. So did countries that, like some Latin American republics, earned large amounts of dollars during the war and then when the war was over went on a spree of reckless spending from which they woke up with badly upset balances of payments. As an emergency symptom the dollar shortage had undoubted reality for a few years. The Marshall Plan did a great deal to provide relief, and great progress has been made toward a satisfactory balancing of international accounts. Arguments have of course been advanced in support of the theory of a chronic and enduring dollar shortage; some of these are rather crude,[26] while others are learned and subtle.[27] But even the best among them fail to carry conviction, based as they are on the assumption that the American economy will continue indefinitely to be far more productive than that of any other country, and that the principle of comparative costs will continue to be stulti-

[25] On the "British problem" see above, Chapter X, Section 3.
[26] See, for example, Thomas Balogh's *The Dollar Crisis* (Oxford University Press, 1949).
[27] The best of these will be found in the article by Honor Croome, "The Dollar Siege" (*Lloyds Bank Review*, London, July 1950), pp. 25–46.

fied through trade restrictions. Nor do the authors make enough allowance for America's growing demand for imported raw materials, for the increased consumption of foreign-made goods by the American public, or indeed for the dynamic (and often unforeseeable) elements that are likely to be most effective in helping to restore international economic equilibrium in the future.

The economic rehabilitation achieved between 1946 and 1950 should have paved the way for the elimination of exchange controls and import quotas. The dollar shortage, its various rationalizations notwithstanding, actually disappeared—as a world phenomenon—by the end of 1950,[28] in spite of the inflationary policies of many countries.[29] What remains, however, is the fear of removing exchange controls on the one hand, and the desire to maintain them as a part of a socialistic planned economy on the other. The latter attitude has been a very important element in the policies of countries such as the United Kingdom, the Labour Government of which believes in the necessity of exchange control as a permanent and normal means of regulating the economic life of the country. At first Labour spokesmen were very discreet on this subject, but in the course of the 1950 election campaign this became an openly admitted principle. How mistaken are those who say: "Nobody likes exchange controls, but

[28] This is borne out by U.S. balance-of-payments figures for 1950 (see *Survey of Current Business,* Department of Commerce, Washington, D.C., March 1951). According to these figures, the U.S. Government extended to the rest of the world grants totaling $4,043 million during 1950. At the same time, the U.S. exported $1,743 million in gold, and foreigners acquired assets in the U.S. (i.e., dollar assets) amounting to $1,869 million. In other words, gold and dollar assets acquired by foreign countries from the United States amounted to 89.3 per cent of the U.S. government grants. This is an indication that there was no longer any real "dollar shortage" in terms of the worldwide situation. The remaining world dollar deficit of $431 million could have been easily compensated through American private foreign investments had these not been discouraged by the prevalence of exchange controls and discriminatory policies. It should be noted that American private foreign investments amounted in 1950 to slightly over one billion dollars, or half of the estimate prepared two years earlier by the National Association of Manufacturers as to the probable size of such investments. Of course, certain areas continued to suffer from a "dollar shortage" while other areas were accumulating dollars in gold—but this was largely due to the prevalence of exchange restrictions and to the absence of multilateral trade and payments.

[29] The demand for imported goods in general, and for dollar goods in particular, depends of course on the credit policies of the various countries. If these policies are expansionist, the demand for imports is easily increased in consequence, and the symptoms of a dollar shortage readily appear—all the more so as national currencies of the countries in question are overvalued behind protective walls of exchange control. Any country can engineer for itself a dollar shortage with the help of inflationary credit policies and an overvalued currency.

circumstances have forced most nations to husband carefully their foreign resources. This is an unhappy necessity, but one that promises to restore these countries to economic health sooner than if they permitted the dissipation of their resources in unbridled imports or in capital flights." [30] Not only has it been expressly stated by British Cabinet members that they "liked" exchange control and regarded it as an indispensable permanent instrument of economic policy, but it has also been proven by the practical experience of countries with sound monetary management (e.g., Belgium) that nothing prevents the "dissipation of their resources in unbridled imports or in capital flights" better than an anti-inflationary—and at times restrictive—domestic credit policy. As for capital flights, these do not tend to occur when a country is well governed. This is a home truth that bears being restated from time to time. It is important to avoid making a bogey out of the fear of capital flight.

A widespread attitude that renders the removal of exchange controls more difficult might be described as "the fear of the market mechanism." Just as a patient who, after a severe accident, is afraid to start walking without crutches, so the government of a war-ravaged country may be afraid of dispensing with the economic crutches provided by exchange control. Such fear stands in the way of a final cure. Great Britain's unhappy experience of 1947 when it prematurely attempted a return to dollar convertibility was another retarding influence. It will be recalled that at the time of the 1945 loan negotiations [31] the United Kingdom had to undertake making sterling convertible by 1947 (in deference to the unreasonably heavy pressure exercised by the United States). Nobody bothered at the time to determine the conditions under which convertibility might endure, and nothing effective was done during the intervening eighteen months to pave the way for the resumption of convertibility. This failure was widely used (and abused) in the years that followed as an argument against the elimination of exchange controls.

[30] Quoted from William L. Clayton's review of *The Economic Munich* by Philip Cortney (*New York Times Book Review*, March 20, 1949). Mr. Clayton had then just retired from the office of Under-Secretary of State for Economic Affairs and the point of view he expressed was (and is) shared by not a few of his former colleagues.

[31] See above, p. 169.

In a sense, every time exchange controls are removed after having been in operation for an extended period of time, their removal may appear to have been premature. For maladjustments as well as resentment and pressures breed freely behind the protective wall of these controls. When the controls are removed and the country's links with the outside world can no longer be minimized or ignored, trouble is almost inevitably in store. Inflationary tendencies tend to develop behind exchange controls, and currencies tend to become overvalued. People who were incommoded by controls will tend to transfer some of their funds abroad as soon as payments have become free again, an attitude that may easily be reversed as the economic position improves and international equilibrium is re-established. Speculators may come out of hiding and try fishing in troubled financial waters. All of this adds up to the simple fact that the removal of exchange controls is more likely than not to result in a "convertibility crisis." Indeed, the various factors listed above may add up to a violent public reaction that, in turn, may produce a crisis far exceeding anything justified by the facts of the case. This is a serious risk and it dictates caution when designing a program for the suppression of exchange restrictions (or import quotas). If a sudden removal of controls, without adequate preparation, is likely to lead to a major crisis, it doesn't follow that one should retain controls indefinitely in order to avoid such a crisis. A sensible and courageous policy will carefully prepare the ground for the removal of restrictions, thereby minimizing the probable scope of a "convertibility crisis," while designing appropriate measures to deal with the crisis when it occurs. Once all the preliminary steps are taken, the "convertibility crisis" may be reduced to the dimensions of a mere phase of economic convalescence.

In recent years "gradualism" has become practically synonymous with "indefinite procrastination," and as such has been the object of considerable criticism on the part of certain observers, including the present writer. There is, however, a legitimate concept of "step by step" solutions; it is one that involves preparation of the ground for the final measures, and acceptance of the risks, thus reduced, of the final move. This kind of carefully thought-out policy ending in a series of consecutive moves, each well timed and all leading to the final goal of suppressing controls, avoids both the risks of excessively precipitate action and those, less spectacular but equally damaging, of unending delays. The following suggestions relate to this middle course of well prepared action.

First: At the same time that exchange controls are being removed, exchange rates should be "unpegged," in order to allow market forces to operate (the orderliness of the market can be maintained and speculation minimized by the use of exchange stabilization funds). This suggestion stands in conflict with a literal interpretation of the Charter of the International Monetary Fund, which provides for parity changes from one fixed rate to another—but not for transitional flexibility. Thus, most of the countries that, following Great Britain's lead, devalued their currencies in relation to the U.S. dollar in the fall of 1949 adopted new fixed rates, while maintaining exchange restrictions. On the other hand countries that, like France and Italy, succeeded in converting their currencies during the postwar years from weakness to strength, have done it by establishing a "free" rate in addition to the official rate of exchange. It must be noted that these countries did in fact interfere with the free market. The "free" rates were never really free, but became more and more so as time went on, and as it was found that their level corresponded to what could be maintained in a really free market. This flexibility was an empiric method of finding an appropriate new parity for the currency in question. This is a matter which cannot be settled *a priori*. Contrary to the beliefs held in the twenties, there is no theoretical way to determine the level of new equilibrium exchange rates or parities, once events have rendered old parities impracticable. Only experience can tell.[31] In order to avoid unilateral action or the use of foreign exchange rates to promote a country's international economic objectives at the expense of other countries, some form of international supervision over flexibility is necessary, and the IMF is well equipped to fulfill that function. The fact that exchange controls sheltering arbitrary exchange rates give rise to the development of vested interests and repressed pressures makes it all the more necessary to apply a period of transitional flexibility, buttressed by the operation of stabilization funds, before setting

[31] Cf. M. A. Heilperin: *International Monetary Economics* (London and New York, 1939), Chapter VII.

a new rate and returning to a completely free foreign-exchange market.

It is sometimes argued, by those who oppose such a transitional period of flexible exchanges, that this approach could in no case apply to the so-called "key currencies"; i.e., currencies that, like the pound sterling or the dollar, are major media for the conduct of international trade. It is argued that it is in the interest of world economic stability that the exchange relations between such currencies should always be fixed rather than be allowed to fluctuate from day to day. Now, the experience of the thirties does not bear out this contention. It will be recalled that after the suspension of the gold standard in England in 1931 the sterling-dollar rate was allowed to fluctuate. The foreign-exchange market was not exactly free, since an exchange equalization account was established for the express purpose of intervening in the market. These interventions were, however, limited to what was necessary for the sake of maintaining orderly and gradual fluctuations. The interventions did not aim at maintaining a sterling-dollar rate that would otherwise have been impracticable. It will also be recalled that it was under that regime that the sterling area was formed and did a very prosperous business until the outbreak of the second world war. Britain's recovery began to gain momentum in the last quarter of 1932, and by the end of 1938 British production substantially exceeded the 1929 level.

The reader may well ask how it happened that the instability of exchange relations between the two key currencies—the dollar and the pound sterling—did not cause any significant disturbances in international trade. The answer will be found in the role of forward exchange. At first the Bank of England only dealt in "spot" exchange transactions, but later it operated in the forward market as well. Now the existence of a forward exchange-market is indispensable if exchange flexibility is to give its best results. This market provided an opportunity for the importer to cover himself, at the time of his purchase, against exchange fluctuations that might take place between the time he placed his merchandise orders and the time of their delivery. Although the forward market offers an opportunity to speculate, it also makes it possible to avoid speculation on the part of importers. Once all this had been realized by the Bank of England, its operations contributed greatly to the stabilization of the conditions under which international trade was conducted. This experience with exchange-equalization accounts (or stabilization funds) during the thirties has a good deal to teach us that is of value in the present period of readjustments.

Thus, we conclude that during the transitional period leading from wartime and immediate postwar disturbances to a future stable condition of the world economy, exchange flexibility, accompanied by the freeing of exchange markets from controls, is by far the preferable solution. Some suggestions are made below for a corresponding revision (or a reinterpretation) of the Charter of the IMF. It hardly needs saying that exchange stability should remain the basic long-term requirement of international monetary relations.[32]

Second: A government that intends to put an end to exchange controls must adopt domestic policies that achieve and maintain equilibrium between the country's economy and the world economy, and that assist the maintenance of confidence both at home and abroad in the currency shortly to be liberated. This involves not only the adoption of certain positive policies but also, and very importantly, the avoidance of certain types of error in domestic policy. Among these errors to be avoided one should mention domestic overconsumption and overconstruction, both of which lead to inflation. In certain quarters today the view is prevalent that the main condition for avoiding inflation is the government's balancing its budget. Although important, this step is insufficient. The greatest inflation the United States has experienced in modern times took place in the twenties *in spite* of the fact that the budget was small and balanced and that prices of many important goods were falling. What caused the inflation was an expansion of bank credit, interfering with the price decline that otherwise would have taken place as a result of the spectacular growth of productivity during that period. Similarly, after World War II there was a steady inflation in

[32] An unwelcome plea for flexibility has come, in May 1951, from the United Nations' Economic Commission for Europe. In Chapter 5 of its *Economic Survey of Europe for 1950,* the Research and Planning Division of ECE advocates flexible parities *but without the restoration of free foreign-exchange markets.* What this would amount to is unilateral manipulation of exchange rates as an instrument of national economic planning behind the walls of trade and payment restrictions. These recommendations, if followed, would contribute to the growth of economic nationalism and to a further breakup of the world economy into insulated units.

Great Britain, although it was hidden by the use of food subsidies and vast social services. This inflation was no less damaging to the international position of the pound sterling than would have been an open inflation of the more orthodox type. Sweden also experienced an inflation, first stimulated by wartime "neutral" trade with both belligerent camps, and, since the war, fed by a policy of capital expansion on the part of the government, a policy continued with arbitrarily and excessively low interest rates. A balanced budget is not enough to avoid inflation; restrictive credit policies are at times indispensable; eventually it must be realized that "cheap money" has an inflationary influence. If exchange controls are to be eliminated domestic inflationary tendencies must be curtailed. In addition to antiinflation policies, broadly conceived, some encouraging gestures toward foreign investors would help, as well as the funding or temporary blocking of the country's floating foreign debt (in countries where there is a large outstanding debt of this kind, such as Great Britain, with her "sterling debts" inherited from the war).

Third: Before relinquishing exchange controls, the government should obtain assurances that any needed foreign assistance will be available to it in the form of stabilization loans or lines of short-term credit in foreign central banks. The EPU already operates to a certain extent as a "central bank of central banks." It is conceivable that an enlarged payments union combined with a reorganized IMF might become a source of such credits. These facilities should be adequate to accommodate such "hot money" as might still wish to migrate (even temporarily) in spite of all the previously indicated measures.

It will be noted that before re-establishing the convertibility of sterling in 1947, the British Government completely failed to prepare the country for the "convertibility crisis." [33] Nor did the government of the United States exercise any helpful influence

[33] This failure had, undoubtedly, deep and varied reasons. The task of restoring Britain's international balance was stupendous and appeared to many to call for a *long* period of transition. As early as December 13, 1945, Mr. Winston Churchill said in the House of Commons that "this convertibility proposal within 15 months appears to be a proposition so doubtful and perilous that the best hope is that in practice it will defeat itself. . . ." (Hansard, 13 December 1945. Column 714). The Labour Party consistently regarded exchange control as one of the basic and *permanent* instruments of economic planning, although it wasn't till the 1950 elections that members of the Labour Cabinet stated this view explicitly and in public.

in the matter. Once the British crisis developed, no major effort was made to keep the sterling convertible by means of (1) devaluing it; (2) restricting credit; (3) advancing U.S. monetary aid to the Bank of England. It is one of the disastrous omissions of the past five years that, instead of following such a course, with America's aid and blessing, the British Government reinstated exchange control—with full American consent. It went further: on the strength of the "convertibility crisis," the British delegation to the ITO conference then meeting in Geneva was quick to request a provision in the ITO Charter allowing a country in balance-of-payments difficulties to use *discriminatory* trade restrictions. This provision was duly adopted and its revised text now forms Article 22 of the Havana Charter.

Properly handled the British "convertibility crisis" might have helped to achieve international monetary reconstruction well before 1950. Handled as it actually was, the crisis placed a serious obstacle in the path of an early restoration of multilateral trade and payments. Already the Bretton Woods Agreement of 1944 accepted control over capital movements as a permanent feature of the peacetime economy. The British crisis resulted, in addition, in a great reluctance to remove payment restrictions on current transactions. The notion came to be widely accepted that a country's balance of payments must be in equilibrium before exchange controls and import quotas can be removed. This, however, is a mistaken notion that ignores the large body of past experience concerning the restoration and maintenance of equilibrum in international payments.[34]

By contrast, it seems well worth while to quote the concluding paragraphs of the pamphlet "Liberating World Trade," published in June 1950,[35] the Second Report on the Operations of the General Agreement on Tariffs and Trade:

". . . Many of the controls on trade, even though they may appear to be indispensable, have secondary effects which retard recovery. The existence of one control necessitates another, and if the first is removed the need for the second may fall away. Moreover, restrictions maintained by one country may aggravate the difficulties of others,

[34] For an analysis of "re-equilibrium mechanisms," see the writer's *International Monetary Economics* (London and New York, 1939), Chapter VIII.

[35] Published by the Interim Commission for the International Trade Organization, located at the United Nations European Headquarters in Geneva.

so that the removal of any one restriction may lead to the abolition of many.

". . . it is part of the doctrine of the General Agreement that as recovery progresses import restrictions shall be discarded. This progressive dismantling of restrictions is not simply an end in itself, or even a mere accompaniment of economic recovery; it is an important contribution to the cure.

"When, therefore, a point is reached where balance-of-payments Q.R.s [Quantitative Restrictions] can be relaxed, more will be lost in the struggle for recovery by an excessive timidity in scrapping controls than by a policy of calculated boldness in measures of liberation.

". . . a few experiments in liberation, even by governments which are not positive of their ability to bear the risks involved, would provide a stimulus which, coming at a crucial moment, could tip the scales in favor of recovery. Experiments in liberation would shift the emphasis from restrictions to expansion in international economic policy."

Although this quotation deals with import quotas only, its wise observations apply with equal force to exchange control.[36] Had a frontal attack been made on both quantitative trade restrictions and on exchange control—these evil twins, children of national collectivism and international crisis—there is a good chance that well before 1950 the world economy might have recovered the vigor which it still lacks.

In summing up the foregoing discussion, it may be helpful to observe that exchange adjustments that are needed in a disturbed situation like that inherited from the war can be obtained either by administrative measures or by economic pressures. The former lead in practice to an unnecessary degree of "gradualism" and may even result in a perpetuation of exchange controls. On the other hand, economic pressures may lead to unnecessarily acute crises, bankruptcies, and other disturbances prolonging the period of adjustments. At the end of the war it would have been impossible to restore overnight the freedom of markets, on account of the extraordinarily high measure of

---

[36] See the *Second Annual Report on Exchange Restrictions* (International Monetary Fund, Washington, D.C., April 1951), cited and commented upon in footnote 24 above.

demand created by wartime economies. After a few years the opposite danger is enlarged, namely that of indefinite procrastination. One of the great achievements of judgment and skill in the field of economic statecraft is the combining of both approaches, using both administrative measures and free economic forces. It would seem that five years after the end of the war a good deal of progress has been made in Western Europe along both lines, so that by 1951 we have reached the final phase, when decisive action would appear to be both possible and necessary.

Before concluding this brief survey of the monetary inhibitions and frustrations of recent years, let us turn once more to the International Monetary Fund. It has already been noted that during the period 1945–50 the Fund remained on the sidelines watching events, frequently disapproving but rarely, if ever, playing an active role. It has also been noted that in 1951 the Fund has become a leading champion of the liquidation of exchange controls. The lessons of the past five years lead to the following suggestions:

(1) The rigid provisions of its Charter concerning adjustments of exchange rates might have been appropriate to a world that has recovered its balance, where postwar inflations have been stopped, and where international markets have recovered their full scope. But that was *not* the world of 1949–50, and far more flexible arrangements were necessary. The treatment of the so-called "transition period" in the Bretton Woods Agreement did not prove adequate. Soon after the end of the war a good case might have been made for a revision of the IMF Charter. The Bretton Woods system of parity adjustments depends upon the correct determination of "initial parities"; but no mechanism is provided for deciding what these parities should be in terms of existing economic conditions. This is an important gap in the Bretton Woods Agreement, and its filling is an urgent need. Only when initial parities have been correctly set—by applying, under appropriate safeguards, the test of the market mechanism—can the procedure provided by the Fund's Charter operate in a satisfactory manner.

(2) Although the scarce-currency provisions [37] of the IMF Charter were never applied to the dollar, largely owing to assist-

[37] Article VII of the Articles of Agreement of the International Monetary Fund.

ance provided under the Marshall Plan, the dollar shortage has been invoked throughout as an excuse for exchange controls and discriminatory trade practices. The scarce-currency provisions adopted at Bretton Woods are in need of careful revision, considering that (a) there is no reference in them to rates of exchange, and (b) whenever there appear widespread inflationary tendencies in the world, these automatically tend to make scarce the currencies of countries that resist these inflationary pressures. Thus the latter countries would, most unfairly, be placed at a disadvantage. The entire concept of scarce currencies seems not to have been carefully examined either before the Bretton Woods Conference or at the Conference itself. It should certainly be closely studied at the earliest possible time. If a currency is scarce, the condition may be ascribed either to the rate at which it exchanges for other currencies or to the failure of the country in question to "play the game" of monetary internationalism in accordance with the well-known (albeit unwritten) rules. Article VII of the IMF Charter fails to take note of either of these considerations, and proposes instead a system of control and rationing which, without contributing in any way to a basic improvement of the situation, opens the door to new exchange restrictions. Actually, the existence of scarce currencies should be looked upon as a particular application of the notion of fundamental disequilibrium (Article IV, Section 5 of the Fund's Charter) and treated accordingly.

(3) By ruling that a member "may not make net use of the Fund's resources to meet a large or sustained outflow of capital" and that "the Fund may request a member to exercise controls to prevent such use of the resources of the Fund," (Article VI, Section 1(a) of the Articles of Agreement), the Bretton Woods Agreement accepted exchange control as a permanency—for it is impossible to control capital movements without controlling all other transactions as well. This feature of the IMF Charter has already been questioned in Chapter III; the experience of recent years shows that this basic weakness altered the entire approach of the Western world to the problem of world economic reconstruction. To say this is not to ignore the disruptive effect of capital flights upon the monetary stability of countries in which they occur. But capital flights are an occasional and marginal phenomenon. Is it then wise to forego the benefits of

fully convertible currencies and free international payments in order to prevent the recurrence of these occasional and marginal disturbances? Is it not time for another method of handling "hot money"? As has often been observed, it is not the money that is "hot" but the place from which it takes flight, and the heat is increased rather than reduced by the insulating effects of exchange restrictions. What is usually needed is an appropriate change in domestic policies, to improve the prevalent condition of confidence. On occasion, especially when the crisis is due to such international causes as the danger of war, outside assistance may be needed. This would involve appropriate arrangements between central banks—a problem so far unsolved, and one in urgent need of solution. In actual practice, exchange control has proven to be much more effective in disrupting international economic relations than in keeping "hot money" at home.[38] International economic relations are allowed to disintegrate in order to provide a bad solution to the problem of capital flights.

As these words are written it clearly appears that the "key currency" approach to the problem of monetary reconstruction advocated by many authorities in 1943 and 1944 as an alternative to the IMF (which was then under active consideration), should have been followed even after the establishment of the Fund. After the passage of six years full sterling convertibility has not yet been achieved, and this failure represents the main roadblock in the path of monetary reconstruction. Its achievement should be the first item on the international agenda. In spite of the new wave of insecurity sweeping the world in 1951, and in spite—or maybe because—of the economic consequences of rearmament, the time seems now to be ripe for a determined frontal attack on exchange restrictions and for the restoration of free payments.

In the last analysis, the success of any present and future action toward the restoration of an international monetary system will depend upon the willingness of the governments concerned to

---

[38] A careful reader of these pages may be struck by an apparent contradiction between these views and the statement made at the bottom of page 60 to the effect that "the most effective way to check a flight of capital is to establish exchange control." Now, there can be no doubt about exchange control checking a flight of capital in the short run, but it doesn't solve the problem of "hot money" in the longer run because it fails to remove the causes of capital flights. In the longer run, exchange control is not even effective in checking the symptoms.

adopt appropriate "rules of the game" and thereafter to adhere
to the spirit as well as to the letter of these rules.[39]

6.

There can be no doubt that the Marshall Plan was the boldest
and most constructive of all the postwar economic programs and
proposals. Beginning with Secretary Marshall's Harvard speech
of June 1947, the speed of economic reconstruction throughout
Western Europe was given a new and great momentum, and by
the end of 1950 the major purposes of the program were nearly
completed. Within the brief compass of this survey it is of course
impossible to do more than indicate the highlights of the program, its accomplishments, and the limits of its results. The
reader may be directed to the comprehensive recent study of
Professor Howard S. Ellis and associates, entitled *Economics of
Freedom* and issued under the auspices of the Council on Foreign Relations in New York, to Paul G. Hoffman's book, *Peace
Can be Won,* and, of course, to the *Quarterly Reports to Congress* of the Economic Cooperation Administration.

The basic concept of the program—officially known as ERP,
or European Recovery Program, and administered by the ECA
or Economic Cooperation Administration—was to stimulate
economic co-operation among European countries by providing
them with American assistance. An organization of European
countries eligible for ERP assistance was founded under the
name of Organization for European Economic Cooperation
(OEEC). At first, the organization limited itself to the task of
distributing among its member countries the aid obtained from
the U.S. Government. With the passage of time, and as the first
impact of the Marshall Plan upon European reconstruction

[39] The difficulties encountered by the European Payments Union in the last quarter
of 1950 and the first half of 1951 serve to re-emphasize the need of governments not
to violate the spirit of the rules they have adopted, while apparently following their
letter. Nowhere, perhaps, is the basic conflict between economic nationalism and the
world economy more clearly apparent than in the monetary field. So long as collectivist policies call for the economic insulation of a country from the world economy,
exchange control will be maintained under any pretext whatever, and the requirements
of international equilibrium will be subordinated to the whims of national governments. It is to be hoped that a growing realization of the extent to which national
well-being depends upon a well-functioning world economy will bring about the
revival of an internationalist approach to national policies. The record of the recent
past and the challenge of the immediate future lend support to such hopes.

began to be felt, other steps were taken to promote closer co-operation among members of the OEEC. The most important steps were a program for progressive relaxation of import quotas within Western Europe, and a series of successive, increasingly flexible and comprehensive clearing systems to facilitate intra-European payments, culminating in the establishment, in summer 1950, of the European Payments Union (EPU).

Both the over-all size of the American assistance and its distribution among the members of OEEC were based on balance-of-payments projections; i.e., advance estimates of what balances of payments of the various countries separately and of the whole group taken jointly were likely to be, especially in their relations with the United States. On that basis, and subject to the limitations of Congressional appropriations, dollar grants were made to the OEEC and, through it, to individual countries.[40] The actual Marshall Plan assistance, however, was not extended in the form of free dollar balances to be used at the discretion of the recipient countries but in the form of actual supplies of goods shipped from the United States.[41]

This method of extending aid—in goods rather than in free dollars—had several important consequences:

(1) It gave rise to a considerable amount of centralized economic planning, since the material needs of the various countries had to be ascertained by the governments of those countries on the basis of some blueprint of the immediate economic future. Paradoxically, ERP may have—up to a point—stimulated economic planning while aiming at a revival of private enterprise.

(2) Since the grants were made to governments and not to the immediate recipients of the goods, and since the ultimate receiver of the goods had to pay for them regardless of their origin, the governments of the recipient countries would accumulate funds of local currency corresponding to the proceeds of their sales of merchandise received from the United States. These

[40] Later the system was revised and the U.S. determined the grants to each country directly, based on the OEEC's distribution formula and on the shrinking amount of Congressional appropriations.

[41] This should be qualified by a reference to the so-called conditional aid, an arrangement by virtue of which some particular country would undertake to supply other members of OEEC with agreed-upon quantities of specified goods on a grant basis and would receive from ECA a corresponding dollar payment. Belgium, for example, received most of its ECA dollars conditionally; a part of ECA's assistance to the United Kingdom was also conditional, and so forth.

were the so-called counterpart funds. These funds, administered by mutual agreement between the government of the country and the respective ECA Mission, were instrumental in promoting the country's reconstruction. To be precise, one should say that it is not the goods shipped from the United States which represented the American gift to the recipient country; these goods were paid in their domestic currency by the people for whom they were intended. The actual grant consisted, in reality, of the counterpart funds that, instead of simply accruing to the credit of the United States Government, were made available for the reconstruction and development of the respective OEEC countries. Had the U.S. Government maintained the ownership of the sterling, franc, and lira balances, the Marshall Plan would have simply been a method of supplying the various countries with dollars against balances in their own currencies, at the official rates of exchange; i.e., rates at which the required amounts of dollars were then unobtainable in free foreign-exchange markets. No real grant or gift would have been involved in such a transaction. The way ECA worked, the U.S. grants or gifts consisted essentially of the counterpart funds—a fact not always understood abroad and almost never realized in the United States.[42]

(3) The Marshall Plan aid has been primarily directed toward the restoration and modernization of the productive equipment of the various countries; considerably less attention was paid to the operation of markets and to the monetary aspect of the problem. Thus, while a spectacular recovery of production was achieved by the end of 1950, the liberalizing of intra-European trade and payments lagged very much behind, and the reintegration of Western European countries into a network of unrestricted world trade had made relatively little progress. These three points explain why ECA has been more successful in

[42] There was of course a second, even less clearly visible, "gift" element in ECA transactions, namely the disposition on the part of the U.S. Government to accept local currencies at their overvalued official rates. The mechanism of the ECA grants was exceedingly interesting in that it helped to overcome simultaneously balance-of-payments difficulties and shortages of capital in the recipient countries. Its drawback in many cases is that the American contribution cannot be clearly identified when counterpart funds are applied to balancing national budgets, or (which is a far sounder plan) to reducing a country's national debt. In either case the man in the street does not quite know what he has been getting from the United States. And, the American legislator is frequently confused about the nature of the aid for which he is asked to vote credits.

restoring production than in liberating trade and payments.

The Marshall Plan was designed for Europe; it was narrowed down to Western Europe by virtue of the Soviet reactions to it. It has been instrumental in checking the drift toward Communism in Western Europe by putting an end to the hopelessness of the first postwar years, by facilitating economic reconstruction and thereby fortifying people's confidence in their individual and national future, and by creating an environment favorable to the growth of co-operation among Western European countries. Although ECA at first stimulated economic planning, the rapid improvement in economic conditions was favorable to the revival of liberal tendencies throughout most of Continental Western Europe. As expressed by commercial and monetary policies, this liberal revival was limited to the internal life of Western Europe. In its basic concept the Marshall Plan was too exclusively European: Europe depends so heavily upon multilateral world trade that the regionalism of ECA and OEEC reduced the Plan's effectiveness. Had it aimed more expressly at the restoration of free economic intercourse between Western Europe and the rest of the non-Soviet world, the Marshall Plan might have achieved even greater results. The trade-liberalizing program of OEEC and the operations of the European Payments Union illustrate the consequences of this regional approach.[43] Both are to be welcomed, but neither promises too much under the present geographic limitations.

The same kind of comment must be made about the concept of European "integration" which has been promoted by ECA since the fall of 1949.[44] What are we to understand by "integration"? If it means the elimination of trade and payment barriers, then it is just another word for free or freer trade. If that is intended, then there is no reason why it should be limited to Western Europe alone. On the other hand, the notion of integration might be associated with political union, about which so much has been said in Western Europe since the end of World

[43] ECA's regionalist predilections also expressed themselves in the fostering of customs unions within Western Europe. Too much was expected from that approach, and little came of it in actual practice. Even Benelux—the most successful customs union project of the postwar years—ran into serious difficulties. For the best available discussion of these questions, see *The Customs Union Issue*, by Professor Jacob Viner (Carnegie Endowment for International Peace, New York, 1950).

[44] For a more detailed discussion of the problem of European economic "integration," see Appendix II.

War II. So interpreted, however, integration is likely to prove a misleading objective. Indeed, by predicating economic integration upon political unity, one may retard the progress of liberalization of trade and payments instead of stimulating it.

The ambiguity that beclouds the concept of integration has made it easier for the Labour Government of the United Kingdom to minimize the degree of its co-operation with the other OEEC countries. The Labour Party's statement on *European Unity,* issued in May 1950—one of the most controversial documents of that year—is exceedingly candid when it says that Great Britain's participation in a movement toward European unity must be limited by the requirements of its internal socialist program. Since, however, socialist planning requires trade and payment controls, one can hardly see the Labour Party participating wholeheartedly in any program of European economic integration. It is conceivable that another government in the United Kingdom might prove far more co-operative on purely economic grounds.[45] In any event, what is badly needed is a clear definition of the phrase: "European economic integration." Great Britain's conflict of loyalties between Europe and the Commonwealth will tend to disappear once integration is equated with freer trade; the conflict will tend to grow, however, with any attempt to combine the political objective of European unity with the economic objective of freer trade.

If an all too exclusive concentration on production and an excessive faith in regionalism limited the otherwise considerable success of the Marshall Plan, that program has also been handicapped by three other factors. One is the acceptance of the balance-of-payments approach to the problems of the various countries, combined with implications of the dollar-shortage theories. This has led to much too tolerant an attitude toward exchange controls, and even toward trade discrimination against the United States. Another is that the ECA and OEEC have adopted a "gradualistic" approach to the removal of trade and payment barriers; there are good reasons to believe that such an approach is doomed to failure and that only a frontal attack on these impediments to international economic intercourse can succeed. And the third factor is the too great emphasis that has

---

[45] *See* Richard Law's *Return from Utopia* (London, 1950), for the view of a well-known, liberally minded member of the Conservative Party.

been placed on institutional arrangements, while too little confidence is shown in the spontaneous forces of free markets.
Integration, for instance, should have been interpreted as meaning less restrictions rather than more institutional arrangements.

Space forbids going into many other aspects of the Marshall
Plan. But let it be noted that by the end of 1950 the aim of the
Plan has been largely accomplished not only in production terms
but even in the condition of balances of payments. It is noteworthy that in 1950 the ERP countries received U.S. grants for
$3,250 million, but acquired from the United States $1,358 million in gold, and dollar assets for $534 million.[46] In other words,
nearly 60 per cent of the Marshall aid has gone into strengthening the gold and dollar holdings of the various countries, a
development to be welcomed both as a proof of continuing improvement in the condition of ERP countries and because it
foreshadows the possibility of a return to free convertibility of
currencies not only within Western Europe but also in relations
with the dollar area.

7.

Before closing this chapter, let us turn to the foreign-trade policies of the United States. The views expressed on that subject
in Chapters XIII and XIV stand in no need of revision at the
present time—five years after they were originally put on paper
—but a restatement might be useful. Below is a description of
how the foreign-trade policies of the United States appeared to
me at the beginning of 1950, a few months before the outbreak
of the Korean War and the advent of rearmament in the
Western World.[47]

There are five basic propositions:

1. If we consider the interests of the American public at large,
there is no economically valid reason why we should have any
tariff at all. The only valid reason is a political one: the national-
security argument.

2. It is open to serious question whether protection of indus-

---

[46] Figures published in the *Survey of Current Business* (U.S. Department of Commerce, Washington, D.C., March 1951).

[47] The paragraphs that follow are drawn from my article, "The Missing Key to
U.S. Policy," reprinted from the February 1950 issue of *Fortune* magazine by special
permission of the Editors. Copyright 1950 by Time Inc.

tries needed for our national defense should not be obtained through specific subsidies rather than through tariffs.

3. The disproportion between American exports and American imports, the so-called trade gap, can best be closed by opening the American market to foreign goods, by making greater use of foreign services such as shipping, and by spending more in foreign travel.

4. The transition to a quasi-free trading system must be accomplished gradually, and established industries should be adequately compensated through the public treasury for losses suffered in the process.

5. The virtual suppression of our tariff should not be a unilateral act by the U.S. but should be used as a means of breaking down obstacles that exist abroad to multilateral trade and free international payments.

Having thus climbed out to the far end of a limb, let us look into the considerations that prompted this climbing. The Reciprocal Trade Agreements Act was very welcome at the time it was passed, as an indication that the U.S. had turned away from the high-tariff trend and that it was beginning to realize the need for a progressive liberalizing of its commercial policy. As time went on this procedure proved less and less satisfactory. It suffered from three shortcomings. In the first place, tariff reductions could be made only where they didn't hurt any special interests that were big enough, or well enough organized, to be heard; this means that as soon as the program threatened to become effective red lights would be flashed all over the place to stop it. In the second place, the program related only to tariff rates and not to customs procedures, yet the latter are at least as great an interference with imports as are the rates themselves. Finally, the program, by being limited to tariff rates, was ineffective when it came to breaking down import quotas and exchange control, by means of which the trade of many of the other countries was and is restrained. All in all, reciprocal trade agreements amount to little more than a tariff truce on the part of the U.S., associated with ineffectual nibbling at our protective system.

Clearly we need a national debate on the tariff; we need as a result of such a debate an alignment of domestic free-trade forces that would lead to the passage of a new tariff act coming as close to a free-trade act as the exigencies of national security will allow; and we need a clear concept of how the adoption of the new tariff act could be used in our foreign negotiations to promote the major purposes of our foreign economic policy. On the basis of a new and low U.S. tariff one could revive the concept of a selective or nuclear approach to the reconstruction of multilateral trade. The U.S. could then conclude new comprehensive treaties of commerce, whose quasi-free trade terms would be made available not to everybody but only to those countries which would commit themselves to the abandonment of import quotas, exchange control, and discriminatory practices of all kinds toward the U.S. and the other members of the group. Investment treaties, previously discussed, would become part of these new comprehensive treaties of commerce. The now virtually useless most-favored-nation clause would henceforth be limited to these new treaties, and would thus be endowed again with its full meaning and effectiveness.

Such treaties will not be easy to enter into either for ourselves or for our foreign partners. Since the new tariff act would really break down the protective walls that still surround the American market, a number of particular interests would suffer. Since injury would be done to some industries in the name of the greater good for the greater number of citizens, it is only fair that the damage should be compensated through taxpayers' money. Hence, as was suggested a few years ago in the first edition of *The Trade of Nations*,[48] the transition from our present tariff to a very low one should become a process of subsidized liquidation, thereby softening the blow for investors, employees, and workers.

Great difficulties would also be faced by our foreign partners, both in terms of their domestic situation and in terms of their international balance. The question would undoubtedly be asked: "Can they *afford* a multilateral trading system?" A better question is this: "Can they afford *not* to have a multilateral system?" Without U.S. aid none of the larger beneficiaries of postwar loans and of ECA grants would have been able to survive even under their existing methods of bilateralism. The combination of U.S. aid with bilateralism or Schachtianism has created the dangerous illusion that economic nationalism can

[48] See above, pages 230–1.

help countries in distress. We must dispel these illusions by linking our further aid to the principle of increasing economic liberty through multilateralism. But once it is so defined our aid must be forthcoming—and must be generous. Only then will countries that wish to work with us be able to do so.

The stakes are high in terms of our own future and in terms of the prosperity and the peace of the world. The next move is ours. To take it we must decide to direct all our economic efforts toward one objective: the restoration of multilateral trade and free international payments.

split—no logical demonstration is needed of what is an ascertainable fact. The split between the totalitarian, Soviet-controlled part of the world and the rest is almost complete. As to countries that are not totalitarian but have adopted a certain degree of collectivism, their ability to co-operate with other countries has in the past stood in reverse relation to the scope of their national collectivism.[2] It is a fact that centralized national economic planning leads to collectivism; actually, such planning is possible only in a collectivist society. A society that wishes to remain free quickly abandons such elements of planning—as has been demonstrated by the experience of a number of countries in continental Western Europe and is currently being demonstrated by growing British dissatisfaction with the policies of the Labour Government. A society that, on the other hand, accepts national planning by the central government sinks more and more deeply into collectivism—as has been demonstrated by a number of Latin American and Asian countries. A careful observer of the contemporary scene will now recognize that the incompatibility of economic collectivism and political democracy is far more than a mere assertion. The same is true of collectivism and bilateralism. Multilateral trade is essentially a *liberal* trading system; it has its fullest flowering when trade is conducted exclusively by private individuals and corporations; it disappears completely when trade is monopolized by governments. This again, far from being a mere assertion, is abundantly confirmed by contemporary realities.

A number of critics of *The Trade of Nations* considered its author too reluctant to accept compromise and to acquiesce in "middle course" solutions. The following quotation is typical:[3]

"Mr. Heilperin has been carried too far by his zest for the defense of free enterprise economy of classical purity. With the world as it is today three-quarters of a loaf is likely to be the most that we can realistically hope for, and decidedly worth having at that. Mr. Heilperin overlooks the fact that some champions of limited national planning are at the same time the most fervent advocates of interna-

---

[2] The reader may refer to the above-quoted pamphlet, *European Unity*, published in May 1950 by the British Labour Party.

[3] Professor Arthur D. Gayer in the *New York Herald Tribune* Weekly Book Review (August 31, 1947).

tional economic cooperation. Keynes himself after all was one of the architects of the International Bank and Fund."

So is another comment: [4]

"The conflict between national planning and liberal foreign trade policies is certainly a real one. Mr. Heilperin has delineated the dangers well. But we cannot yet say that there is no compromise, that would foreclose a crucial issue before practical experiments have been made. Furthermore, it is dangerous doctrine for one who wants freer multilateral trade to present this issue as 'either . . . or . . .' For most countries the answer to that choice would be, 'National planning, and we will manage to trade somehow.' . . . The danger is of giving an impression of irreconcilability that will lead the general reader to call compromise failure, before it is tried."

Both *The Trade of Nations* and the two reviews quoted above were written before the drafting of the Havana Charter. Does not the record of the ITO Conferences lend support to the point of view adopted in the first fourteen chapters of this book? On the basis of my assumptions the failure of the ITO Conferences was anticipated in Chapter XI and the reasons for it were indicated in advance of the fact. Professor Gayer, in the first of the two quotations above, expresses his willingness to accept "three quarters of a loaf." Why three quarters? Why not one half, one quarter, or one tenth? Who is to say, and where are we to draw the line? (The metaphor of the loaf is, by the way, quite misleading, for compromise in this field tends to be far more qualitative than quantitative. We don't get *part* of a loaf—what we get is a different thing altogether.) If some "champions of limited national planning" also advocate international economic co-operation, this does not by itself prove that the two objectives are consistent. It may be that the "champions" simply contradict themselves. The record of experience is certainly against them. As for Keynes, his work on the International Bank and Fund belongs to a later period of his life than does his advocacy of national economic planning. As was observed earlier in this book: "It would seem that towards the end of his career Keynes was no longer a Keynesian in good standing." [5] Due to his intel-

[4] William Diebold, Jr., in *Political Science Quarterly* (December 1947), p. 608.
[5] See above, page 94.

productive as possible, to increase the mobility of labor, to en-hance the growth of productivity—all of these objectives are less important in a defense economy than they are in normal peace-time.

There are certain elements at present that are prejudicial to the revival of multilateral trade, and others that are helpful. The main negative factors are the following:

1. The requirements of defense production may reduce the ability of various countries to enlarge or even to maintain their export trade; on the other hand, their import requirements in terms of raw materials may be increased. Hence the defense effort may upset the precarious equilibrium of the balance-of-payments of certain countries. The fear of future balance-of-payments difficulties will militate against an early removal of exchange-control machinery, though actual restrictions may be relaxed.

2. A defense economy calls for a number of controls, some monetary and fiscal, and others such straight physical controls as the licensing of imports and exports and the allocation of raw materials. The existence of these controls will tend to narrow down the area of free-enterprise trade and widen the scope of state trading.

3. Inflationary pressures have always been the greatest enemy of international monetary equilibrium; they have frequently led to the adoption or strengthening of exchange controls and to policies of national insulation. These pressures have been getting stronger since Korea and are likely to keep growing.

In contrast to these unfavorable factors, all of them effects of rearmament, we must note some other factors that are likely to speed up the reconstruction of world trade:

1. The disappearance of the world dollar shortage in the course of 1950 [6] was caused primarily by the large foreign pur-chases of raw materials by the United States Government. These purchases are certain to continue as long as defense needs are high, and will result in a relative abundance of dollar exchange in raw-material-producing countries.

2. In connection with the development of the raw-materials resources of the world, there is likely to be an expansion of for-eign investment, both private and public; this will further in-

[6] See Chapter XV, p. 253.

crease the availability of dollars in certain areas.

3. The ability of the United States to supply manufactured goods to raw-material-producing countries will be curtailed by the diversion of an important part of American productive capacity to military output. Yet these countries will have more dollars and their demand for manufactured goods will grow. The balance can be at least partially restored by importing from other industrial countries, in Western Europe particularly. Countries of Western Europe will thus be able to earn dollars outside of the United States, thereby improving the condition of their monetary reserves.

4. There will be two results: First, the triangular trade pattern involving Europe, North America, and the raw-material-producing areas (Latin America in particular) will be restored far more quickly than might otherwise have been the case, and second, the European countries will be better able to liberalize their exchange controls and trade policies.

The balance between the unfavorable repercussions of rearmament and the favorable ones will vary from country to country. It is hazardous, therefore, to engage in predictions concerning the impact of rearmament upon the monetary and financial position of individual countries. But it can be said with considerable assurance that the over-all effect is likely to be favorable to multilateral trade.

This conclusion is important; if confirmed by future events it will mark an almost revolutionary departure from past experience. It is because defense is now looked upon as a common enterprise, its economics calling for the best possible utilization of available resources, that its net impact upon international economic relations may prove to be so favorable. Much has been written in the past about collective security. Now we are learning about the importance of collective defense. We are discovering, by trial and error, that the pattern of world trade which favors Opulence—multilateral trade—can also, when adopted by a group of friendly nations, be favorable to Defense.

4.

Reference has already been made to the value of the European Payments Union in making arrangemetns for the clearance,

282 The Trade of Nations

among NATO countries, of accounts resulting from the mutual supplies of arms and equipment in connection with the common rearmament program. There arises the question of the possible geographical expansion of the scope of the Payments Union. As has been pointed out in the preceding chapter, the main reason for having a clearing union at all must be looked for in the prevalence of exchange control. Rearmament now makes a complete elimination of these controls unlikely for a number of years to come, irrespective of any liberalizing of their use. The need for a clearing system will therefore last longer than could have been anticipated prior to Korea. But it must be noted that the geographic limitations of EPU greatly reduce its usefulness. Even before it was six months old, its lopsidedness became apparent: the sterling area, an important source of raw materials for Western Europe, belongs indirectly to the EPU, through the instrumentality of London, while oversea areas that have been in the past, and are likely to be in the future, markets for Western Europe's manufactured exports (such as Latin American countries) are outside the Union.

It would be logical to include the Latin American republics within the scope of the EPU—this would imply, of course, the abandonment of the first initial. It was one of the original aims of EPU to expand inter-European trade and thereby reduce the dollar requirements of that area. In practical terms this was never a very sound objective, nor were the discriminatory features of it attractive to the United States; the justification for it lay in the dollar shortage. But since that shortage seems to have disappeared of late, and is likely not to become a real issue again for some time, there is no reason why the United States (as well as Canada) should not become members of the broadening Payments Union, along with Western Europe, the sterling area, and the Latin American Republics. Should all this happen, the non-Soviet world would be endowed with a Payments Union sufficiently comprehensive in scope to be really favorable to the expansion of multilateral trade and really effective in facilitating international payments.[7] Eventually, the Payments Union might be merged with the International Monetary Fund.

[7] See my article: "A Clearing System for the Free World" (*Fortune*, May 1951).

5.

In conclusion, let us look beyond the emergency, toward a more distant future. Supposing the world is spared the ordeal of a third world war, supposing that the non-Soviet world will grow strong enough to discourage aggression, and supposing further that when rearmament reaches the necessary level a declining proportion of national incomes will have to be devoted to military expenditures; what will then happen to the trade of nations?

Problems of readjustment will arise. The transition from rearmament to armed peace would, of course, be less dramatic than the transition from general war to assured peace. In either case the answer to the adjustment problem lies in economic expansion of civilian production and civilian requirements; i.e., of output and income. A war or defense economy inevitably breeds maladjustments. The most serious of these arise in the fields of production of primary products (raw materials and foodstuffs) because these are fields in which adjustments are most difficult. Through development programs, through the expansion of foreign investments, and through the maintenance of economic activity in the industrial countries, it will be possible to minimize the extent of overproduction and the scope of necessary correctives. Therein lies the future importance of such ventures as the Colombo Plan or Point Four. Therein, too, lies the opportunity for private foreign investments. As in the past, so also in the future the great enemy of progress will be economic nationalism. Shall we learn from the many painful experiences of the past that economic nationalism must be fought with utter determination, both from within nations and from without? No quarter must be given in the fight, if international co-operation and partnership are to be achieved and if the trade of nations is to be allowed to produce rising living standards for people throughout the world. This is the challenge and the hope.

APPENDIXES AND INDEX

APPENDIX I

An Appraisal of the Havana Charter for an International Trade Organization

DURING the long debate over the Havana Charter (1948–50) defenders of the document often argued that the International Trade Organization should be supported by all those who favor the free-enterprise system and who realize the importance of world trade. They claimed that the International Trade Organization would help the free-enterprise system as well as serve the best interests of the United States and of world prosperity.

Now, a careful study of the document shows—to my mind, conclusively—that an International Trade Organization based on the Havana Charter would achieve results exactly the opposite of those anticipated by its advocates, and that it would jeopardize the free-enterprise system, the future of world trade, and America's position in the world economy. An International Trade Organization to promote better international economic relations and freer trade throughout the world is very desirable—if the national policies of the member governments aim at a well-knit multilateral world economy, ruled by the mechanism of free markets and prices and affording full scope to private initiative and free enterprise. An International Trade Organization would follow such policies almost as a matter of course and, without being really indispensable—as the experience of the second half of the nineteenth century shows—it would nevertheless perform important functions and render valuable services. The charter of such an organization would be very clear and simple and readily understandable to even the lay reader; it would be the exact opposite of the cumbersome, uncandid, and ambiguous document agreed upon at Havana, intelligible only after protracted and painstaking study.

The charter of a "good" ITO would prohibit the use of import quotas, exchange controls, subsidies of all kinds, and all discriminatory trade practices. It would declare it a duty of every country to make itself economically solvent without the use of restrictive and discriminatory commercial and monetary policies. It would provide for an emergency procedure by which a country faced with exceptional difficulties beyond its own control would be given appropriate assistance in overcoming these difficulties without resorting to measures that disrupt the network of international trade. The charter of an ITO of which the United States would really want to be a member would place multilateral trade and free private enterprise first on its list of desirable objectives. Indeed, whenever privately conducted trade is

[287]

allowed to proceed without major govermental interference its world-wide multilateral pattern develops as a matter of course.

The Havana Charter bears no resemblance to the hypothetical document I have tried to outline here. It is true that the Charter contains provisions that prohibit import quotas, subsidies, and discriminatory practices, but these provisions are so thoroughly qualified by exceptions, reservations, and special directives as to lose all practical significance. It is possible for advocates of the Charter to point to these provisions in support of their contentions. Opponents of the Charter, however, can point to a multitude of provisions that go the other way and that, unlike the first group, are operating provisions, leading to—or permitting to take place—action that is in sharp conflict with the alleged objectives of the ITO and the obligations of its members. An obligation that one is at liberty to neglect ceases to be a true obligation.

It will be readily objected that the kind of ITO described above would find few adherents today. This is a valid observation. At the time of drafting the Havana Charter there were not more than half a dozen countries really devoted to principles of economic liberalism. All the others had governments that believed in the virtues of nationalistic economic planning and in the notion that it is a proper function of government to regulate a country's foreign trade and foreign payments (as well as its domestic economy). They attached the greatest possible importance to maintaining unlimited sovereignty in their national economic planning. It was obvious that the kind of ITO the United States desired to set up was not then practical. We should thereupon have shelved this project until the condition of the world and of national tempers would permit genuine international economic co-operation.

But no such wise course was pursued by the American negotiators. It became apparent early in the ITO Conferences that the U.S. delegates had set their hearts on establishing an ITO—*any* ITO—and that they were willing to go to great lengths of compromise in reaching a universally acceptable agreement. It was my good fortune to observe from a close position both the Geneva and Havana Conferences of 1947–8, and to follow at first hand the negotiations leading to the adoption of the Havana Charter. I have since recounted the story of the Charter's progressive deterioration [1]; I concluded by quoting the following passage from the famous essay *On Compromise* written in the last quarter of the nineteenth century by Great Britain's statesman and philosopher, Lord Morley:

"A principle, if it be sound, represents one of the larger expediences. To abandon that for the sake of some seeming expediency of the hour,

[1] "How the U.S. Lost the ITO Conferences," *Fortune*, September 1949).

is to sacrifice the greater good for the less, on no more credible ground than that the less is nearer. It is better to wait, and to defer the realization of our ideas until we can realize them fully, than to defraud the future by truncating them, if truncate them we must, in order to secure a partial triumph for them in the immediate present. It is better to bear the burden of practicableness, than to stifle conviction and to pare away principle until it becomes mere hollowness and triviality. What is the sense, and what is the morality, of postponing the wider utility to the narrower? Nothing is so sure to impoverish an epoch, to deprive conduct of nobleness, and character of elevation."

Unfortunately the concept of limits of compromise was not recognized by our negotiators, and they so far overstepped these limits as to put their signatures eventually upon a document that is the negation of American aims and that can truly be described, in my opinion, as a charter of economic nationalism. Indeed, one title of distinction of that document is that it is probably the first International Charter of Economic Nationalism ever written in the long history of the civilized world.

2.

It was suggested at the beginning of this discussion that an ITO based on the Havana Charter would jeopardize both free private enterprise and America's position in the world economy. Now a third count can be added to this double indictment. The Havana Charter, instead of setting the stage for a revival of multilateral world trade, makes the attainment of such a goal very difficult indeed. Instead of promoting world trade the rules of the Charter would promote its disintegration.

The Charter is a long and intricate document, but by careful study one can discover several provisions of basic significance, which by themselves define the kind of world in which we would have to live should an ITO ever be established on the basis of the Havana Charter.

The first and most important of these provisions is buried in paragraph 4(b) of Article 21:

"The Members recognize that, as a result of domestic policies directed toward the fulfilment of a Member's obligations under Article 3 relating to the achievement and maintenance of full and productive employment and large and steadily growing demand, or its obligations under Article 9 relating to the reconstruction or development of industrial and other economic resources and to the raising of standards of productivity, such a Member may find that demands for foreign exchange on account of imports and other current payments are absorbing the foreign exchange resources currently available to it in such a manner as to exercise pressure on its monetary reserves which would justify the institution or maintenance of restrictions under paragraph 3 of this Article. Accordingly,

(i) no Member shall be required to withdraw or modify restrictions which it is applying under this Article on the ground that a change in such policies would render these restrictions unnecessary;

(ii) any Member applying import restrictions under this Article may determine the incidence of the restrictions on imports of different products or classes of products in such a way as to give priority to the importation of those products which are more essential in the light of such policies."

This establishes a priority of national—and nationalistic—economic planning over the requirements of good international economic relations. A country is free under the Charter to pursue domestic policies that inevitably lead to balance-of-payments difficulties and, once these difficulties occur, it is free to adopt import quotas, to control by government regulations the composition of its import trade, and to engage in various discriminatory practices. The Organization, on the other hand, is allowed neither to object nor to point out that a change in that country's domestic policies would make it internationally solvent, thereby removing the need for the use of import quotas and the rest. In the words of Mr. Walter Nash, formerly Deputy Prime Minister and Finance Minister of New Zealand, and one of the principal authors of the Havana Charter: "When a conflict arises between the desirability of pursuing policies of economic development and full employment on the one hand and the desirability of avoiding quantitative restrictions on the other, the domestic policies will take precedence." [2]

Should there remain any doubt as to the Charter's intent, we find in Article 6 a broad directive to the ITO to "have regard, in the exercise of its functions under other Articles of this Charter, to the need of Members to take action within the provisions of this Charter to safeguard their economies against inflationary or deflationary pressure from abroad." This means that a member government is free to surround its country with trade barriers in order to insulate it from the world economy. It is well to remember, however, that such policies of economic insulation considerably aggravated the economic depression of the thirties, and substantially contributed to the breakup of international economic relations during that distressing decade. Thus, for the first time in an official document, collectivist national planning is given precedence over international order, while policies of economic insulation obtain the right-of-way over the operating requirements of a well-functioning world economy.

[2] "Report by New Zealand Delegation on the Conference Held at Havana, Cuba, From 21 November 1947 to 24 March 1948," Department of External Affairs Publication No. 58.

As I have indicated in Chapter XV, the Havana Charter deals not only with matters of commercial policy but also with problems of full employment and economic development. To be sure, an international agreement on principles of commercial policy was the original American objective; but leadership in the drafting of the Charter has passed, in the course of the successive ITO Conferences,[3] from the United States to countries governed, at that time, by state socialistic governments![4] Consequently, chapters on full employment and economic development acquired a very important place in the Charter. Delegates of these countries would openly assert that they regarded the employment and development provisions of the Charter as being the two main pillars of the ITO. When we read these two chapters, however, what do we find? Constructive proposals for maintaining national prosperity and employment amongst increasingly abundant international trade, or ways of promoting the growth of backward areas within the context of an expanding world economy? By no means. All we find is that these chapters are abundant sources of exceptions to the rules that prohibit quantitative restrictions and discriminatory practices. Indeed, as one of the delegates who fought for a "good" charter remarked in a committee meeting towards the close of the Conference, the ITO should be called "An Organization for the Restriction of International Trade in the Name of Employment and Economic Development"!

These aberrations notwithstanding, it is the restoration and preservation of multilateral trade that remains the main objective of an International Trade Organization worthy of its name. And this calls for the adoption of a domestic policy that assists the maintenance of a country's international solvency. Such is the unambiguous lesson from past experience. This was the core of the unwritten rules of the gold standard, and it could easily be shown that this must be so under any system of international economic equilibrium. The Articles of Agreement of the International Monetary Fund also erred by not stipulating explicitly that this principle be revived. There, however, we find at least this redeeming provision: a member country that runs into balance-of-payments difficulties obtains relief—but, unless it improves its balance-of-payments position, it is certain in the end to become ineligible for further use of the Fund's resources. In other words, a country neglectful of its international solvency will end by losing its good standing with the Fund. There is no parallel stipulation in the Havana Charter. On the contrary, a country in persistent balance-of-payments difficulties can obtain freedom of action to adopt

[3] London, October–November 1946; Geneva. April–September 1947; Havana, November 1947–March 1948.

[4] Among them the United Kingdom, Australia, New Zealand, France, India.

restrictive and discriminatory commercial policies—a freedom not available to countries whose international solvency has been better guarded. Considering that many countries are concerned more with preserving their freedom of action in terms of national economic planning than with maintaining their international solvency, and that these countries would accept falling into bad standing with the International Monetary Fund rather than forego their freedom of action under the ITO, there can be but little doubt that an ITO based on the Havana Charter would have spelled the doom of the Fund.

There is no reference in the Charter to multilateral trade; and that omission is one of the most candid features of this uncandid document. During the closing phase of the Havana Conference some consideration was given in certain circles to the possibility of attaching to the document a general resolution in favor of multilateral trade. But that idea was given up completely when it became clear that the Conference would never agree to a forthright statement in favor of multilateralism.

3.

The present discussion does not cover the entire contents of the Havana Charter. That document includes very worthwhile technical provisions on the administration of customs duties and similar matters, a well-intentioned, albeit innocuous, attempt at drafting international antitrust laws, and provisions concerning intergovernmental commodity agreements. Here we are concerned with those provisions which define the nature of the world economy-to-be. These basic provisions are a triumph of nationalistic economic planning over expanding world trade, while private trade is placed in a precarious and inferior position. The Havana Charter represents the negation of a free-world economy. Worse still: had an ITO actually been established, membership in that organization would have rendered it impossible for the United States to exercise any further leadership in the direction of restoring multilateral trade. Our hands would be tied: we could neither object to trade restrictions and discriminatory practices adopted by countries invoking balance-of-payments difficulties or economic development to justify their actions, nor could we retaliate in kind because of our own solvency and our high degree of economic development. Under the Havana Charter we are obliged to apply the most-favored-nation treatment to all ITO members in good standing, even those who by their policies discriminate against the United States. In this connection, it should always be remembered that import quotas are by their very nature discriminatory, and that to speak of a nondiscriminatory administration of such import quotas is simply absurd.

The universalist approach having failed to restore the world economy to its former health—witness the contents of the Havana Charter—the U.S. Government might wish some day to seek the reconstruction of multilateral trade by other means, namely through bilateral negotiations with a small group of countries of like mind with us. Our bargaining power in such negotiations would be based upon granting these countries lower tariff rates and most-favored-nation treatment. Membership in an ITO based on the Havana Charter would have meant throwing this bargaining power away. The Havana Charter having been found wanting, it is important to consider an alternative approach to the reconstruction of world trade. Such an approach has been indicated in Chapter XII above,[5] and is further explored in a recent article of mine.[6]

One further matter calls for attention in the present note. According to the Havana Charter, the United States, like every other member of the ITO, would have only one vote. This one-country-one-vote system, superficially "democratic," in fact creates the absurd situation of placing the large trading nations of the world in the position of a permanent minority while the majority is permanently held by a large number of countries whose stake in world trade is small, experience in the art of commercial policy recent, and who are animated by a fierce spirit of nationalism, economic and otherwise. It is true that the United States was not often outvoted in the course of the ITO negotiations. But this was due exclusively to the fact that American delegates always accepted damaging compromises in advance of a ballot.

Adherents of the Charter denied in debate that the one-country-one-vote system would have the bad effects mentioned above. Their arguments were based upon three considerations: first, a country's position in international organizations is not measured merely by its numerical vote—the United States would always exercise an influence greater than the one vote it would formally possess; second, countries other than the United States have conflicting interests, and to anticipate that they would, all of them, "gang up" on the United States would be taking an unduly dim and unrealistic view of the actual probabilities; and finally, adherents of the Charter considered that the fear of the one-country-one-vote system assumed bad faith on the part of other countries in accepting commitments under the Charter. The defenders of the Charter, on the contrary, assumed throughout that other governments would always act in complete good faith.

[5] See Section 4 of that Chapter, pages 194–7.
[6] "The Missing Key to U.S. Policy" (*Fortune*, February 1950).

These arguments are hardly convincing. True, the influence of a country in international councils is not measured by its numerical vote. But the fact remains that the influence of the United States upon the final shape of the Havana Charter was very small—as might have been expected in view of the minority position we had in the councils that drew up the Charter. This is perhaps obscured by the fact that our delegates were far too prone to recede from their earlier positions and to rationalize the unhappy compromises they accepted; but we have before us the Charter as a conclusive proof of the weakness of America's position in the ITO Conferences.

Second, let us examine the alleged diversity of interests of the other fifty-odd countries. These countries may have many interests at variance but they are all at one in their desire to have practically complete freedom in the use of quantitative trade restrictions and discriminatory practices. They are also at one in their wish not to be exposed to unfavorable American reactions when they use these instruments of policy, to which the United States is supposed strongly to object. The defenders of the Charter have often referred to the "miracle" of agreement that took place among these fifty-odd countries. But looking at it more closely, one cannot help wondering whether there was any miracle at all. What did these countries agree upon in the end? On their right to do as they please, a right that only two among them (Switzerland and the United States) would be deprived of because these two countries are both economically developed and financially solvent. That all the other countries should have agreed to the Havana Charter was not at all miraculous. The only miraculous thing is that the American signature should appear at the bottom of the Havana text!

As to the question of good or bad faith, that is largely a matter of definition. Is a country acting in good faith if it accepts the principle of eliminating import quotas but sees to it that its own right to retain them is safeguarded by escape clauses and special provisions? It might be better not to go too deeply into this.

These then are the principal reasons why in my opinion the Havana Charter was a misbegotten agreement and why an ITO based on it would have helped economic nationalism instead of furthering the cause of world economic co-operation.

APPENDIX II

Notes on the Economic Integration
of Western Europe

IN ITS BASIC CONCEPT the Marshall Plan had two closely related aims: one to assist the economic reconstruction of European countries, the other to promote economic co-operation and mutual assistance among them. At first the OEEC—Organization for European Economic Cooperation—limited its functions largely to the distribution of American aid among the participating countries; later on it moved in the direction of promoting the liberalization of trade and payments within Western Europe.[1] The change started to take place in the last quarter of 1949, and the new slogan that came to be adopted was that of "integration." It is the purpose of this Appendix to enlarge more fully upon this shift within OEEC, and upon the problem of integration itself.

By early fall of 1949 the dissatisfaction with OEEC was getting rather general, not only in the United States but in Europe as well. *The Economist* of London, for example, had in its October 29, 1949 issue an important article on the future of OEEC. The article noted that:

"At this juncture in the history of Europe . . . the failures of the OEEC are, perhaps, of greater importance than its achievements. . . . The economic unification of Europe has, in theory, been desired by most, but not desired enough for any positive steps to be taken to achieve it. . . . policy has drifted into the disastrous position of accepting an objective which it does not intend to achieve. As a result, for the Americans at least, the failure of the OEEC nations to move toward closer association has been a profound disappointment."

The Economist went on to analyze critically the policies of Great Britain, which they blamed, to a considerable extent, for the failure of OEEC to promote closer economic co-operation among its members: "British policy has left the universal impression, especially in the sphere of international trade and finance, that its attachment to bilateralism and airtight domestic plans is deeper than its determination to co-operate in a return to convertibility and multilateralism."

The crisis of OEEC was, of course, giving considerable cause for concern at ECA headquarters in Washington, so much so that at the end of October 1949 Paul G. Hoffman flew to Paris to deliver a major address before the Council of the OEEC. This speech marked a

[1] See above, Chapter XV, pp. 266–269.

turning-point in the history of the Marshall Plan. Mr. Hoffman emphasized the need for the European Recovery Program to devote its fullest energies to two major tasks. The first of these was to balance Europe's dollar accounts. As for the other, let us quote Mr. Hoffman's remarks verbatim:

"The second [task]—and to say this is why I'm here—is to move ahead on a far-reaching program to build in Western Europe a more dynamic, expanding economy which will promise steady improvement in the conditions of life for all its people. This, I believe, means nothing less than an integration of the Western European economy. . . .

"The substance of such integration would be the formation of a single large market within which quantitative restrictions on the movement of goods, monetary barriers to the flow of payments and, eventually, all tariffs are permanently swept away. . . .

". . . This would make it possible for Europe to improve its competitive position in the world and thus more nearly satisfy the expectations and needs of its people.

"This is a vital objective. It was to this that Secretary Marshall pointed in the speech which sparked Europe to new hope and new endeavor.[2] It was on this promise that the Congress of the United States enacted the ECA act. This goal is embodied in the convention of the OEEC. . . .

. . . While pressing forward to the broader objective of economic integration of all the participating countries, we should not slacken our efforts toward establishment of close economic arrangements within one or more smaller groups of countries—always with the intention that these should contribute toward, and not be turned against, the integration of the whole of Western Europe and its overseas territories." [3]

Mr. Hoffman wound up his speech by requesting that the OEEC have ready early in 1950 "a record of accomplishment and a program which together will take Europe well along the road toward economic integration."

This notion of European economic integration was very stimulating to the mind, but when it came to practical interpretation Mr. Hoffman's speech, as was only natural under the circumstances, raised more questions than it answered. After reading it I ventured to formulate certain implications of the concept of integration and to submit them to the *New York Times* in the form of a "Letter to the Editor." That letter appeared on November 6th, 1949, and its text is reproduced below.

[2] Reference is evidently made to Secretary Marshall's speech delivered at the Harvard Commencement exercises on June 5, 1947.

[3] This refers, of course, to the formation of customs unions, which for a time was an objective actively encouraged by the U.S. Government. As has been noted in Chapter XV, these endeavors were unsuccessful.

2.

To the Editor of The New York Times:

Paul Hoffman's brilliant and important speech of Oct. 31 and the report of *The New York Times* correspondent, Harold Callender, concerning European reactions to it raise several issues of considerable importance for the future of the European recovery program.

The term "economic integration" frequently used by Mr. Hoffman in his address is perhaps a new term to be used on the political scene, but the realities which it covers are not in the least novel. Western Europe (and more than Western Europe) was very effectively integrated during most of the fifty years preceding the outbreak of World War I. This integration was due to the prevalence of free trade or low and stable tariffs, and of free international payments predicated upon the acceptance of a common international monetary system. This was achieved in spite of the existence of separate states, many of which were animated by a spirit of political but not economic nationalism.

RISE OF BARRIERS

Disintegration started setting in by the revival of protectionism, the operation of international cartels, etc. In the last quarter of the nineteenth century and in the early part of the twentieth, Germany was the main source of disintegrating influences, although the contagion spread. Since World War I England gradually gave up the liberal economic doctrines which helped to create a world in which she could be prosperous, and started to lay foundations under her present difficulties.

Contrary to the views reported by Harold Callender in his dispatch from Paris dated Oct. 31, "integration" is not an American doctrine nor is it a doctrine that "had been superimposed upon the mutual engagements made when the Marshall Plan began." The Marshall Plan was always predicated upon an effective get-together of the OEEC countries; while the word "integration" was not used, the concept underlies the entire design for ERP.

The United States never embraced the doctrine of international economic integration. This is witnessed by the traditional attachment to the tariff and the almost insuperable difficulty to get away from the protectionist outlook. Such integration as we have achieved relates to the large domestic market of the United States, and as such it represents nothing new in the world.

When Paul Hoffman urges Western Europe to integrate, he is bringing back to the Europeans something which is not a theoretical concept alone but something which should spell to them a memory of a very prosperous past.

The principal source today of international economic disintegration is to be found in the policies of socialistic economic planning, which by its very nature tends to be national and nationalistic. Import quotas, bilateralist deals and exchange control, plus all kinds and manner of discriminatory practices, are unavoidable features of nationalistic planning. This is further emphasized by the spread of the doctrine of economic "insulation" of a country from inflationary or deflationary tendencies originating abroad.

ENDING CONTROLS

Mr. Hoffman has rightly observed that: "Trade and payments cannot long continue free among countries in which there are widely divergent degrees of inflationary or deflationary pressure. . . . Unless individual countries accept the necessity for some coordination of domestic financial policies, the prospects for eliminating even the most restrictive types of controls over international trade will be dim indeed."

This is a wise application of the lessons of a long experience and makes a great deal more sense than the hope so frequently expressed by state socialistic economists and statesmen that they can best serve the economic interests of their respective countries by policies of economic insulation from the rest of the world.

The Organization of European Economic Cooperation's recommendation that half of existing import quotas be removed by Dec. 15 is hedged by an important escape clause. This is a poor augury for the future. As time goes on it appears increasingly that only drastic and radical methods of removing import quotas and exchange control will create economic unity in Western Europe. A "gradualistic" approach to the removal of trade barriers must fail. Nor must this elimination be limited to Western Europe alone. This area cannot be economically solvent otherwise than within a much wider network of multilateral trade based on the same absence of major restrictions upon trade and payments. Latin America in particular is a very important area from the point of view of European reconstruction.

TRADE IMBALANCES

Countries that would effectively remove trade and payment restrictions have to face a period of serious balance-of-payments difficulties. If we want a program of restoring a liberal world economy to succeed, we must find ways for the United States effectively to assist the cooperating countries in overcoming that unavoidable period of possibly acute difficulties. It may very well be that from now on the great service ECA could render is to help Western European countries to weather the financial storms incident in their return to an integrated world economy.

My letter to the *New York Times* gave rise to correspondence with Mr. Hoffman, in the course of which I developed several points in greater detail. The following is quoted from my letter of November 29th, 1949, to Mr. Hoffman:

"The more I think about the implications of your Paris speech the more I am convinced that it should mark the opening of a second phase of the Marshall Program. . . .

"There is, in this connection, one line of thought to which I have come to attach very much importance. . . .

"There seems to be a certain amount of disagreement as to what is exactly intended by the term 'integration' as applying to the policies you urged the OEEC countries to adopt. One concept would define 'integration' in terms of the suppression of all those barriers which prevent the price mechanism and the market system to operate freely; this means, most of all, the elimination of import quotas and of exchange control, and of various kinds of bilateral deals. As a later development there should also be a progressive reduction, and, if possible, an eventual elimination, of customs barriers as well. However, tariffs, if they are stable and are not prohibitively high, do not interfere with the price mechanism nor with the kind of integration which was characteristic of Europe before the First World War and would be most helpful in solving her economic difficulties were it to be revived in the near future.

"The second concept of integration involves the establishment of a complete economic union throughout Western Europe, leveling off all barriers as well as eliminating all other arrangements, mostly of a domestic character, which interfere with the free mobility of 'factors of production' across national boundaries. Defined in that way, integration would amount to an economic merger of the several countries and would have far-reaching implications in terms of political federation as well.

"There are undoubtedly intermediate positions between these two concepts of integration, but the definitions I have just given seem to express the basic divergencies of views which, I think, are very significant. For my part I think that only the first approach is practicable and that it offers certain very specific advantages which the second does not:

(1) Integration via the re-establishment of the price mechanism and market system (but not accompanied by an economic 'merger' with strong political undertones) can embrace not only Western Europe but Britain *and* the sterling area, and can be extended to North America and eventually to Latin America. (I will say more on this last point presently.)

(2) It excludes the theoretical possibility of Western Eurpoe exclusive of Great Britain organizing itself on an autarchic basis and using bilateralist techniques in dealing with the rest of the world.

(3) It helps to emphasize the fact that Western Europe is not economically curable within its own limits and that what is needed is not only its economic integration but also its *re-integration* with a far wider area of multilateral trade within which alone Western European countries can balance their economic accounts.

"Of course, wherever customs unions would spontaneously tend to spring up, like Benelux and the now often-mentioned Fritalux, they should be encouraged. However, should a comprehensive union be susceptible to achievement in Continental Western Europe it would certainly not be joined by Great Britain and the sterling area at large, and thereby would not assist a return to multilateral world trade.

"I wonder if I am correct in my reading of your Paris speech when I think that you endorse integration of the first kind while leaving the doors open to regional customs unions. Coordination of fiscal and monetary policies, of which you emphasize the need, is, of course, the integral part of any liberal economic program since without such a coordination international monetary stability cannot be maintained. On the other hand, experience with the gold standard shows that such a coordination can be achieved without any necessary establishment of a currency union.

"Two recent dispatches, appearing in the *New York Times,* makes me wonder whether; (a) my reading of your speech is correct, and (b) other people's reading of that speech is correct. I refer in particular to the Washington dispatch of James Reston which appeared on November 14th, from which I quote the following:

'The United States Government is now developing several new themes about the "integration" of Europe. But even in the highest levels of the Government there is no agreement about what "integration" means or what the United States should do to bring it about.'

The other is a letter from Harold Callender (Paris correspondent of The *New York Times*) appearing in Section 4 of the Sunday issue of November 20th in answer to my letter of the 6th, from which I quote the following passage:

'Mr. Heilperin is right in saying that, in the American view, the concept of "integration"—for which we are still awaiting a definition in terms of the immediate as distinct from the remote future— "underlies the entire design for ERP." Mr. Hoffman holds that it is implicit in the written undertakings already given by European states. It became explicit, but only "in principle," as the French like to say when they do not want to commit themselves, when the Marshall Plan Council here agreed on Nov. 1 that a single European market was desirable. These uses of language have some intellectual interest. But they hardly affect the fact that Americans are asking something they call "integration" which, if the word means what Mr. Hoffman said it meant (a single European market without any tariffs or other barriers), is realizable, if at all, only in a somewhat distant future.'

"May I say in concluding this overly-long letter that I greatly believe that an authoritative statement defining the concept of integration would be most timely at the present time as it would put an end to a lot of confusing speculations and clear the way for constructive discussion.

May I also submit my personal hope that when that concept is defined it may be defined in what I have called the first meaning of the word 'integration,' namely elimination of import quotas, exchange controls and bilateralism, and the restoration of the market and price system not only in Western Europe but throughout the sterling area and in the Americas. In this connection I come increasingly to the conclusion that to solve the problem of the economic balance of Western Europe, it is essential to deal much more effectively with the problem of Latin America than has been done to date so that this area also can be re-integrated in the network of multilateral trade. I think there are very obvious implications of this in terms of the future policies based on 'Point 4.' "

In his answer to my letter Mr. Hoffman equated "integration" with the elimination of quantitative restrictions on the movement of goods and the removal of tariffs and other trade barriers. He also indicated his belief that the best approach to integration was through regional arrangements within Europe.

Actually, as has been indicated in the main body of this book,[4] the OEEC made two major moves following Mr. Hoffman's challenge: one was the program of progressive and gradual elimination of import quotas, and the second the establishment of the European Payments Union. Although no official elaboration or clarification of the concept of "integration" has come forth, there can be no doubt, in retrospect, that Paul Hoffman's speech of October 31, 1949 did open a new phase of the Marshall Plan.

3.

Almost two years have now passed since the word "integration" has become a slogan for action.[5] Partly on account of its ambiguity, partly due to the prevalence of economic nationalism, it has never been fully accepted by those to whom Mr. Hoffman addressed his speech. Because of its political overtones the phrase was not very happily chosen: "European free trade" would have been better. But European free trade is only possible within a liberal economic framework far wider than Europe. Western Europe may well become, in due course, a free-trade area within a multilateral world economy, but it is doubtful, with the benefits of hindsight we now have, whether Europe's economic unity can be achieved on a purely regional basis. Yet the ECA and the OEEC have maintained their regional approach.

The gradualistic approach to either trade liberalization or customs

[4] See Chapter XV, p. 31.
[5] General Eisenhower's London address of July 3, 1951 would indicate that "integration" remains America's slogan for Western Europe.

unions has also stood in the way of "integration." Really significant results by way of removing economic barriers can only be achieved through well-prepared, bold, and drastic moves and only if the parties involved are willing to make the necessary adjustments in their domestic policies and conditions. It is pretty much like jumping into a cold lake and warming oneself up by the exercise of swimming—against standing on the shore and shivering as one timidly ventures one foot in the cold waves and eventually decides to go home for a hot cup of coffee. By and large, European nations have ventured a bit, shivered a great deal, and still stand undecided on the shore, neither going in nor quite daring to go home. There are, however, forces at work now—in mid-1951—which, as has been indicated in Chapter XV, work for the suppression of quantitative controls and for the expansion of triangular trade between Western Europe and the Americas. These developments may pave the way for a genuine free-trade movement in Western Europe, along with the rehabilitation of multilateral trade throughout the non-Soviet world.[6]

[6] A discussion of European integration would be incomplete without a reference to the Schuman Plan. This Plan, which aims at the establishment of a coal and steel "community" in Western Europe, under the administration of a supranational authority, has given rise to many discussions, as well as to successfully completed negotiations between the governments of France, Germany, Italy, and the Benelux countries. At the time of this writing the treaty concluded in April 1951 has not yet been ratified by the respective governments. The Schuman Plan is an economic project with a definitely political aim, the latter being to assist the political organization of Western Europe and the establishment of the closest possible relations between Germany and France. The economics of the Schuman Plan are, on the whole, unclear and subject to very considerable reservations. In any case, only the actual operation of the scheme will make it possible to form a definitive judgment concerning it. This is why only this incidental reference to it is made in the present edition of *The Trade of Nations*. One general comment, however, should be added: the philosophy of the Schuman Plan; i.e., that of placing two basic industries, taken out of their economic context, under the authority of a supranational agency, is at variance with the liberal attitude that would reduce governmental barriers and controls to international economic relations and aim at private-enterprise free trade. The latter is, of course, the basic philosophy of the present book.

INDEX

INDEX

to Book Five and Appendixes

[viii]

PRINTER'S NOTE

This book is set on the Linotype in GRANJON, *a type named in compliment to Robert Granjon, type-cutter and printer — 1523–90, Antwerp, Lyon, Rome, Paris. Granjon, the boldest and most original designer of his time, was one of the first to practice the trade of typefounder apart from that of printer.*

Linotype GRANJON *was designed by George W. Jones, who based his drawings upon a face used by Claude Garamond (1510–61) in his beautiful French books.* GRANJON *more closely resembles Garamond's own type than do any of the various modern faces that bear his name.*

The book was composed, printed, and bound by H. Wolff, New York.